The Triune Godhead

The Triune Godhead

When Three Equals One

Tarita Wright

RESOURCE *Publications* · Eugene, Oregon

THE TRIUNE GODHEAD
When Three Equals One

Copyright © 2022 Tarita Wright. All rights reserved. Except for brief quotations in critical publications or reviews, no part of this book may be reproduced in any manner without prior written permission from the publisher. Write: Permissions, Wipf and Stock Publishers, 199 W. 8th Ave., Suite 3, Eugene, OR 97401.

Resource Publications
An Imprint of Wipf and Stock Publishers
199 W. 8th Ave., Suite 3
Eugene, OR 97401

www.wipfandstock.com

PAPERBACK ISBN: 978-1-6667-3767-7
HARDCOVER ISBN: 978-1-6667-9738-1
EBOOK ISBN: 978-1-6667-9739-8

06/08/22

Scripture quotations marked (KJV) are taken from The Authorized (King James) Version. Rights in the Authorized Version in the United Kingdom are vested in the Crown. Reproduced by permission of the Crown's patentee, Cambridge University Press

Images sourced from: (1) Wikimedia Commons under the Creative Commons Agreement and (2) Libreshot.com, permission granted by owner of website Martin Vorel.

Permission granted by Ellen G. White Estate for quotations and extracts by Ellen G. White

Contents

Preface | vii
Introduction: Understanding God | ix

1   3 Yet 1 | 1
2   3 Persons, 1 Godhead: Mystery of the Godhead and the Tree | 7
3   3 Roles, 1 Mission: Mission Possible | 18
4   3 Persons, 1 Name: Je.Ho.Vah | 23
5   3 Sons, 1 Man: Jesus | 29
6   3 Phases, 1 Court: Judgment | 41
7   3 Mouths, 1 Truth: Three Witnesses | 54
8   3 Architects, 1 Design: The Godhead's Creation | 70
9   3 Lies, 1 Truth: Fall of Man | 81
10 3 Temptations, 1 Escape: Deception and Restoration | 90
11 3 Heads, 1 Tail: The Archenemy of the Godhead | 103
12 3 Rooms, 1 Way in: The Godhead in the Sanctuary | 119
13 3 Traits, 1 Personality: Christian Character | 151
14 3 Wrappings, 1 Gift: Righteousness | 168
15 3 Final Breaking News, 1 Channel: Three Angels' Messages | 181
16 3 Verbs, 1 Action: Love | 252
17 3 Thoughts, 1 Emotion: Fear | 261
18 3 Keys, 1 City: Kingdom of the Godhead | 268

Appendix A: Events and Occurrences with the Number Three | 279
Appendix B: Trees and the Roles They Played | 290

Appendix C: Comparative Look at Revelation 14 and Psalms 96 | 293
Appendix D: The Investigative Judgment | 297
Appendix E: Timeline of the 2300 Year Prophecy | 302
Appendix F: The First, Second, and Third Temple | 303

Bibliography | 307

Preface

This book explores the mystery of the triune Godhead—the Father God, the son Jesus Christ, and the Holy Spirit. All three are distinct yet equal. All three are God within themselves—divine, holy, and eternal.

From the existence of the world, mankind has sought for an understanding of God. This search has led many to seek internally, digging deep within the recess of their own internal thoughts. But if we start a journey by searching inward for answers, doesn't that lead back to where we already started?

Many search externally, looking out and etching out man-made gods of gold, silver, wood, or even the worship of nature. External gods to fill an internal vacuum. The prophet Jeremiah who lived in the seventh century BC, lamented that these man-made gods would eventually "perish from the earth" (Jer 10:11 KJV.) Jeremiah admonished that these were false gods and the only true God is the God who made the heavens, the earth, and the seas (Jer 10:10–16.) The same lament holds true for us today.

The King James Version of the Bible is used extensively in this book, both the Old and New Testaments, to show the consistent continuity of God's Word. Although written by forty human agents over a fifteen-hundred-year span, the Bible is inspired by the Holy Spirit (2 Pet 1:20–21; 2 Tim 3:16.) This book is saturated with many Bible verses to show the harmony of God's word and to allow those seeking for truth to search the scriptures for themselves. Each verse is like a puzzle piece that fits together to reveal the whole picture. The Bible ought to be studied line upon line, precept upon precept, here a little and there a little (Isa 28:13.) Each piece paints a picture of the Godhead and unfolds the testimony of Jesus Christ, earth's physical ambassador of the Godhead (John 5:36–39.) This book also explores the profound themes of threes, that not only reveals the unified sovereign governance of the Godhead but validates its triunity.

The Bible is not just a book, it is a library. It is the encyclopedic living Word of God. Let's embark into this library that will reveal the mystery of this triune Godhead.

Introduction

Understanding God

Giant sequoias are called nature's skyscrapers. They are one of the largest and tallest trees in the world. They are the third longest lived species and can grow to a diameter of thirty feet and some have recorded heights of three hundred and eleven feet. How can a gigantic three-hundred-foot sequoia redwood tree come from such a small sequoia seed pod the size of a pinhead, 0.16–10.20 inches?

As we ponder this perplexing enigma, we can ask another mysterious question. How can such a huge cosmic God who created the infinite vastness of the visible and invisible universe and galaxies also be an unseen divine Spirit? How could an infinite God become a tiny, finite baby born in a manger pod?

Ponder this . . . God became a tiny baby.

Understanding God is to understand the mystery of a seed. A seed is an infinity of trees. It is planted, it grows into a tree and bears fruits with seeds. The "new" seeds are planted, they grow into trees and bear fruits with seeds. Those seeds are planted, they grow and bear fruits with seeds. The cycle is never ending. A seemingly intrinsic origin with no extrinsic birth. There is no inherent beginning and no inherent end.

Jesus Christ, the finite man, yet was a minute infinity of the Godhead when he walked the earth. He was fully man, yet fully divine, and fully God. The infinite, immeasurable, vastness of divinity in a concentrated vessel of a human capsule.

"I am Alpha and Omega, the beginning and the ending, saith the Lord, which is, and which was, and which is to come, the Almighty" (Rev 1:8.)

— 1 —

3 Yet 1

Can you identify these trees without their fruits?

Can you now identify these trees?

What does a tree have to do with the Godhead? Would you be able to identify the tree without the fruit? Even if you were able to identify the tree, you perhaps had seen it before laden with its fruits. The fruit revealed the tree. Likewise, Jesus said that he came to reveal the Father (Matt 12:33.) God, the heavenly Father is like the tree. Jesus is like the fruit.

> Matt 12:33—"Either make the tree good, and his fruit good or else make the tree corrupt, and his fruit corrupt, for the *tree is known by his fruit.*"
>
> Luke 6:44—"For every *tree is known by his own fruit.*"
>
> John 16:28—"*I came forth from the Father* and am come into the world."

John 17:5,8—"And now, O Father, glorify thou me with thine own self with the glory which I had with thee before the world was. For I have given unto them the words which thou gavest me, and they have received them, and have known *surely that I came out from thee*, and they have believed that thou didst send me."

A tree has three key components:

- tree (the trunk with limbs and branches)
- fruit
- seed

It is interesting to note that the word *tree* is found in the word *three*. The Godhead is also a triunity—three in one.

- Father (God)
- Son (Jesus Christ)
- Holy Spirit (Holy Ghost/Comforter)

Can Three Be One?

If a tree has three components, likewise the Creator who made the tree, can and does exist in three components. If a tree is one cohesive whole, likewise the Godhead is a cohesive whole. All three are one.

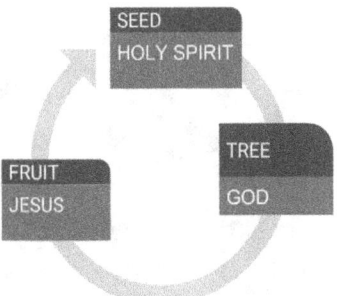

A seed is infinitude packaged into a minute finite capsule. The seed holds all three from the beginning—the seed itself, the tree, and the fruit. It takes on a finite form, yet it is infinite. The finite seed is buried in the ground, but it gives of itself, i.e., it transforms itself to become a tree which births fruits that hold more seeds. This infinite cycle is repeated over and over and over again. One seed but there are three co-existing components in this never-ending infinite cycle. Each component visibly unfolds at different stages and takes on separate forms, yet each can and does exist together at the same time—co-existing and codependent and co-eternal. They exist at the same time because we see a tree in full bloom laden with fruits with seeds in it and the remnants of the unseen seed lay deep in the hearth of the earth. They take on separate forms as a seed, a tree, and a fruit, yet they are one.

Such is the Godhead—three yet one. The Holy Spirit is like the unseen seed force. The Father is the paternal tree structure. Jesus, the son is the fruit, the visible representative of the Godhead. He became a finite man although he was eternal and divinely infinite. Jesus lived in human form for thirty-three years. He died and was buried in the "heart of the earth" (Matt 12:40.) He died temporarily, rose on the third day, became the "firstfruits of them that slept," and returned to heaven to reunite with the heavenly Father (1 Cor 15:20.) While on earth, Jesus was a minute infinity of God—and yet Jesus was God.

If the rational deductive mind accepts that the seed is the tree is the fruit, then the same must hold true that the Holy Spirit is God is Jesus. Similarly, the triune Godhead in wisdom has coded and pre-programmed elements of nature, plants, animals, birds, humanity, and its own self to be three in one—a cohesive trinity. The triune cycle of life is replicated throughout creation.

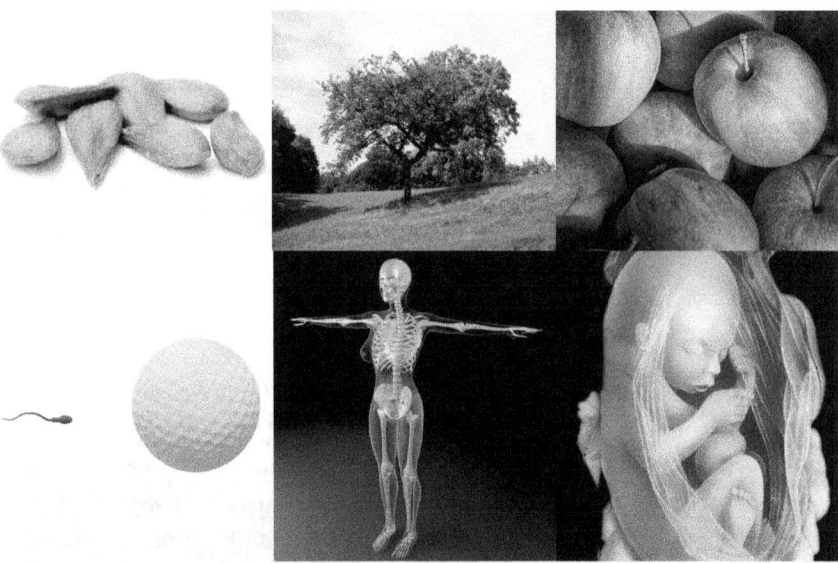

Gen 1:29—"And God said, behold, I have given you every herb bearing seed, which is upon the face of all the earth, and every tree, in the which is the fruit of a tree yielding seed, to you it shall be for meat."

The seed incubates the tree. The tree incubates the fruit. The fruit incubates the seed. The sperm (semen) and egg incubate human life. The human body incubates a baby. The baby incubates the same cyclical reproductive system. This is the infinite triune cycle of life.

> Fun Facts: Translation of seed in different languages: Latin (semen), German (samen), Finnish (siemen), Italian (seme), Portuguese (semente), Russian (semya), Spanish (semilla), Bulgarian (cemeha), Croatian (sjeme), Slovak (semeno.) Semen originated from Latin and means seed or sowing. Words such as insemination, seminar, seminary, and disseminate originated from this root word "sem," which means to impart or plant inside of someone or something, whether that means seeds, genetic matter, words, exchange of knowledge or ideas etc. The etymology or the study of the origin of words profoundly reveals that "sem" means one, as one, together with, same, equal like, likeness. It is from "sem" that words such as assemble, ensemble, similar, and simultaneous originated.

Here are some biblical references for seed:

- Seed = embryonic plant, Gen 1:11 or offspring Matt 22:24 (literal interpretation)
- Seed = semen, Gen 38:8–9 (literal interpretation)
- Seed = word of God, Luke 8:11; Matt 13:19 (spiritual interpretation)

The triunity of the seed capsule is potent evidence of superior construct and engineering. The omniscient, omnipotent, omnipresent Godhead, in wisdom created infinity in finite ways—inside finite capsules lies infinite creative force. This same triune Godhead created something out of nothing. This is the mysteries of the Godhead. Three creative forces existing together as one—three yet one.

> Fun Facts: The sun is divided into three regions; the interior, the solar atmosphere (chromosphere and corona), and the surface (photosphere.) The interior has three main parts; the core, the radiative zone, and the convective zone.

— 2 —

3 Persons, 1 Godhead

Mystery of the Godhead and the Tree

(Father. Son. Holy Spirit: Tree. Fruit. Seed)

Mystery of the Tree

seed ↔ tree ↔ fruit
Without the seed there is no tree. Without the tree there is no fruit.
fruit ↔ seed ↔ tree
Without the fruit there is no seed. Without the seed there is no tree.
tree ↔ fruit ↔ seed
Without the tree there is no fruit. Without the fruit there is no seed.

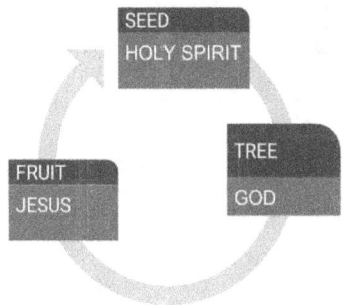

If a fruit were to say that it came into existence on its own or through some evolutionary process over time or epochs of change, it would be denying that it came from the tree. It accepts that it has flesh and seeds, as this is impossible for it to deny, but how can it deny the tree? If a tree were to say that it came into existence on its own or through some evolutionary process over time without its seed, it would be impossible to rationalize how it knew what kind of tree it would be or what fruit to bear. If a seed said it came into existence on its own or through some evolutionary process over time, then it would be denying its connection to the tree and the fruit. If it evolved over time, what was it before it became a seed? How did it determine what seed it would be? What would be its purpose if it only remained a seed? Then, there would be no trees nor fruits. A fruit that looks at itself and assumes that it evolved by itself, denying that it came from a tree or that the tree even exists, is like someone who assumes that they evolved by themselves and denies that they were created by God and denies that God exists. This would be akin to Adam and Eve, the first parents denying that they were created. A tree that looks at itself and assumes it evolved by itself, denying its connection to the seed or fruit is like someone who accepts that they have a body and accepts that God created them—however they deny the existence of Jesus and deny the existence of the Holy Spirit.

A seed that looks at itself and assumes it evolved by itself and denies that it came from a tree and a fruit is like a person who denies that he or she has parents. Spiritually, this is akin to someone denying that God or Jesus exists yet believe in a mystical spirit being.

The stem of a fruit is nature's umbilical cord connecting the fruit to the branch where it gets its nourishment. Same premise with humans, we have an umbilical cord connecting us in the womb, enabling us to get nourishment while we develop. When we are born, the cord is severed leaving a belly button (navel) which is a mark showing our connection to our mother. Not only are we connected to our earthly mothers, but we are connected to our heavenly Father through Jesus Christ. "I am the vine, ye are the branches, he that abideth in me, and I in him, the same bringeth forth much fruit, for without me ye can do nothing" (John 15:5.) The psalmist David beautifully pens an homage to the wise divine designer in Ps 139:13–17:

> "for thou hast possessed my reins, thou hast covered me in my mother's womb. I will praise thee, for I am fearfully and wonderfully made, marvelous are thy works, and that my soul knoweth right well. My substance was not hid from thee, when I was made in secret, and curiously wrought in the lowest parts of the earth. Thine eyes did see my substance, yet being unperfect, and in thy book all my members were written, which in continuance were fashioned, when as yet there was none of them. How precious also are thy thoughts unto me, O God! how great is the sum of them!"

Why Three? Why is the Number Three so Significant?

If you only had the fruit and its seed, then the assumption is that the seed evolved into a fruit without a tree. How then could the fruit exist without a tree on which to hang and nourish itself? If you only had the fruit and the tree, how would the tree evolve without the seed? If you only had the tree and the seed, then where did the seed come from? Then the fruit would never exist.

- In order to have the fruit, you need the tree and the seed.
- In order to have the seed, you need fruit and the tree.
- In order to have the tree, you need the seed and the fruit.

One must have the two others to exist, all three are needed to function as a whole. It is equally impossible to think of the Godhead as only one eternal person. The Godhead must therefore be composed of three co-eternal beings—God the Father, Jesus Christ the Son, and the Holy Spirit.

Mystery of the Seed

The mystery of the triune Godhead is wonderfully perplexing as the mystery of a seed. What is in the seed that determines what it will be? God, the all-wise Creator brilliantly programmed and coded the seed. How does a pumpkin seed know that it will become a pumpkin and not a squash?

A seed is finite yet infinite. Finite because it will die when it is planted in the soil, but this is not death but the beginning of a miraculous transformation of its former self (shell.) It begins to release and disseminate the precoded signals like antennas sending out signals to grow roots, stems, trunk, branches, leaves, and eventually becomes a tree that bears fruit. It is infinite because it reproduces itself in this unending cycle of continuous life. There is no difference between the seed, the tree, or the fruit except that they took on different forms but inherently they are the same. They work together to accomplish one goal.

Jesus came to earth in human form; a finite man who lived thirty-three years. Yet, he was fully divine. Thirty-three and the number three within themselves are profound numbers. When Jesus died and laid in the tomb, it was the beginning of the transformative process of preparing to return to heaven in a transformed body. After he rose from the dead, he told Mary not to touch him as he had not yet ascended to the Father (John 20:17.) God, Jesus, and the Holy Spirit took on different roles and forms to accomplish one divine mission—yet they are one. Likewise, the seed, tree, and fruit have different forms, roles, emergence—yet they function together for the same unified purpose. There are many vast mysteries in God's creation to contemplate. Here are just a few.

Fragrance

If trees, plants, fruits, and flowers evolved over time as the theory of evolution ascribes, how could an intangible element as fragrance evolve over time? A rose is perfumed with fragrance. A mango has a strong sweet distinct redolence. Fragrance is not influenced by its external environment; it smells like a rose regardless of external influences. If the external environment is hot, cold, dry, or humid, the rose still smells like a rose. A rose smells the same a hundred years ago as it does today. Different flowers have different fragrances and different herbs have their own unique aroma. How can fragrance be programmed into a seed? Fragrance is invisible, intangible, yet it brings potent evidence of a wise creative designer. It is God's signature on nature which man cannot create. Man can only attempt to replicate in a lab through trial and error.

Color

Fruits, flowers, trees, and herbs have vastly different colors. How can color be programmed into a seed, that regardless of the soil it is planted in, it still inherently maintains the color it was programmed to be? How does a fruit, flower, plant, tree, or herb know what color it will be?

Nutritional Content

Fruits, vegetables, and herbs have a vast variety of nutrients needed for the human body. There are thirteen essential vitamins. How is this programmed into different seeds? Why do different fruits, vegetables have different vitamins, minerals, and nutritional content?

Taste

Every fruit, vegetable, herb, nut, and grain have their own unique taste and flavor. Some are sweet, some sour, some are spicy, some are bitter etc. Taste receptors in the mouth's taste buds triggers a sensory explosion of flavor.

Animal Instincts

Animals have innate instincts—a bird instinctively knows how to fly and make nests, bees make hives, and beavers build dams. Animals exhibit these similar behaviors regardless of the varying and diverse geographic regions they are in. These instincts could not be the result of evolution.

Human Emotions and Talents

Humans are created with a variety of emotions and talents. God has precoded every person with unique gifts and talents to be used for his glory. You cannot tell by just looking at someone what those gifts or talents are. If humans came into being by evolution, how could emotions and talents evolve over time? If humans evolved over time, did emotions and talents start at a lower base level and then evolved over time? How would it have known that it reached its highest level?

Fragrance, color, taste, texture, nutrition, emotions, talents, instincts, are clear proof of a superior, supremely wise designer. God in wisdom created these additional intangible components that no human effort can perfectly replicate. God is the all-knowing, all-wise Creator!

> Ps 19:1—"The heavens declare the glory of God and the firmament sheweth his handywork."

> Job 12:7–10—"But ask now the beasts, and they shall teach thee, and the fowls of the air, and they shall tell thee or speak to the earth, and it shall teach thee, and the fishes of the sea shall declare unto thee. Who knoweth not in all these that the hand of the Lord hath wrought this? In whose hand is the soul of every living thing, and the breath of all mankind."

Creation points to the Creator. The magnificent engineering of a simple yet complex seed is the handiwork of the triune Godhead. Understanding the mystery of the seed, the tree, and the fruit will unveil the mystery of the Godhead. We will now examine these parallels using the Bible.

How is the Seed Likened to the Holy Spirit?

Q: Who or what is the Holy Spirit?

A: The Comforter

> John 14:26—"But the Comforter which is the Holy Spirit which the Father will send in my name."

Q: Who is the Comforter?

A: The Spirit of Truth

> John 14:16–17—"And I will pray the Father, and he shall give you another Comforter, that he may abide with you forever, even the Spirit of truth, whom the world cannot receive, because it seeth him not, neither knoweth him but ye know him, for he dwelleth with you, and shall be in you."

John 15:26—"But when the Comforter is come, whom I will send unto you from the Father, even the Spirit of Truth, which proceedeth from the Father, he shall testify of me."

Q: Who is the Spirit of Truth?

A: The Word (Holy Word of God)

John 17:17—"Sanctify them by the word; thy word is truth."

Eph 1:13—"In whom ye also trusted, after that ye heard the word of truth, the gospel of your salvation, in whom also after that ye believed, ye were sealed with that holy Spirit of promise."

Q: What or who is the Word?

A: Liken to a seed

Luke 8:11—"Now the parable is this, the seed is the word of God."

Mark 4:14—"The sower soweth the word."

1 Pet 1:23—"Being born again, not of corruptible seed, but of incorruptible, by the word of God, which liveth and abideth forever."

Summary: Holy Spirit → Comforter → Spirit of Truth → word → seed. Therefore, the Holy Spirit is likened to the seed.

How is the Fruit Likened to Jesus?

Q: How was Jesus conceived?

A: Of a virgin by the Holy Spirit

Luke 1:35,42—"And the angel said unto her the Holy Ghost shall come upon thee, and the power of the Highest shall overshadow thee; therefore, also that holy thing which shall be born of thee shall be called the Son of God. Blessed are thou among women and blessed is the *fruit* of thy womb."

The Holy Spirit was the spiritual seed that overshadowed Mary and she conceived and gave birth to the fruit, which was Jesus. Therefore, the fruit is likened to Jesus. Although Jesus is primarily the fruit, parallels to the seed can also be drawn.

How is the Seed Likened to Jesus?

Q: How does Jesus describe himself?

A: The way, the truth, and the life

> John 14:6—"Jesus said, I am the way, the truth, and the life; no man cometh to the Father, but by me."

Q: What is truth?

A: The word (which is likened to a seed)

> John 17:17—"Sanctify them by the word; thy word is truth."

Q: Who or what is the word?

A: Likened to the seed

A: Likened to Jesus

> Luke 8:11—"Now the parable is this, the seed is the word of God."
>
> John 1:1,14—"In the beginning was the Word, and the Word was with God, and the Word was God. And the Word was made flesh, and dwelt among us, and we beheld his glory, the glory as of the begotten of the Father, full of grace and truth."
>
> Rev 19:13—"And he was clothed with a vesture dipped in blood and his name is called the Word of God."

If the seed is the word of God and that Word became flesh (Jesus); therefore, the seed is also likened to Jesus. If Jesus is likened to the seed and the Holy Spirit is also likened to the seed, therefore Jesus is one with the Holy Spirit. Jesus is the same in purpose with the Holy Spirit.

How is a Tree or Plant Likened to Jesus?

Q: What is Jesus' self-description?

A: A vine

John 15:1-6—"I am the true vine, and my Father is the husbandman. Every branch in me that beareth not fruit he taketh away, and every branch that beareth fruit, he purgeth it, that it may bring forth more fruit. Now ye are clean through the word which I have spoken unto you. Abide in me, and I in you. As the branch cannot bear fruit of itself, except it abide in the vine, no more can ye, except ye abide in me. I am the vine, ye are the branches, he that abideth in me, and I in him, the same bringeth forth much fruit, for without me ye can do nothing. If a man abide not in me, he is cast forth as a branch, and is withered, and men gather them, and cast them into the fire, and they are burned."

Isa 53:2—"For he shall grow up before him as a tender plant, and as a root out of a dry ground, he hath no form nor comeliness, and when we shall see him, there is no beauty that we should desire him."

Note: Isaiah prophesied the coming Messiah, seven hundred years before his birth.

How is God and the Kingdom of God Likened to the Seed, Fruit, and Tree?

Mark 4:30-32—"And he said, 'whereunto shall we liken the kingdom of God or with what comparison shall we compare it? It is like a grain of mustard seed, which, when it is sown in the earth, is less than all the seeds that be in the earth. But when it is sown, it groweth up, and becometh greater than all herbs, and shooteth out great branches, so that the fowls of the air may lodge under the shadow of it.'"

Mark 4:26-29—"And he said, 'so is the kingdom of God, as if a man should cast seed into the ground and should sleep, and rise night and day, and the seed should spring and grow up, he knoweth not how. For the earth bringeth forth fruit of herself; first the blade, then the ear, after that the full corn in the ear. But when the fruit is brought forth, immediately he putteth in the sickle, because the harvest is come.'"

If the kingdom of God is likened to seed, fruit, and tree and Jesus is also likened to the same, and the Holy Spirit is likened to seed; therefore, they are all equal—sharing the same experience, purpose, and mission. Jesus outrightly proclaimed that he is one with the Father, in response to Philip's request to show them the Father.

John 14:9-11,20—"Jesus saith unto him, 'have I been so long time with you, and yet hast thou not known me, Philip, he that hath seen me hath seen the Father, and how sayest thou then, show us the Father? Believest thou not that I am in the Father, and the Father in me? The words that I speak unto you I speak not of myself, but the Father that dwelleth in me, he doeth the works. Believe me that I am in the Father, and the Father in me, or else believe me for the very works' sake. At that day ye shall know that I am in my Father, and ye in me, and I in you.'"

More Bible references and declarations of Jesus being one with God, the Father:

John 10:30,38—"I and my Father are one. But if I do, though ye believe not me, believe the works, that ye may know, and believe, that the Father is in me, and I in him."

John 17:11—"And now I am no more in the world, but these are in the world, and I come to thee. Holy Father, keep through thine own name those whom thou hast given me, that they may be one, as we are."

John 16:27-28—"For the Father himself loveth you, because ye have loved me, and have believed that I came out from God. I came forth from the Father, and am come into the world; again, I leave the world, and go to the Father."

1 Tim 3:16—"And without controversy great is the mystery of godliness, God was manifest in the flesh, justified in the Spirit, seen of angels, preached unto the Gentiles, believed on in the world, received up into glory."

John 5:18—"Therefore the Jews sought the more to kill him, because he not only had broken the sabbath, but said also that God was his Father, making himself equal with God. That all men should honor the Son, even as they honor the Father. He that honoreth not the Son honoreth not the Father which hath sent him."

Col 2:8-9—"Beware lest any man spoil you through philosophy and vain deceit, and after the tradition of men, after the rudiments of the world, and not after Christ. For in him dwelleth all the fullness of the Godhead bodily."

1 Cor 15:45-47—"And so it is written, the first man Adam was made a living soul; the last Adam was made a quickening spirit. Howbeit that was not first which is spiritual, but that which is

natural, and afterward that which is spiritual. The first man is of the earth, earthy; the second man is the Lord from heaven."

2 Cor 4:4—"In whom the god of this world hath blinded the minds of them which believe not, lest the light of the glorious gospel of Christ, who is the image of God, should shine unto them."

Symbiosis

The seed is in the fruit. The fruit is in the tree. The tree is in the seed. You cannot separate the seed from the fruit. You cannot separate the fruit from the tree. You cannot separate the tree from the seed. Similarly, you cannot separate the Holy Spirit from Jesus. You cannot separate Jesus from God. You cannot separate God from the Holy Spirit. You cannot approach the tree without also approaching the fruit and vice versa. You cannot access the seed without accessing the fruit. You cannot partake of the fruit without encountering the seed. Similarly, you cannot encounter the Father without encountering the Son, Jesus Christ and vice versa. You cannot encounter the Holy Spirit without encountering Jesus. You cannot partake of a sustaining symbiotic relationship with Jesus without encountering the abiding Holy Spirit.

> 1 John 2:22-23—"Who is a liar but he that denieth that Jesus is the Christ? He is antichrist, that denieth the Father and the Son. Whosoever denieth the Son, the same hath not the Father, but he that acknowledgeth the Son hath the Father also."

Summary

Holy Spirit ↔ God ↔ Jesus

Without the Holy Spirit there is no God and without God there is no Jesus.

Jesus ↔ Holy Spirit ↔ God

Without Jesus there is no Holy Spirit and without the Holy Spirit there is no God.

God ↔ Jesus ↔ Holy Spirit

Without God there is no Jesus and without Jesus there is no Holy Spirit.

— 3 —

3 Roles, 1 Mission
Mission Possible

This chapter explores the roles and core mission of the Godhead in the context that each member is revealed at different stages and phases—yet they participate and exist together at the same time. In the context of human understanding, we see separate beings existing at different stages but from the perspective of the Godhead, they exist at the same time.

By way of recapping:

Jesus ↔ Holy Spirit ↔ God

fruit ↔ seed ↔ tree

Without Jesus there is no Holy Spirit and without the Holy Spirit there is no God and without God there is no Jesus. Without a fruit there is no seed and without a seed there is no tree and without a tree there is no fruit. The Holy Spirit was sent after Jesus left earth but was also on earth before Jesus was born. The Holy Spirit also played an active role in Jesus' ministry but was not dispatched to aid the disciples until Jesus was about to depart. Can a seed come after the fruit and also before the fruit? The answer is yes. When Jesus was about to leave the disciples (physical realm) and return to heaven (spiritual realm), he imparted to them the promise of the coming of the Holy Spirit.

> John 16:7—"Nevertheless I tell you the truth, it is expedient for you that I go away, for if I go not away, the Comforter will not come unto you, but if I depart, I will send him unto you."

John 7:38–39—"He that believeth on me, as the scripture hath said, out of his belly shall flow rivers of living water. But this spake he of the Spirit, which they that believe on him should receive, for the Holy Ghost was not yet given, because Jesus was not yet glorified."

Jesus departed so that the Comforter (Holy Spirit) could make its appearance. Similarly, it is impossible for a seed to come into view without the fruit first being stripped and peeled away—outer flesh removed to reveal the seed. It was impossible for the Holy Spirit, in a physical aspect, to be revealed to the disciples until Jesus departed to continue the spiritual intercessory work in heaven. Jesus wanted the disciples to recognize that the Holy Spirit was an integral part of the triune Godhead, whose work was distinct, yet in complete harmony with the mission. The mission was the great plan of salvation to save mankind. "And I will pray the Father and he shall give you *another Comforter*, that he may abide with you forever" (John 12:16.) Jesus identified himself as a Comforter, in that he would ask the Father for *another* type of Comforter, in the form of the Holy Spirit. He identified himself as one in purpose with the Holy Spirit. The Holy Spirit is another member of the Godhead that would be given to mankind in a more omnipresent role. Jesus was limited to the small geographical surrounding areas where he lived but the Holy Spirit would not be limited to space, time, or region. In John 14:17–18, Jesus identified who the Holy Spirit is—"even the Spirit of truth, whom the world cannot receive, because it seeth him not, neither knoweth him, but ye know him, for he dwelleth with you, and shall be in you. I will not leave you comfortless, I will come to you." Jesus tells the disciples that the Holy Spirit will abide in them forever, i.e., the Spirit of truth. Then explicitly tells them that he himself will come to them in the form and conduit of the Holy Spirit.

Who is this Spirit of truth? Jesus in a few verses earlier had proclaimed to the disciples that, "I am the way, *the truth*, and the life; no man cometh unto the Father but by me" (John 14:6.) He expounded to them that, not only was he abiding *with* them in the physical realm, but he shall be *in* them via conduit of the Holy Spirit, in the spiritual realm. He is one with the Holy Spirit in mission and purpose and will continue to share in the same experience in the plan of salvation.

The Holy Spirit was revealed more clearly after Jesus' departure yet interacted with mankind before Jesus' birth. Jesus was born of the Holy Spirit to the virgin Mary. Elisabeth, Mary's cousin, also had an encounter with the Holy Spirit. Her unborn child was said to be filled with the Holy Spirit from the womb (Luke 1:15.) Her unborn son John would become the forerunner of Jesus.

Herein is another mystery—a seed is revealed more clearly when the fruit is peeled and exposed; yet the seed inherently existed before the fruit because it was the genetic blueprint of the seed that became the tree that bore that fruit, that now holds the seed. The seed is from the beginning and yet also is the end. The same is true for the triune Godhead—it is alpha and omega, beginning with no immanent end.

> Matt 1:18–20—"Now the birth of Jesus Christ was on this wise, when as his mother Mary was espoused to Joseph, before they came together, she was found with child of the Holy Ghost. Then Joseph her husband, being a just man, and not willing to make her a public example, was minded to put her away privily. But while he thought on these things, behold, the angel of the Lord appeared unto him in a dream, saying, 'Joseph, thou son of David, fear not to take unto thee Mary thy wife, for that which is conceived in her is of the Holy Ghost.'"

> Luke 1:35—"And the angel answered and said unto her, 'the Holy Ghost shall come upon thee, and the power of the Highest shall overshadow the, therefore also that holy thing which shall be born of thee shall be called the Son of God.'"

The Holy Spirit was sent by God at conception and Jesus was born "of the Holy Spirit." It was the same Holy Spirit that guided and aided Jesus throughout his earthly ministry. Jesus imparted the Holy Spirit to the disciples and by extension to all mankind when he returned to heaven. The Holy Spirit is eternal. Jesus identified himself as another Comforter, showing that he is one in power and purpose with the Holy Spirit. If the Holy Spirit is eternal, then Jesus is also eternal.

There are different phases, stages, and roles of the Holy Spirit. The Holy Spirit was sent by God and was supernaturally buried into Mary's womb; no human eyes saw this. Perhaps God spoke a word into Mary's womb. God's word is life. It is the same Holy Spirit that was present at the creation of the earth. "And the Spirit of God moved upon the face of the waters" (Gen 1:2.) Jesus was also present at creation, he was the Word that became flesh and dwelt among us (John 1:1–3.) The trinity of the Godhead were active in the creation of the world and in the plan of salvation. Each taking on different roles at different times but all sharing jointly in the same experience.

A tree does not immediately bear fruit, it bears fruit in the fullness of time, in its seasons. Jesus is like the fruit and God is like the tree. Jesus was the fruit that came to bear witness of the Father and of God's word (truth) in the fullness of time.

> Gal 4:4—"But when the fulness of the time was come, God sent forth his Son, made of a woman, made under the law."

> John 18:37—"Thou sayest that I am a King. To this end was I born, and for this cause came I into the world, that I should bear witness unto the truth. Everyone that is of the truth heareth my voice."

Each member of the Godhead has a distinct role. Yet the mission is the same. They were revealed at different times and stages to humanity but they were always coeval—existed at same time throughout eternity. They work in perfect cohesive harmony to accomplish this mission.

> 1 John 5:6-8—"This is he that came by water and blood, even Jesus Christ; not by water only, but by water and the blood. And it is the Spirit that beareth witness because the Spirit is truth. For there are three that beareth witness in heaven, the Father, the Word, and the Holy Spirit, and these three are one. And there are three that bear witness in earth, the spirit, and the water, and the blood, and these three agree in one."

God (the Father), the Word (Jesus Christ), and the Holy Spirit are one. God sent Jesus to earth aided by the Holy Spirit. The Spirit, the water, and the blood are also spiritual witnesses in this mission. A seed is not seen unless it is unveiled in the fruit. The same is true with the Holy Spirit; it is the unseen member of the Godhead. Strong's Concordance defines seed as a masculine noun which means offspring, descendant, or sowing. The Latin for seed is *semen*. The seed (Holy Spirit), came upon Mary and overshadowed her, sparking the birth of the spiritual fruit, Jesus. This is another divine mystery of the Godhead.

Accepting the Father, Accepting the Son, Accepting the Holy Spirit

Can a fruit be picked from a tree without approaching the tree? How can you then approach God without also acknowledging the fruit, Christ Jesus or vice versa? When we eat a fruit, are we not eating of the tree? Is this what Jesus meant when he said, "no man cometh unto the Father, but by me" (John 14:6.) You cannot accept God without accepting Jesus. You cannot accept Jesus without accepting God. Likewise, you cannot accept that a tree exists if you deny that its fruit is real. If you believe a tree exists, then you inherently must also accept that its fruit is real. How can one believe that a tree exists but still deny that its fruit is real or deny that the fruit came from the tree? Accepting Jesus means to inherently accept God. Accepting God means inherently accepting Jesus and by extension the Holy Spirit. No one can come to an understanding and an acceptance of who God is without an understanding and acceptance of who Jesus is. Jesus came by the Holy Spirit in the flesh.

Can you eat a fruit without encountering the seeds or deny that the seeds exist? Likewise, we cannot accept Jesus without also encountering the Holy Spirit. God is a Spirit and those that worship him must worship him in spirit and truth—the spirit is the Holy Spirit, and the truth is Jesus (John 4:24.) The worship of God embodies the trinity. The Godhead took on different forms to accomplish one divine mission, and that ultimate mission is to save mankind and for mankind to encounter this coeval trinity.

— 4 —

3 Persons, 1 Name

Je. Ho.Vah

(Je = Jesus Ho = Holy Spirit Vah = God)

> Exod 6:2–3—"And God spake unto Moses, and said unto him, 'I am the Lord, and I appeared unto Abraham, unto Isaac, and unto Jacob, by the name of God Almighty, but by my name JEHOVAH was I not known to them.'"
>
> Ps 83:18—"That men may know that thou, whose name alone is Jehovah, art the most high over all the earth."
>
> Fun Fact: Jehovah appears seven times in the Bible (KJV); this includes Jehovahjireh and Jehovahnissi, Jehovahshalom. Seven is God's number that represents perfection and completeness.

It cannot be by chance or coincidence that the name Jehovah incorporates the three members of the Godhead—Jesus, Holy Spirit, and God (Vah.) They are three persons sharing one name. The oneness of their name reflects the oneness of their nature, character, and mission.

What is the Meaning of Vah?

Vah is from the Hebrew word *ahavah*. Hebrew is not just the original language of the Bible but of the Creator. Ahavah, like most Hebrew words, is composed of three consonant root words that reveals the true meaning of the word. The root word "ahav" is spelt "aleph, hei, bet." Ahav means to give and ahava means love. You cannot love without giving.[1] "For God so loved the world that he gave his only begotten son" (John 3:16.) God is love, that is why he gave.

> "Love or 'ahava' in the Hebraic mind is very different in today's culture. In the Hebrew, love is connected directly with action and obedience. Strong's Exhaustive Dictionary defines ahava as 'to have affection, sexually or otherwise, love, like, to befriend, to be intimate.' It brings to mind the idea of longing for or breathing for another. Hebraically ahava is a verb and a noun, it is an act of doing. Ahava is not just a feeling. To get a clear understanding of ahava, let's examine the Hebrew word itself and learn how to love hebraically. First, most Hebrew words can be broken down to a three-consonant root word that contains the essence of the word's meaning. The root word of ahava is 'ahav.' The term ahav in Hebrew means, 'to give.' True ahava, true love, is more concerned about giving than receiving. Being the center of someone's attention isn't love. And love isn't about getting some feeling or fix. Ahava is about giving devotion and time. Giving is the vehicle of love. YHWH so loved the world that he gave His only Son. Meaningful relationships have mutual giving. Love may focus on receiving, but ahava is all about giving. There is a difference. Consider that the Hebrew word 'ahava' is not an emotion but an action. It is not something that happens 'to you' but a condition that you create when you give. You don't 'fall' in love—you give love!"[2]

Beautifully captured in this summary and bears repeating, ahava in Hebrew means love; "breathing for another," action, obedience, and giving. Our human understanding of love focuses on receiving but ahava is all about giving. Giving true unconditional love, giving devotion, and time. You don't fall in love but you give love. God demonstrated his immense love for mankind when he gave Adam his own breath. God breathed into Adam's nostrils and man became a living soul (Gen 2:7.) God gave us life by giving us his breath of life.

> Fun Facts: The first letter of the Hebrew alphabet, aleph, has a numerical value of one. The first letter of the English alphabet is "A" and has a value of one. Aleph is the first letter of ahava. God's

1. Rendelman, "Ahavah," para. 6–7.
2. Rendelman, "Ahavah," para. 6.

self-title is Alpha and Omega. God told Moses that his name is I AM. Jesus called God, "Abba" which means Father. God's love for mankind is agape love. Interesting to note, "A" is the first letter of the English alphabet and "M" is the thirteenth letter.

Ahavah which means love is connected to another Hebrew word, *echad* which means one. The numerical value of their letters is thirteen and it implies oneness; unity is the aspiration of love and love emerges from a perception of unity.[3] Though echad means one, its deeper meaning is that of a single entity with more than one part—one and the same; a unified oneness. This is profound—the numerical value of ahavah which means love is thirteen. The numerical value of echad which means one is also thirteen. Thirteen appears to be an important number to the triune Godhead. One in unity and one in love. The number thirteen consists of one and three. Therefore, triune Godhead means, one who are three, and three who are one—(1=3 and 3=1)!

Jesus pleaded with the disciples to be one just as he is one with the Father. John 17:21-23, "that they all may be one; as thou, Father, art in me, and I in thee, that they also may be one in us, that the world may believe that thou hast sent me. And the glory which thou gavest me I have given them, that they may be one, even as we are one. I in them, and thou in me, that they may be made perfect in one; and that the world may know that thou hast sent me, and hast loved them, as thou hast loved me."

Love can only be accomplished when there is oneness. The essence of God and of the name JEHOVAH, is love. Christ even implored us to love our enemies (Matt 5:44.) How do you love your enemies? Forgive them—love is to give, so when we forgive, we are giving forgiveness, which is an act of love. "Giving is the vehicle of love."[4] There are three commands to love in the Torah; "love your neighbor as yourself" (Lev 19:18), "love the stranger as yourself" (Lev 19:34), and "you shall love the Lord your God with all your heart, soul, and strength" (Deut 6:5.)"[5]

---

3. The Jewish Chronicle, "Ahavah," para. 1.
4. Rendelman, "Ahavah: Hebrew Word Study," para. 6.
5. The Jewish Chronicle, "Ahavah," para. 3.

God is Love

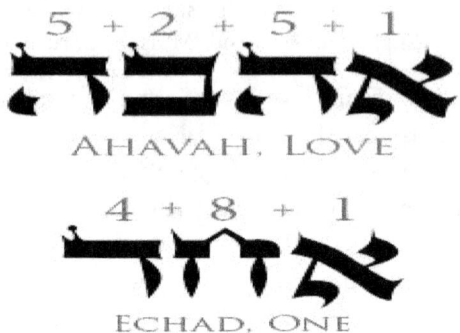

Ahavah = love = 13; Echad = one = 13. Therefore, Ahavah = Echad and love = one.

If God is love, therefore God is one. The triune Godhead is one in unity and love. One entity with three persons. True love is the common thread that binds all forms of relationships to the Godhead.

Marriage—One Rib, One Flesh, One Name

> Gen 2:21-24—"And the Lord God caused a deep sleep to fall upon Adam, and he slept, and he took one of his ribs, and closed up the flesh instead thereof; and the rib, which the Lord God had taken from man, made he a woman, and brought her unto the man. And Adam said, 'this is now bone of my bones, and flesh of my flesh; she shall be called woman, because she was taken out of man.' Therefore, shall a man leave his father and his mother, and shall cleave unto his wife, and they shall be one flesh."

Marriage was created in the garden of Eden as an intimate and sacred institution, a communal relationship with God at the center. So intimate was the creation of marriage that God took a piece of Adam, a rib that protected his heart and created the bond of love in the form of Eve. The Godhead qualifies a married couple as one flesh. Two people not just taking on one name, but one in love and purpose. The wife surrenders her maiden name and takes on the name of her husband. The husband gives her his name. True love seeks to serve. In a marriage a couple should always seek to serve each other; not self-seeking. Marriages should reflect the love and oneness of the Godhead.

Pentecost—One Day, One Place, One Accord

> Acts 2:1–4—"And when the day of Pentecost was fully come, they were all with one accord in one place. And suddenly there came a sound from heaven as of a rushing mighty wind, and it filled all the house where they were sitting. And there appeared unto them cloven tongues like as of fire, and it sat upon each of them. And they were all filled with the Holy Ghost, and began to speak with other tongues, as the Spirit gave them utterance."

On the day of Pentecost, the Holy Spirit fell upon the disciples because they were on one accord and in one place. Unity in mind, focus, and goal allows love to grow which allows for the manifestation of the Godhead and unification with their purpose.

The Church—One Lord, One Faith, One Baptism

> Eph 4:1–6—"I therefore, the prisoner of the Lord, beseech you that ye walk worthy of the vocation wherewith ye are called, with all lowliness and meekness, with longsuffering, forbearing one another in love; endeavoring to keep the unity of the Spirit in the bond of peace. There is one body, and one Spirit, even as ye are called in one hope of your calling; one Lord, one faith, one baptism, one God and Father of all, who is above all, and through all, and in you all."

The church, the bride of Christ must be spiritually married to Christ to be one with the Godhead. Having the Father's name engraved in their foreheads. One union with the Godhead; of one faith and of one baptism. As Jesus was about to depart for heaven, he gave the great commission and charged the disciples to "go ye therefore, and teach all nations, baptizing them in the name of the Father, and of the Son, and of the Holy Ghost" (Matt 28:19.) Spiritual marriage takes place at baptism; sinners symbolically receive a new name. It is the name of the triune Godhead—three persons, sharing one name. This name has equal weight, equal power, equal influence and is used with non-exclusive rights by each member of the Godhead.

Jesus confirmed this in the following declarations—"I am come in my Father's name" (John 5:43); "the works that I do in my Father's name, they bear witness of me" (John 10:25); "but the Comforter, which is the Holy Ghost, whom the Father will send in my name" (John 14:26); "whatsoever ye shall ask the Father in my name, he will give it you" (John 15:16); "Holy Father, keep through thine own name those whom thou hast given me, that they may be one, as we are" (John 17:11.) Scripture also declares—"and he was clothed with a vesture dipped in blood, and his name is called The Word of God" (Rev 19:13.) Jesus proclaimed, "I have declared unto them thy name, and will declare it, that the love wherewith thou hast loved me may be in them, and I in them" (John 17:26). That name is JEHOVAH. Their name is JEHOVAH!

— 5 —

3 Sons, 1 Man

Jesus

(Son of God. Son of Man. Son of David)

Matt 1:21—"And she shall bring forth a son, and thou shalt call his name Jesus, for he shall save his people from their sins."

Isa 7:14—"Therefore the Lord himself shall give you a sign, behold, a virgin shall conceive, and bear a son, and shall call his name Immanuel."

The name Jesus is the Greek derived version of the Hebrew *Yehoshua*, which means, "the Lord is salvation." The name Immanuel means "God with us." God took on the form of a man, born of a virgin through the power of the Holy Spirit, to dwell with man, to save mankind. The prophecy given to Isaiah, who lived 700 years before Christ, is just one of many messianic prophecies that foreshadowed and heralded the coming of the Messiah. The word Messiah is from the Hebrew *mashiach* which is translated as "Anointed One." The prophet Micah, who also lived 700 years before Jesus, prophesied of the place where Jesus would be born. "But thou, Bethlehem Ephratah, though thou be little among the thousands of Judah, yet out of thee shall he come forth unto me that is to be ruler in Israel, whose goings forth have been from of old, from everlasting." (Mic 5:2.) Ephratah is the ancient former name for Bethlehem, and it means abundance, fruitfulness, bearing fruit. Bethlehem means "house of bread." Jesus was the fruit of the Godhead who described himself as the living bread from heaven (John 6:32–35.) Throughout his earthly journey, Jesus was called by many names and titles. There were three specific titles that were commonly used and were ascribed to him to validate his heavenly origin, to define his earthly birth, and to underscore his mission. These titles were, "Son of God," "Son of Man," and "Son of David." Many used these titles to acknowledge his authority, while some used it with disdain, derision, and doubt.

Son of God

"Son of God" was the title bestowed upon Jesus before his birth. The angel Gabriel visited the virgin Mary and announced the immaculate conception. "And the angel answered and said unto her, 'the Holy Ghost shall come upon thee, and the power of the Highest shall overshadow thee; therefore, also that holy thing which shall be born of thee shall be called the Son of God'" (Luke 1:35.) He was the Son of the heavenly Father and yet he was one with the Father (John 10:30.) Jesus used this title as his own self-designation to validate his heavenly origin. It was an authoritative title. Jesus himself declared that even the "dead shall hear the voice of the Son of God, and they that hear shall live" (John 5:25.) The disciples proclaimed him to be the Son of God when they saw him walk on water (Matt 14:33.) Peter declared that he was the Son of the living God in response to Jesus' question, "who do men say that I the Son of Man am?" (Matt 16:16.) John bore witness that he was the Son of God when he saw the Holy Spirit in the form of a dove descend upon him at his baptism and heard the voice of God from heaven declaring that Jesus was his beloved son (John 1:34.) Nathanael confessed Jesus' pre-eminence that he was the Son of God when Jesus revealed to him that he saw him supernaturally under a fig tree. Martha confessed that he was the Son of God when he reminded her that he was the resurrection and the life and shortly thereafter brought Lazarus back to life. Jesus credited the resurrection of Lazarus to the glory of God so "that the Son of God might be glorified" (John 11:4,27.) The Ethiopian eunuch (finance minister) was baptized and confessed with his mouth that, "I believe that Jesus Christ is the Son of God" (Act 8:37.) The centurion standing guard at the foot of the cross, watching Jesus suspended above, when he saw the earthquake, and observed the three hours of unexplained darkness, and heard Jesus cried out before dying, had to proclaim that "truly this man was the Son of God" (Mark 15:39.) Even the mouths of unclean spirits declared that he was the Son of God when they beheld Jesus' healing power (Mark 3:11.) The demoniac of Gadarenes (east shore of Sea of Galilee), cried with a loud voice and confessed that Jesus was the Son of God before Jesus cast the demons from him and sent them into a herd of pigs (Mark 5:7–13.) Paul, after his conversion, preached and proclaimed throughout many cities and synagogues that Jesus was the Son of God (Acts 9:20.)

"Son of God" appears forty-eight times in the New Testament. Many believed and proclaimed that Jesus was the Son of God, but some used this title with doubt, skepticism, and disdain. While Jesus was in the wilderness fasting and praying, the devil, with disdain, tempted him and sought to cast doubt upon this title. "If thou be the Son of God," was the clause used twice by Satan in a futile attempt to plant a seed of doubt (Matt 4:3–6.) During Jesus' trials before Caiaphas, Pilate, and the council of scribes and elders, they skeptically asked if he was indeed the Son of God (Matt 26:63; Luke 22:70.) The jeering crowd at the foot of the cross mocked with derision, "if thou be the Son of God, come down from the cross" (Matt 27:40.) Skepticism, disdain, derision, and doubt did not thwart Jesus' mission nor diminish the power of his title. It is a title that is acclaimed with divine transformative power. "Whosoever shall confess that Jesus is the Son of God, God dwelleth in him, and he in God" (1 John 4:15.)

Son of Man

"Son of Man" appears eighty-six times in the New Testament and was the title ascribed to Jesus to define and validate his earthly birth and mission. He was fully God, fully divine, yet fully man, born of a woman through the power of the Holy Spirit. He was born to die, to save mankind. He suspended his divinity and humbled himself in human form. He identified with mankind, with the challenges and frailties of the human experience. "For we have not a high priest which cannot be touched with the feeling of our infirmities but was in all points tempted like as we are, yet without sin" (Heb 4:15.) Who did people say was the Son of Man? This is a question Jesus pointedly asked the disciples. This question implied and inferred that he was more than the substance of an earthly man. The answers varied; from John the Baptist, Elijah, Jeremiah, or one of the prophets. Jesus then promptly asked another pointed question, "but whom say ye that I am?" (Matt 16:13–15.) The answer came from Peter, who declared that Jesus was the Christ, the Son of the living God. The connection of the titles, "Son of God" and "Son of Man" was made with Peter's answer—Jesus was of a heavenly origin veiled in human flesh. A heavenly king born as a baby in a manger pod. A twelve-year-old boy having engaging and challenging discussions with doctors in the temple whilst his earthly parents sought him for three days; to whom he retorted that he must be about his Father's business. A carpenter with the hammer of divine authority. A son whose mother prodded him to turn water into wine at a wedding feast. When the title "Son of Man" was used, it was used to highlight one or both of these two dichotomies—his earthly connections to people and the human experience, and his heavenly origin and divine authority.

The Human Experience—Jesus declared that "the Son of Man came eating and drinking" and yet was accused of being a glutton, winebibber, friend of publicans, and sinners (Matt 11:19.) He came to minister to human needs; "the Son of Man came not to be ministered unto, but to minister" (Mark 10:45.) He related his affinity to Jonah's experience of being in a whale's belly for three days, "so shall the Son of Man be three days and three nights in the heart of the earth" (Matt 12:40.) He was without a home and felt as an outcast when he declared, "foxes have holes, and the bird of the air have nests, but the Son of Man has nowhere to lay his head" (Matt 8:20.) He was betrayed by a companion; "Judas betrayest thou the Son of Man with a kiss?" (Luke 22:48.) He would die; "the Son of Man is delivered into the hands of men, and they shall kill him" (Mark 9:31.)

Divine Authority—Jesus used the self-title of "Son of Man" to validate his divine authority and power. He declared, "that the Son of Man hath power on earth to forgive sins" (Matt 9:6.) The Son of Man was Lord of the Sabbath (Luke 6:5.) The Son of Man came to save lives (Luke 9:56.) The Son of Man had authority over heavenly angelic beings and will dispatch them to gather those who are sinners (Matt 13:41.) "The tribes of the earth shall mourn, and they shall see the Son of Man coming in the clouds of heaven" (Matt 24:30.) The Son of Man has authority to execute judgment (John 5:27.) The Son of Man has the power to give eternal life (John 6:27.) The Son of Man stands at the right hand of God (Acts 7:56.) The "Son of Man" is a title that is acclaimed with salvific power—"for the Son of Man is come to save that which was lost" (Matt 18:11.)

Son of David

The title "Son of David" appears fourteen times in the New Testament and authenticates the earthly genealogy of Jesus. He was born on earth and lived on earth; he had an earthly family tree. However, this title with a familial name did not diminish his divine authoritative power. The miracles and works that he performed, he ascribed to the credit and for the glory of the heavenly Father. Blind men, including Bartimaeus, cried out for healing, "thou Son of David, have mercy on us" (Matt 9:27; Mark 10:46.) The woman of Canaan, cried out, "have mercy on me, O Lord, thou Son of David, my daughter is grievously vexed with a devil" (Matt 15:22.) As he made the triumphant entry into Jerusalem, the crowd cried, "hosanna to the Son of David, blessed is he that cometh in the name of the Lord" (Matt 21:9.) However, after witnessing the many miracles, some used the title with skepticism to discredit his divine authority. "Is not this the Son of David?" they asked. The Pharisees accused him of casting out demons using the power or influence of devils. Jesus challenged their narrative by quizzically asking, "what think ye of Christ? whose son is he?" "They say unto him, the Son of David." Jesus then retorted, "if David then calls him Lord, how is he his son?" (Matt 12:23-24—22:42,45.) This conversation highlighted the paradox of his genealogy.

How was he one man, yet three sons? In contemporary colloquialism, he was the Son of God, born of the Holy Spirit, intravenously to earthly surrogate parents, Mary and Joseph, whose genealogy was of David. Divinity wrapped in the earthly genetic swaddling clothing of temporal flesh. Infinity in a human capsule; concentrated glory but equally as potent with power as the heavenly Father.

Messianic Prophecies

There were many prophecies that pointed to the coming Messiah. As noted in the introduction, the prophet Isaiah, who lived 700 years before Jesus, prophesied his birth. The circumstances surrounding Mary and Joseph's flight into Egypt to save baby Jesus from the decree by Herod to kill all the babies two years and under, was prophesied by Hosea who lived about 700 years before Christ and Jeremiah about 600 years (Hos 11:1; Jer 31:15.) These prophecies were corroborated in the New Testament account in Matt 2:13-18. The time of Jesus' baptism, his anointing as Messiah and the start of the priestly ministry was prophesied by Daniel, who lived about 600 years before Christ (Dan 9:24-25.) His method of teaching would be in parables (Ps 78:1-2) and was fulfilled in the account of Matt 13:34-35. The rejection of his priestly ministry by the people, and the sorrow he was to bear was prophesied by Isaiah (Isa 53:2-4.) His humble yet triumphant entrance into Jerusalem riding on a colt (donkey) was prophesied by Zechariah, who lived 500 years before Christ (Zech 9:9.) This prophecy was fulfilled and corroborated in the New Testament accounts of Mark 11:7-11, Matt 21:7-11, and Luke 19:35. His betrayal by Judas at the Last Supper and the price paid in this plot was prophesied by David and Zechariah (Ps 41:9; Zech 11;12-13.) David lived about 1000 years before Christ. These prophecies were corroborated in the New Testament accounts of John 13:2 and Matt 27:3. The trial and crucifixion was prophesied with specific details—his beard would be plucked out, he would be smitten, whipped on his back, he would be spat upon, gambling for his clothes, he kept silent during his trial, given vinegar to drink, crucified between two thieves, hands and feet pierced, none of his bones would be broken, buried with the rich, his body would not see corruption, he would rise from death (Isa 50:6—53:7-12; Zech 12:10; Ps 6:10—22:16-18—34:20—69:21.) These prophecies were corroborated in the New Testament verses of John 19:32-33; Luke 24:6-7; Matt 26:67—27:34-38,57-60.

Theme of Threes in the Life of Jesus

The profound theme of threes was evident throughout the life of Jesus. His earthly journey was paved with threes, an evidence of the spiritual presence of the heavenly Father and the abiding Holy Spirit. He was heaven's ambassador representing the triune Godhead. All three coexist together, sharing the same earthly experience through Jesus.

Birth—4 BC in a manger in Bethlehem, a city in Jerusalem which has an elevation of 777 meters. The number seven is a profound number within itself. Seven is God's number for perfection. Three wise men brought gifts of gold, frankincense, and myrrh (Matt 2:11)

Childhood—At the age of twelve his parents brought him to Jerusalem for Passover. Returning home they realized that we was not with them, and after searching for three days, he was found in the temple reasoning with the doctors, who were amazed by his wisdom (Luke 2:46-47)

Years on earth—thirty-three years

Baptism (beginning of ministry)—AD 27 at the age of thirty (Luke 3:21–23)

Length of ministry—three and a half years (Dan 9:26–27)

Temptation in wilderness—three temptations (Matt 4:1–11; Luke 4:1–12)

Replied to temptations—three responses of "it is written" (Matt 4:4,7,10; Luke 4:4,8,12)

Ministry (areas)—three key areas of teaching, preaching, and healing (Matt 9:35)

Witnesses—Jesus identified three witnesses that validated his authority—the Father, his work, and John the Baptist who was the forerunner of Jesus (John 5:36–37)

Prophecies—Jesus identified three things that fulfilled the prophecies of him—the law of Moses, the prophets, and the psalms (Luke 24:44)

First miracle performed—third day at a wedding in Cana (John 2:1)

Raised the dead—three accounts—son of the widow of Nain, Jairus' daughter, and Lazarus (Luke 7:14—8:54–55; John 11:43)

Walked on water—the disciples were at sea about twenty-five to thirty furlongs, which is three nautical miles from shore. It was the "fourth watch" which is between 3 am to 6 am. Three disciples recorded this (Matt 14:25; Mark 6:48–49; John 6:19)

Jesus wept—three accounts in Scripture—Lazarus' death, over Jerusalem, and nearing the crucifixion (John 11:35; Luke 19:41; Heb 5:7)

Transfiguration—three disciples as witnesses; Peter, James, and John (Mark 9:2–3)

God spoke audibly—three times recorded in New Testament that God spoke from heaven to Jesus in an audible voice that was heard by witnesses—Jesus' baptism, mount of transfiguration, and the final week before crucifixion (Matt 3:17; Mark 9:7; John 12:28)

Garden of Gethsemane—three disciples chosen from the disciples to accompany him while he prayed (Peter, James, and John.) He prayed for three specific things (himself, the disciples, and the church.) He prayed at three intervals (Mark 14:33,41; John 17:1–26)

Betrayal—Judas betrayed Jesus for thirty pieces of silver (Zech 11:12–13; Matt 27:3,9–10)

Crucifixion—AD 31 at the age of thirty-three. Jesus took the final 600-meter journey to Calvary bearing the cross along a processional passage called Via Dolorosa ("Sorrowful Way.") Three nails pierced his body to a cross made of three types of wood—fir, pine, and cypress (box wood.) A crude plaque written in three languages Greek, Latin, and Hebrew, was affixed to the top of the cross; it read "Jesus of Nazareth the King of the Jews." He was crucified at the "third hour," around 9 am. Three hours later, around noon, there was unexplained darkness throughout the land, for a duration of three hours, until 3 pm (the ninth hour.) He prayed three prayers, crying out to God—asking to forgive those that were crucifying him; asking why he was forsaken; commending his Spirit unto God (Dan 9:26–27; Isa 60:13; Luke 23:34–46; John 19:20; Mark 15:25,33–37; Matt 27:45–50)

Resurrection—three days in the tomb and rose on the third day. Three women came to tomb and was alerted by an angel (Matt 17:22–23; Acts 10:40; Mark 9:31—16:1–6; 1 Cor 15:4; Luke 9:22—24:46)

Three appearances to earth—first as a baby/died on cross/went to heaven; second as King from heaven to take the righteous to heaven/execute judgment/punish wicked; third will be after the millennium (one-thousand-year in heaven), Christ returns with the righteous (Luke 2:11; Acts 1:9–11; John 19:17–20; 1 Thess 4:16–17.) Note: In the second coming, Christ will not physically touch the earth but will be in the air and the saints will be "caught-up" to meet him.

"I come quickly"—three declarations by Jesus in the book of Revelation that he is coming quickly (Rev 22:7,12,20)

The Seventy-Week Prophecy

The seventy-week prophecy in the book of Daniel spans the anointing of Jesus as the Messiah, i.e., baptism, up to the time of the crucifixion. Daniel was a Jewish exile taken captive from Jerusalem during the invasion by Nebuchadnezzar, the Babylonian king in 605 BC. Although Daniel was schooled in the Babylonian culture and rose in the ranks, he never lost his connection with God. He obediently kept the commandments, even in the face of death. He received many prophetic dreams, visions, and interpretations from God and one of the most profound was the seventy-week prophecy.

Daniel 9:21-27

21. Yea, whiles I was speaking in prayer, even the man Gabriel, whom I had seen in the vision at the beginning, being caused to fly swiftly, touched me about the time of the evening oblation.

22. And he informed me, and talked with me, and said, O Daniel, I am now come forth to give thee skill and understanding.

23. At the beginning of thy supplications the commandment came forth, and I am come to shew thee, for thou art greatly beloved, therefore understand the matter, and consider the vision.

24. Seventy weeks are determined upon thy people and upon thy holy city, to finish the transgression, and to make an end of sins, and to make reconciliation for iniquity, and to bring in everlasting righteousness, and to seal up the vision and prophecy, and to anoint the most Holy.

25. Know therefore and understand, that from the going forth of the commandment to restore and to build Jerusalem unto the Messiah the prince shall be seven weeks, and threescore and two weeks; the street shall be built again, and the wall, even in troublous times.

26. And after threescore and two weeks shall Messiah be cut off, but not for himself, and the people of the prince that shall come shall destroy the city and the sanctuary, and the end thereof shall be with a flood, and unto the end of the war desolations are determined.

27. And he shall confirm the covenant with many for one week, and in the midst of the week he shall cause the sacrifice and the oblation to cease, and for the overspreading of abominations he shall make it desolate, even until the consummation, and that determined shall be poured upon the desolate.

Understanding the Seventy-Week Prophecy

The revelation of this astounding prophecy was made more clearly to early church pioneers of the Seventh-day Adventist Church in the 1800s. It was intertwined with the revelation of the heavenly sanctuary.

> "The burden of Christ's preaching was, "the time is fulfilled, and the kingdom of God is at hand; repent ye and believe the gospel." Thus, the gospel message, as given by the Savior himself, was based on the prophecies. The "time" which he declared to be fulfilled was the period made known by the angel Gabriel to Daniel. "Seventy weeks," said the angel, "are determined upon thy people and upon thy holy city, to finish the transgression, and to make an end of sins, and to make reconciliation for iniquity, and to bring in everlasting righteousness, and to seal up the vision and prophecy, and to anoint the most holy" (Dan 9:24.)
>
> A day in prophecy stands for a year (see Num 14:34; Ezek 4:6.) The seventy weeks, or four hundred and ninety days, represent four hundred and ninety years. A starting point for this period is given; "know therefore and understand, that from the going forth of the commandment to restore and to build Jerusalem unto the Messiah the prince shall be seven weeks, and threescore and two weeks," sixty-nine weeks, or four hundred and eighty-three years (Dan 9:25.) The commandment to restore and build Jerusalem, as completed by the decree of Artaxerxes Longimanus (see Ezra 6:14—7:1,9) went into effect in the autumn of 457 BC. From this time four hundred and eighty-three years extend to the autumn of AD 27. According to the prophecy, this period was to reach to the Messiah, the Anointed One. In AD 27, Jesus at his baptism received the anointing of the Holy Spirit, and soon afterward began his ministry. Then the message was proclaimed, "the time is fulfilled." Then, said the angel, "he shall confirm the covenant with many for one week [seven years.]" For seven years after the Savior entered on his ministry, the gospel was to be preached especially to the Jews; for three and a half years by Christ himself, and afterward by the apostles. "In the midst of the week He shall cause the sacrifice and the oblation to cease" (Dan 9:27.) In the spring of AD 31, Christ the true sacrifice was offered on Calvary. Then the veil of the temple was rent in twain, showing that the sacredness and significance of the sacrificial service had departed. The time had come for the earthly sacrifice and oblation to cease. The one week—seven years—ended in AD 34. Then by the stoning of Stephen the Jews finally sealed their rejection of the gospel;

the disciples who were scattered abroad by persecution "went everywhere preaching the word" (Acts 8:4), and shortly after, Saul the persecutor was converted, and became Paul, the apostle to the Gentiles. The time of Christ's coming, his anointing by the Holy Spirit, his death, and the giving of the gospel to the Gentiles, were definitely pointed out."[1]

Timeline of Seventy-Week Prophecy

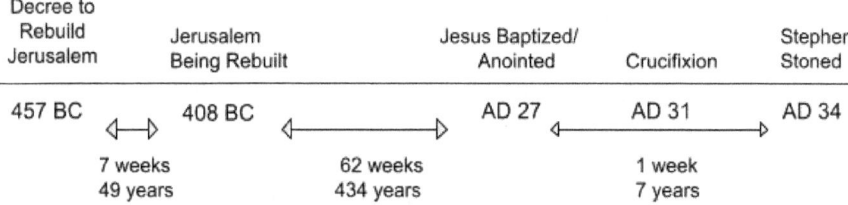

Baptism and Anointing

Jesus was baptized as prophesied in AD 27 at the age of thirty. It was common for a levitical priest to enter the ministry at the age of thirty. Therefore, it was fitting that Jesus was baptized at thirty years old to commence his ministry.

> Luke 3:21–23—"Now when all the people were baptized, it came to pass, that Jesus also being baptized, and praying, the heaven was opened. And the Holy Ghost descended in a bodily shape like a dove upon him, and a voice came from heaven, which said, 'thou art my beloved Son, in thee I am well pleased.' And Jesus himself began to be about thirty years of age, being (as was supposed) the son of Joseph, which was the son of Heli."

Birth

Jesus was thirty years old in AD 27 at his baptism; therefore, he was born in 4 BC.

---

1. White, *Desire of Ages*, 233–34.

Crucifixion

After Jesus was baptized, he immediately began his official ministry after being anointed by the Holy Spirit. As prophesied, his ministry would abruptly come to an end as he was to be "cut off" in the midst of the week. "In the midst of the week he shall cause the sacrifice and the oblation to cease" (Dan 9:27.) In prophetic language, one day is equal to one year (Num 14:34; Ezek 4:6.) Therefore, one week is seven years. Jesus was crucified in the middle of the final seven-year timeline. This meant that Jesus was crucified three and a half years after he was baptized, which would be the spring of AD 31. He was thirty-three years old.

The evidence is overwhelming, the list of witnesses is extensive, and the prophecies irrefutable. Jesus was born on time, he was baptized on time, he began his ministry on time, he died on time, he rose from death on time, and he returned to heaven on time. Jesus, the ambassador of the triune Godhead, who transcended time, came to a sinful world, and was constrained and subjugated to time. He was obedient to time and often noted, "my time is not yet come," as he waited patiently for prophecy to be fulfilled and for his ministry to come to fruition. "The time is fulfilled" heralded the beginning of his ministry. "My time is at hand" were his words as the crucifixion approached. "It is finished" were his last words on the cross. Though no man knows the day or the hour of the second coming, the evidentiary conclusion is clear—Jesus will also return on time.

— 6 —

3 Phases, 1 Court
Judgment

(Investigative. Sentencing. Executive)

There are three phases of judgment; investigative, sentencing, and executive. A tribunal court wherein all three members of the Godhead are involved in all phases.

The Garden of Eden—Breaking of the Law

Investigative: This involves asking questions, gathering, and reviewing evidence, interviewing alibis and witnesses, interrogation etc. Adam and Eve broke God's command (law.) They disobeyed God and ate the fruit from the tree of knowledge of good and evil. God came down to visit them. The investigative judgment began with God asking Adam three questions.

1. *"Where art thou?"* (Gen 3:9.)

    When an investigator begins the line of questioning, it usually begins with the question, "where were you the night/day of . . . ?" Although God knew where Adam was physically, this question was not about geographical location but a spiritual question, requiring Adam to recognize that he was now outside of the will of God, and of what God spiritually required and expected of him.

2. *"Who told thee that thou was naked?"* (Gen 3:11.)

As the investigation continues, the investigator wants to know who you were with; do you have an alibi or an accomplice? Adam confessed that he ran because he heard God's voice. He was afraid and naked, so he went into hiding. Was Adam afraid before he heard God's voice or only after he realized he was caught? We are sometimes sorry when we are caught and not sorry for the sin committed. True repentance or remorse should lead us to God, not away.

3. *"Has thou eaten of the tree, whereof I commanded thee that thou shouldest not eat?"* (Gen 3:11.)

A bold investigator then pointedly would ask, "did you commit this crime?" God did just that, and asked this pointed question, seeking a confession. Adam then pointed the finger at God and Eve by rebutting, "the woman who thou gavest to be with me, she gave me of the tree, and I did eat" (Gen 3:12.) This investigative discourse between Adam and God shows Adam trying to distance and disassociate himself from his accomplice, his wife, by depersonalizing her to "the woman." This was the beginning of the greatest whodunit the earth had ever seen. The first court case on earth began with three questions.

God then turned the attention to Eve. God asked her one question which was more of a rhetorical, introspective question than an investigative one; *"what is this that thou hast done?"* (Gen 3:13.) Eve replied by deflecting responsibility and blamed the serpent. God did not continue the line of questioning with the culprit, the serpent. A lesson for believers and Christians, who are tempted into engaging the devil with conversation. Jesus himself, while tempted by the devil in the wilderness, only replied by quoting scripture. The next phase of judgment was the sentencing of Adam, Eve, and the serpent.

Sentencing is the pronouncement of punishment. The serpent was the first to receive the ruling of conviction. "And the Lord said unto the serpent because thou hast done this, thou art cursed above all cattle, and above every beast of the field; upon thy belly shalt thou go, and dust shalt thou eat all the days of thy life. And I will put enmity between thee and the woman, and between thy seed and her seed; it shall bruise thy head, and thou shalt bruise his heel" (Gen 3:14–15.) This was earth's first restraining order—though not a physical restraint but rather a spiritual one. Enmity was wedged between the serpent and woman. The woman, spiritually, is God's church. Enmity means hatred or hostility. Sentencing was then handed down to Eve. "Unto the woman he said, I will greatly multiply thy sorrow and thy conception; in sorrow thou shalt bring forth children, and thy desire shall be to thy husband, and he shall rule over thee" (Gen 3:16.) Adam would be the last to receive sentencing and was given the longest reprimand of the three. God verbalized the charges, so that Adam and all witnesses could see the transparency of the court. "And unto Adam he said, 'because thou hast hearkened unto the voice of thy wife and has eaten of the tree of which I commanded thee, saying, thou shalt not eat of it, cursed is the ground for thy sake; in sorrow shalt thou eat of it all the days of thy life; thorns and thistles shall it bring forth to thee, and thou shalt eat the herb of the field. In the sweat of thy face shalt thou eat bread, till thou return unto the ground, for out of it wast thou taken, for dust thou art, and unto dust shalt thou return'" (Gen 3:17–19.)

The third phase of judgment is the executive. This is the act of carrying out the sentencing—the beginning of punishment. Before God handed down executive punishment, the triune Godhead conferred and deliberated the case and read out for the court, perhaps the unfallen worlds, why they reached their fair and just verdict. "And the Lord God said, 'behold, the man is become one of us, to know good and evil, and now lest he put forth his hand and take also of the tree of life and live forever.' Therefore, the Lord God sent him forth from the garden of Eden, to till the ground from whence he was taken. So, he drove out the man, and he placed at the east of the garden of Eden, cherubims and a flaming sword which turned every way, to keep the way of the tree of life" (Gen 3:22–24.)

Eden, paradise lost became the venue for the first court session on earth by a just judge. God, in the closing argument before executing judgment, outlined why Adam and Eve had to leave the garden. Before the first tenants were evicted, God made them new attire. "Unto Adam also and to his wife did the Lord God make coats of skins, and also clothed them" (Gen 3:21.) Adam and Eve were given new garments; they were no longer clothed in the righteousness of God and could no longer walk naked in the garden as pure sinless creations partaking of Eden's wholesome food. In the modern-day judiciary system, convicted inmates are given new garments before they are led away "to do hard time." Adam and Eve were given coats of skin and banished from Eden to their new life of toil and hard labor. The question is often asked as to why Adam and Eve did not die immediately after they had eaten the fruit. Afterall, God did say that they would surely die if they ate of it (Gen 2:17.) In our modern-day judicial system, when a judge sentences an offender to death, that individual does not immediately die; however, the punishment begins, and they are taken to jail or death row to begin the death sentence. Adam and Eve did not immediately die but the downward progression towards death began—their physical lifespan was shortened and spiritually, they no longer had access to the tree of life and to God's daily visible presence.

In the first court case on earth, the triune Godhead were all active in carrying out judgment. The role of the Holy Spirit is to convict and reprove of sin, righteousness, and judgment (John 16:7–8.) It is the internal interrogator and investigator that pricks at the conscience. Adam and Eve were convicted of sin because they disobeyed God and did not believe God's word. The Holy Spirit had reproved or rebuked them, so they made garments of fig to cover up their shame instead of immediately repenting and turning to God.

God the righteous judge and prosecutor, investigated, pronounced sentencing, and executed judgment. Jesus was the defense lawyer pleading their case to the Father. The whole human race was being defended. Jesus was also placed in the midst of the sentencing phase. In the great plan of salvation, enmity was placed between the woman and the serpent. "It shall bruise thy head, and thou shall bruise his heel" (Gen 3:15.) This prophetic disclaimer made by God foreshadowed the coming Messiah that would free the world from death row. Jesus was the plan of salvation for humanity from the creation of the world.

> "Sorrow filled heaven, as it was realized that man was lost, and that the world which God had created was to be filled with mortals doomed to misery, sickness, and death, and there was no way of escape for the offender. The whole family of Adam must die. I saw the lovely Jesus and beheld an expression of sympathy and sorrow upon His countenance. Soon I saw Him approach the exceeding bright light which enshrouded the Father. Said my accompanying angel, He is in close converse with His Father. The anxiety of the angels seemed to be intense while Jesus was communing with His Father. Three times He was shut in by the glorious light about the Father, and the third time He came from the Father, His person could be seen. His countenance was calm, free from all perplexity and doubt, and shone with benevolence and loveliness, such as words cannot express. He then made known to the angelic host that a way of escape had been made for lost man. He told them that He had been pleading with His

Father, and had offered to give His life a ransom, to take the sentence of death upon Himself, that through Him man might find pardon; that through the merits of His blood, and obedience to the law of God, they could have the favor of God, and be brought into the beautiful garden, and eat of the fruit of the tree of life to which they had now forfeited all right."[1]

Cain—Fratricide

Earth's first murder case—Cain killed his brother, Abel. God, the investigator asked Cain two direct questions; "where is Abel thy brother?" and "what has thou done?" (Gen 4:9–10.) Similarly, to Eve, God asked the rhetorical, introspective question, "what has thou done?" The Holy Spirit had already convicted Cain of this sin, so he attempted to hide the evidence by burying Abel's body in a shallow grave. Like his parents who ran from God and hid themselves, Cain sought to hide the sin he had committed instead of submitting to the conviction of the Holy Spirit. The evidence against Cain was compelling. God made his closing remarks before sentencing. "The voice of thy brother's blood crieth unto me from the ground. And now art thou cursed from the earth, which hath opened her mouth to receive thy brother's blood from thy hand. When thou tillest the ground, it shall not henceforth yield unto thee her strength, a fugitive and a vagabond shalt thou be in the earth" (Gen 4:10–12.) This preamble caused Cain to plea bargain, by pleading that, "my punishment is greater than I can bear" (Gen 4:13.) God being a just but merciful judge, then pronounced, "therefore whosoever slayeth Cain, vengeance shall be taken on him sevenfold" (Gen 4:15.) God then "set a mark upon Cain, lest any finding him should kill him." This was equivalent to protective custody or judicial monitoring. The Bible does not state if this mark was a visible marking or some spiritual divine protection. There is also no mention that an animal sacrifice was made to cover or atone for Cain's sin. Perhaps this mark was not just immediate divine protection for Cain, but the foreshadowing to the sacrifice of Jesus who is the propitiation for the sins of the whole world (1 John 2:1–2.) The executive phase of judgment was then carried out and Cain was sent forth out of the presence of the Lord (Gen 4:16.) Like his parents, Cain was driven out from the presence of the Lord which was the beginning of punishment. He dwelt

---

1. White, *Early Writings*, 126

in the city of Nod, which in cruel irony means to hang one's head down in shame or guilt.

Israelites in the Wilderness of Sinai—Breaking the Law

God is a loving, just, and merciful God. He is the supreme law giver and a just judge who requires obedience to his laws, but is also our advocate, ready to forgive our sins when we turn to him with a repentant heart. Nowhere is this more evident in a tangible way than in the earthly courtroom of the sanctuary during the Exodus journey of the children of Israel after they left the bondage of Egypt. The portable sanctuary was also known as Tent of Congregation, Tent of Meeting, or The Tabernacle of Witness. It was the dwelling place of God. It was constructed of white linen curtains placed on standing wood boards overlaid with gold held in place by bars and silver sockets.[2]

God commanded Moses on Mount Sinai to make this earthly replica after the blueprint of the heavenly sanctuary, so that God would be in their midst, to dwell and abide.

> Exod 25:8—"And let them make me a sanctuary that I may dwell among them."

> Heb 8:5—"Who serve unto the example and shadow of heavenly things, as Moses was admonished of God when he was about to make the tabernacle; for, see, saith he, 'that thou make all things according to the pattern shewed to thee in the mount.'"

The sanctuary or tabernacle was also God's blueprint for salvation where sinners atoned for their sins. Daily the children of Israel would

---

2. Wikipedia.org, s.v., "Tabernacle," para. 1.

bring an unblemished animal as a sacrifice for their sins. The sinner was required to place their hands on the animal's head and confess their sins thus transferring their sins onto the sacrifice. The sacrifice was then killed, and the blood was taken by the High Priest into the Holy Place and sprinkled onto the veil (curtain), which separated the Holy Place from the Most Holy Place. It was in the Most Holy Place where the presence of God dwelt, inside the Ark of the Covenant. Once a year on the holy Day of Atonement, the High Priest was allowed to enter the Most Holy Place to perform the services of removing the sins from the sanctuary that had accumulated during the course of the year.

- The sanctuary had three compartments: outer court, Holy Place, and the Most Holy Place.
- The sanctuary represented three stages of salvation: justification, sanctification, and glorification.
- The sanctuary represented the three phases of judgment: investigative, sentencing, and executive.

These will be discussed in the Chapter on the sanctuary, but for now we will explore the three phases of judgment.

Day of Atonement

Atonement means "at-one-ment"—to be reconciled to God. Once a year on this holy day, the High Priest entered the Most Holy Place. He was clad in his holy linen coat with the breastplate of judgment strapped near his heart. The breastplate was fitted with twelve gemstones and had the names of the twelve tribes of Israel (Exod 28:15–21.)

Lev 16:4-11,14-16,19

> "He shall put on the holy linen coat, and he shall have the linen breeches upon his flesh, and shall be girded with a linen girdle, and with the linen miter shall he be attired, these are holy garments; therefore, shall he wash his flesh in water, and so put them on. And he shall take of the congregation of the children of Israel two kids of the goats for a sin offering, and one ram for a burnt offering. And Aaron shall offer his bullock of the sin offering, which is for himself, and make an atonement for

himself, and for his house. And he shall take the two goats and present them before the Lord at the door of the tabernacle of the congregation. And Aaron shall cast lots upon the two goats, one lot for the Lord, and the other lot for the scapegoat. And Aaron shall bring the goat upon which the Lord's lot fell and offer him for a sin offering. But the goat, on which the lot fell to be the scapegoat, shall be presented alive before the Lord, to make an atonement with him, and to let him go for a scapegoat into the wilderness. And Aaron shall bring the bullock of the sin offering, which is for himself, and shall make an atonement for himself, and for his house, and shall kill the bullock of the sin offering which is for himself. And he shall take of the blood of the bullock and sprinkle it with his finger upon the mercy seat eastward; and before the mercy seat shall he sprinkle of the blood with his finger seven times. Then shall he kill the goat of the sin offering, that is for the people, and bring his blood within the vail, and do with that blood as he did with the blood of the bullock, and sprinkle it upon the mercy seat, and before the mercy seat. And he shall make an atonement for the holy place, because of the uncleanness of the children of Israel, and because of their transgressions in all their sins, and so shall he do for the tabernacle of the congregation, that remaineth among them in the midst of their uncleanness. And he shall sprinkle of the blood upon it with his finger seven times, and cleanse it, and hallow it from the uncleanness of the children of Israel."

Like the defense attorney going before a magistrate judge, the High Priest brought the blood of the sacrificed lamb into the Most Holy Place to make atonement for sins. He sprinkled the blood upon the mercy seat which is the lid covering the Ark of the Covenant—akin to the judge's bench. It is the sinner's sins that are being investigated; sins transgressed against the law of God. The shed blood is the evidence of transgressions brought into the judge's chambers to begin the trial. With his own finger, the High Priest sprinkled the blood on the mercy seat. The blood splatter was the silent witness against the sinner. The sinner caused the shedding of innocent blood. It was a spiritual crime scene. As the warm blood stained the golden emblem of God's righteousness and holiness of his laws, the children of Israel were to afflict their souls.

> Lev 16:29-30—"And this shall be a statute forever unto you, that in the seventh month, on the tenth day of the month, ye shall afflict your souls, and do no work at all, whether it be one of your own country, or a stranger that sojourneth among you. For on

> that day shall the priest make an atonement for you, to cleanse you, that ye may be clean from all your sins before the Lord."

This affliction of the soul was the internal investigative phase. A time of personal interrogation and confession of sins under the conviction of the Holy Spirit. The blood, both convicted and exonerated the sinner. It cost the life of an innocent victim, the lamb, yet it freed and redeemed the sinner from the penalty of sins. Justice and mercy were mingled in blood.

In the sentencing phase after the High Priest departed the Most Holy Place, he also made an atonement for the altar that was in the Holy Place (Lev 16:18-19.) He then returned to the live goat and pronounced sentencing by transferring the sins onto the live goat, also referred to as the scapegoat.

> Lev 16:20-22—"And when he hath made an end of reconciling the holy place, and the tabernacle of the congregation, and the altar, he shall bring the live goat. And Aaron shall lay both his hands upon the head of the live goat and confess over him all the iniquities of the children of Israel, and all their transgressions in all their sins, putting them upon the head of the goat, and shall send him away by the hand of a fit man into the wilderness. And the goat shall bear upon him all their iniquities unto a land not inhabited and he shall let go the goat in the wilderness."

The executive punishment saw the banishment of the sin-laden goat. The live goat represented the devil who is the originator of sin. Like Adam, Eve, and Cain, the scapegoat was immediately removed from the presence of God. Sin is the dividing wedge of enmity that causes an immediate separation from God.

The sanctuary was an object lesson pointing to the coming Messiah, who would be the sacrificial Lamb for the sins of the whole world—type would meet anti-type in the judgment and ultimate death of Christ.

The Lamb of God—Sins of the World

The mercy of God to withhold punishment of mankind, is no more evident than in the sacrifice of his only beloved son, Jesus, who was sent to pay the penalty for all sins.

> John 1:29—"The next day John seeth Jesus coming unto him, and saith, 'behold the Lamb of God, which taketh away the sin of the world.'"

> 2 Cor 5:21—"For he hath made him to be sin for us, who knew no sin, that we might be made the righteousness of God in him."

The investigative phase of judgment began in the garden of Gethsemane when the weight of sin was placed upon Jesus. In Hebrew, Gethsemane, means *"gat shemanim"* or oil press. His soul was afflicted with the sins of the world. The heavy weight of sin was pressed against his soul, and he sweated drops of blood.

> Luke 22:42-44—"Saying, 'Father, if thou be willing, remove this cup from me; nevertheless, not my will, but thine, be done.' And there appeared an angel unto him from heaven, strengthening him. And being in agony he prayed more earnestly, and his sweat was as it were great drops of blood falling down to the ground."

Every sin ever committed in the past, present, and future was transferred to Jesus in his willing obedience to pay the penalty for all sins. From personal, internal interrogation to public external interrogation, Jesus was then brought into rushed mock trials. There were six trials—three religious (Jewish/church) and three civil (Roman state.)[3]

First Trial Before Annas approx. 2am, Friday—(Religious)

> John 18:12-13,19-24—"Then the band and the captain and officers of the Jews took Jesus, and bound him, and led him away to Annas first, for he was father-in-law to Caiaphas, which was the high priest that same year. The high priest then asked Jesus of his disciples, and of his doctrine. Jesus answered him, 'I spake openly to the world, I ever taught in the synagogue, and in the temple, whither the Jews always resort, and in secret have I said nothing. Why askest thou me, ask them which heard me, what I have said unto them, behold, they know what I said.' And when he had thus spoken, one of the officers which stood by struck Jesus with the palm of his hand, saying, 'answerest thou the high priest so?' Jesus answered him, 'if I have spoken evil, bear witness of the evil, but if well, why smitest thou me?' Now Annas had sent him bound unto Caiaphas the high priest."

---

3. Rudd, "Six Trials of Jesus," Intro. A.1.

Second Trial Before Caiaphas, approx. 2:30am to 5am Friday—(Religious/Jewish)

John 18:14—"Now Caiaphas was he, which gave counsel to the Jews, that it was expedient that one man should die for the people."

Matt 26:57,59-62—"And they that had laid hold on Jesus led him away to Caiaphas the high priest, where the scribes and the elders were assembled. Now the chief priests, and elders, and all the council, sought false witness against Jesus, to put him to death, but found none, yea, though many false witnesses came, yet found they none. At the last came two false witnesses, and said, 'this fellow said, I am able to destroy the temple of God, and to build it in three days.' And the high priest arose, and said unto him, 'answerest thou nothing, what is it which these witness against thee?'"

John 18:28—"Then led they Jesus from Caiaphas unto the hall of judgment and it was early, and they themselves went not into the judgment hall, lest they should be defiled, but that they might eat the passover."

Third Trial Before Sanhedrin, approx. 6am—(Religious/Jewish)

Luke 22:66-71—"And as soon as it was day, the elders of the people and the chief priests and the scribes came together, and led him into their council, saying, 'art thou the Christ tell us?' And he said unto them, 'if I tell you, ye will not believe. And if I also ask you, ye will not answer me, nor let me go. Hereafter shall the Son of man sit on the right hand of the power of God.' Then said they all, 'art thou then the Son of God?' And he said unto them, 'ye say that I am.' And they said, 'what need we any further witness for we ourselves have heard of his own mouth.'"

Fourth Trial Before Pilate, approx. 6:30am—(Civil/Roman)

Luke 23:1-7—"And the whole multitude of them arose and led him unto Pilate. And they began to accuse him, saying, 'we found this fellow perverting the nation, and forbidding to give tribute to Caesar, saying that he himself is Christ a King.' And

Pilate asked him, saying, 'art thou the King of the Jews?' And he answered him and said, 'thou sayest it.' Then said Pilate to the chief priests and to the people, 'I find no fault in this man.' And they were the more fierce, saying, 'he stirreth up the people, teaching throughout all Jewry, beginning from Galilee to this place.' When Pilate heard of Galilee, he asked whether the man were a Galilaean. And as soon as he knew that he belonged unto Herod's jurisdiction, he sent him to Herod, who himself also was at Jerusalem at that time."

Fifth Trial Before Herod, approx. 7am—(Civil/Roman)

Luke 23:8-11—"And when Herod saw Jesus, he was exceeding glad for he was desirous to see him of a long season, because he had heard many things of him, and he hoped to have seen some miracle done by him. Then he questioned with him in many words, but he answered him nothing. And the chief priests and scribes stood and vehemently accused him. And Herod with his men of war set him at nought, and mocked him, and arrayed him in a gorgeous robe, and sent him again to Pilate."

Sixth Trial and Second Trial before Pilate (Civil/Roman), approx. 7:30am–8am

Luke 23:12-18—"And the same day Pilate and Herod were made friends together, for before they were at enmity between themselves. And Pilate, when he had called together the chief priests and the rulers and the people, said unto them, 'ye have brought this man unto me, as one that perverteth the people and, behold, I, having examined him before you, have found no fault in this man touching those things whereof ye accuse him, no, nor yet Herod, for I sent you to him and, lo, nothing worthy of death is done unto him. I will therefore chastise him and release him.' For of necessity he must release one unto them at the feast. And they cried out all at once, saying, 'away with this man, and release unto us Barabbas.'"

The next phase of judgment was sentencing. "Pilate gave sentence that it should be as they required." It is interesting to note that Pilate voiced his concerns against conviction three times, but then conceded to the demands of the crowd to crucify Christ (Luke 23:20–24.) The final executive phase culminated on Mount Calvary where Jesus was crucified between 9 am (third hour) to 3 pm (ninth hour)—(Luke 23:33; Mark 15:25,34,37.) It was the tradition during Passover that the High Priest would slay the sacrificial lamb at the ninth hour (3 pm.) Jesus, the fulfillment of the sacrificial Lamb, was crucified and died at the ninth hour (3 pm.) Jesus was the fulfillment of prophecy, he was the Lamb of God sent to pay the penalty for sins of the world.

— 7 —

3 Mouths, 1 Truth
Three Witnesses

(The Father. The Word. The Holy Ghost)

(Spirit. Water. Blood)

Gen 1:1—"In the beginning *GOD* created the heaven and earth."

Gen 1:2—"And the earth was without form and void and darkness was upon the face of the deep. And the *SPIRIT* of God moved upon the face of the waters."

Gen 1:3—"And God *said*, 'let there be light,' and there was light."

God "said" was the spoken word, which was *JESUS*. John 1:1 affirms this, "in the beginning was the *WORD*, and the *WORD* was with *GOD* and the *WORD* was *GOD*."

John 1:2—"The same was in the beginning with God."

John 1:3—"All things were made by him, and without him was not anything made that was made."

John 1:14—"And the *WORD* was made flesh, and dwelt among us, and we beheld his glory, the glory as of one begotten of the Father, full of grace and truth."

Trinity means three beings having the same experience—three active witnesses. Three mouths speaking one truth. They were all active in the creation story of earth. The three witnesses are the Father, Son (Jesus/Word), and the Holy Spirit.

> 1 John 5:7-8—"For there are three that bear record in heaven, the Father, the Word, and the Holy Ghost, and these three are one. And there are three that bear witness in earth, the spirit, and the water, and the blood, and these three agree in one."

The three witnesses on earth represented by the spirit, water, and blood all point to Jesus, who was the primary physical witness on earth representing the Godhead.

The Trinity at Creation

> Gen 1:26—"And God said, 'let *us* make man in *our* image, after *our* likeness, and let them have dominion over the fish of the sea, and over the fowl of the air, and over the cattle, and over all the earth, and over every creeping thing that creepeth upon the earth.'"

There are three references to possessive pronouns; "us," "our," "our," confirming that the image of the Godhead has three components.

Similarly, mankind has three components—mind (mental), body (physical), and soul (spiritual.) Similarly, a tree has three components—tree, fruit, and seed. We are indeed made in the image of the Godhead.

God is the mind—likewise man has a mind. Jesus is the body—likewise man has a body. The Holy Spirit is the soul/spirit—likewise man has a spiritual element. Yet, the Godhead is equal, co-eternal, and immortal.

Man is one soul, i.e., the mental, physical, and the spiritual exist together. However, man is not immortal. Mankind lives in an earthly body as mortal beings. The righteous will only receive immortality at the second coming of Christ. Why was mankind made in the image of God? Mankind was made in the image of Godhead to be witnesses of God and to reflect the character of the Godhead. The Father, the son Jesus, and the Holy Spirit are three witnesses in heaven. What does this mean and why is witnessing so important to the Godhead? Let us digress and look at the significance of witnessing and why three is so vital.

The Tabernacle of Witnesses

The tabernacle of witnesses was another name for the portable sanctuary built by Moses for the children of Israel as they journeyed from Egypt to Canaan. God had shown Moses the exact design which was patterned from the real one in the heavenly sanctuary.

> Acts 7:44—"Our fathers had the tabernacle of witness in the wilderness, as he had appointed, speaking unto Moses, that he should make it according to the fashion that he had seen."

> Num 17:1-11—"And the Lord spake unto Moses, saying, 'speak unto the children of Israel, and take of every one of them a rod according to the house of their fathers, of all their princes according to the house of their fathers twelve rods, write thou every man's name upon his rod. And thou shalt write Aaron's name upon the rod of Levi, for one rod shall be for the head of the house of their fathers. And thou shalt lay them up in the tabernacle of the congregation before the testimony, where I will meet with you. And it shall come to pass, that the man's rod, whom I shall choose, shall blossom and I will make to cease from me the murmurings of the children of Israel, whereby they murmur against you.' And Moses spake unto the children of Israel, and every one of their princes gave him a rod apiece, for each prince one, according to their fathers' houses, even twelve rods, and the rod of Aaron was among their rods. And Moses laid up the rods before the Lord in the tabernacle of witness. And it came to pass, that on the morrow Moses went into the tabernacle of witness and behold, the rod of Aaron for the house of Levi was budded, and brought forth buds, and bloomed blossoms, and yielded almonds. And Moses brought out all the rods from before the Lord unto all the children of Israel and they looked and took every man his rod. And the Lord said unto Moses, 'bring Aaron's rod again before the testimony, to be kept for a token against the rebels; and thou shalt quite take away their murmurings from me, that they die not.' And Moses did so as the Lord commanded him, so did he."

> Heb 9:3-4—"And after the second veil, the tabernacle which is called the Holiest of all, which had the golden censer, and the ark of the covenant overlaid roundabout with gold, wherein was the golden pot that had manna, and Aaron's rod that budded, and the tables of the covenant."

The Ark of the Covenant was a wooden chest overlaid with gold and was the most important piece of furniture in the sanctuary. It represented the presence of God. There were three tokens placed inside the Ark; Aaron's rod that budded, the pot of manna, and the tables of the covenant, i.e., the commandments on tables of stone. Aaron's rod that budded served as a witness and reminder against rebellion, doubting, and murmuring. Manna was the coriander seed-like wafer that rained down from heaven to feed the Israelites in their forty-year trek in the wilderness. Manna was to bear witness of God's unfailing provisions and faithfulness. The tables of stone (Ten Commandments) were inscribed by the finger of God and it outlined his unchanging laws. It bore witness to the nature and unchanging character of God. It also bore witness to the standard by which all mankind is judged.

The apostle John who wrote the book of Revelation, was shown in vision by the Holy Spirit, the real heavenly tabernacle. John was imprisoned on the isle of Patmos during the anti-Christian persecution by the Roman rulership during the first century.

> Rev 11:19—15:5—"And the temple of God was opened in heaven, and there was seen in his temple the ark of his testament and there were lightnings, and voices, and thunderings, and an earthquake, and great hail. And after that I looked, and behold, the temple of the tabernacle of the testimony in heaven was opened."

Another word for witness is testimony. The sanctuary was also referred to as the tabernacle of testimony. The earthly tabernacle of witness was a replica of the heavenly tabernacle of testimony. There were three tokens inside the earthly Ark of the Covenant. Likewise, there must also be three emblems in the heavenly Ark, reflecting the triunity of the Godhead. The tables of stones with the inscribed commandments of God must also be one of these emblems, thus signifying that God's law is immutable, unchangeable, and eternal.

Witnessing and the Godhead

To bear record means to witness.

> "This is he that came by water and blood, even Jesus Christ, not by water only, but by water and blood. And it is the Spirit that beareth witness because the Spirit is truth. For there are three

that bear record in heaven, the Father, the Word, and the Holy Ghost, and these three are one. And there are three that bear witness in earth, the spirit, and the water, and the blood, and these three agree in one" (1 John 5:6–8.)

Questions to ponder: Why are there three witnesses in heaven and on earth? What is the significance of three? Why not two or one? Why is witnessing so important?

Answering these vital questions will reveal why the triune Godhead is composed of three members and why witnessing is so important. We will now delve into various Bible verses on witnesses and witnessing from both the New and Old Testaments, which will help to answer these pressing questions.

Mouth of Two or Three

Deut 19:15—"One witness shall not rise up against a man for any iniquity, or for any sin, in any sin that he sinneth; at the mouth of two witnesses or at the mouth of three witnesses, shall the matter be established."

Deut 17:6—"At the mouth of two witnesses, or three witnesses, shall he that is worthy of death be put to death, but at the mouth of one witness he shall not be put to death."

John 8:15–17—"You judge after the flesh, I judge no man. And yet if I judge, my judgment is true for I am not alone, but I and the Father that sent me. It is also written in your law, that the testimony of two men is true."

Matt 18:16—"But if he will not hear thee, then take with thee one or two more, that in the mouth of two or three witnesses every word may be established."

Heb 6:17–18—"Wherein God, willing more abundantly to shew unto the heirs of promise the immutability of his counsel, confirmed it by an oath, that by two immutable things, in which it was impossible for God to lie, we might have a strong consolation."

Additional verses—2 Cor 13:1; 1 Tim 5:19; Matt 26:59–60; Heb 10:28.

Witnessing in Twos or Threes

> Matt 18:20—"For where two or three are gathered together in my name, there am I in the midst of them."

> Luke 24:13-15—"And, behold, two of them went that same day to a village called Emmaus, which was from Jerusalem about threescore furlongs. And they talked together of all these things which had happened. And it came to pass, that, while they communed together and reasoned, Jesus himself drew near, and went with them."

> Luke 10:1—"After these things the Lord appointed other seventy also and sent them two and two before his face into every city and place, whither he himself would come."

> Acts 15:27—"We have sent therefore Judas and Silas, who shall also tell you the same things by mouth."

> John 20:12—"And seeth two angels in white sitting, the one at the head, and the other at the feet, where the body of Jesus had lain."

(Note: The two angels were silent witnesses.)

> Num 7:89—"And when Moses was gone into the tabernacle of the congregation to speak with him, then he heard the voice of one speaking unto him from off the mercy seat that was upon the ark of testimony, from between the two cherubims and he spake unto him."

(Note: The presence of God was in the Ark surrounded by two cherubims. Though inanimate structures in the earthly sanctuary, they represented real angels in the heavenly sanctuary.)

> Luke 23:33—"And when they were come to the place, which is called Calvary, there they crucified him and the malefactors, one on the right hand and the other on the left."

(Note: Even on the cross Jesus was in the midst of two witnesses.)

> Matt 17:1-3—"And after six days Jesus taketh Peter, James, and John his brother and bringeth them up into a high mountain apart, and was transfigured before them, and his face did shine as the sun and his raiment was white as the light. And behold, there appeared unto them Moses and Elias talking with him."

(Note: Peter, James, and John were three disciples chosen to be witnesses. Also, Moses and Elias (Elijah) were two witnesses sent from heaven.)

Witnesses at the Confirmation of Jesus

Simeon and Anna were two witnesses chosen by the Holy Spirit to be witnesses of baby Jesus at his presentation in the temple. Culturally today it is common practice to have witnesses at baby dedications.

> Luke 2:25-30,36,38—"And, behold, there was a man in Jerusalem, whose name was Simeon, and the same man was just and devout, waiting for the consolation of Israel and the Holy Ghost was upon him. And it was revealed unto him by the Holy Ghost, that he should not see death, before he had seen the Lord's Christ. And he came by the Spirit into the temple and when the parents brought in the child Jesus, to do for him after the custom of the law, then took he him up in his arms, and blessed God, and said, 'Lord, now lettest thou thy servant depart in peace, according to thy word for mine eyes have seen thy salvation.' And there was one Anna, a prophetess, the daughter of Phanuel, of the tribe of Aser, she was of a great age, and had lived with a husband seven years from her virginity, and she coming in that instant gave thanks likewise unto the Lord, and spake of him to all them that looked for redemption in Jerusalem."

Witnessing—The Holy Spirit and the Disciples

> Acts 1:8—"But ye shall receive power, after that the Holy Ghost is come upon you and ye shall be witnesses unto me both in Jerusalem, and in all Judaea, and in Samaria, and unto the uttermost part of the earth."

Jesus came in the flesh and was subjected to the limitations of humanity. He had flesh and blood and could be seen with human eyes. He could be seen, so evil men laid hands on him and crucified him. He was fully divine but temporarily suspended divinity to become flesh to accomplish the plan of salvation. There is a record in the Bible where-in Jesus made himself invisible to escape an angry mob who sought to kill him (Luke 4:30.) The supreme wisdom of the Godhead allowed the Holy Spirit to be unseen. Man cannot lay hands on the Holy Spirit, thereby allowing the omnipresence of the Holy Spirit to always have unhindered access to all mankind at all times, in all places. The disciples were commissioned by Jesus to be witnesses after they had received the Holy Ghost. The same holds true for Christians today.

Witnessing in Prophecy

The prophetic book of Revelation highlights two witnesses. These two witnesses represent the New and Old Testament books of the Bible. They also represent Moses and Elijah (the law and the prophet.) During the time of Moses, God had caused the water to turn to blood in Egypt and in the time of Elijah it did not rain for three and a half years. It is interesting to note that these witnesses have the power to turn water to blood. Water and blood are also two key witnesses in the outer court, and by extension, the earth.

> Rev 11:3-7—"And I will give power unto my two witnesses and they shall prophesy a thousand two hundred and threescore days clothed in sackcloth. These are the two olive trees, and the two candlesticks standing before the God of the earth. And if any man will hurt them, fire proceedeth out of their mouth, and devoureth their enemies, and if any man will hurt them, he must in this manner be killed. These have power to shut heaven, that it rain not in the days of their prophecy and have power over waters to turn them to blood, and to smite the earth with all plagues, as often as they will. And when they shall have finished their testimony, the beast that ascendeth out of the bottomless pit shall make war against them and shall overcome them and kill them."

Witnessing and Judgment

> Matt 24:14—"And this gospel of the kingdom shall be preached in all the world for a witness unto all nations, and then shall the end come."

Witnessing and testimony precedes God's judgment. Any fair and just judge calls witnesses to testify before judgment is pronounced. This parallels our modern-day judicial system. Before a judge can carry out sentencing and execute judgment there must be witnesses. Before the final executive phase of judgment upon earth, there must be witnessing. The prophetic book of Revelation mentions an intriguing number of witnesses (Rev 7:3-8—14:1-4.) The one hundred and forty-four thousand sealed servants of God—twelve thousand from each of the twelve spiritual tribes of Israel. This symbolic number of witnesses represents the many who will play a significant role in giving the loud cry of the soon return of Christ. Their witnessing will crescendo with the three angels' messages, then the plagues will fall upon earth (Rev 14:6-12; Revelation chapters 15 to 16.) Revelation spotlights the final and urgent prophetic warning messages of the three angels before judgment is executed. These messages will be the paramount charge given by witnesses in these last days of earth's history.

> Rev 14:6-12—"And I saw another angel fly in the midst of heaven, having the everlasting gospel to preach unto them that dwell on the earth, and to every nation, and kindred, and tongue, and people, saying with a loud voice, 'fear God, and give glory to him, for the hour of his judgment is come, and worship him that made heaven, and earth, and the sea, and the fountains of waters.' And there followed another angel, saying, 'Babylon is fallen, is fallen, that great city, because she made all nations drink of the wine of the wrath of her fornication.' And the third angel followed them, saying with a loud voice, 'if any man worship the beast, and his image, and receive his mark in his forehead, or in his hand, the same shall drink of the wine of the wrath of God, which is poured out without mixture into the cup of his indignation; and he shall be tormented with fire and brimstone in the presence of the holy angels, and in the presence of the Lamb.' And the smoke of their torment ascendeth up forever and ever, and they have no rest day nor night who worship the beast and his image, and whosoever receiveth the mark of his name. Here is the patience of the saints, here are they that keep the commandments of God, and the faith of Jesus."

Before God can pronounce judgment upon the earth, this gospel message must be preached throughout all the world as a witness. These commandment keeping witnesses will also give their personal testimonies, which is another form of witnessing.

The Ten Commandments as a Witness

> Exod 31:18—"And he gave unto Moses, when he had made an end of communing with him upon mount Sinai two tables of testimony, tables of stone written with the finger of God."

Tables of testimony means tables of witnesses. There must be a minimum of two witnesses to establish truth. God could have made them on one or even three tablets, but they were made on two tablets. The word commandment in Hebrew means *mitzvah* (mitz + vah.) Vah means love. God's commandments are laws of love. The first four commandments reflect mankind's love for God and the last six reflect love for our fellow man. They were written with the finger of God and spoken audibly (Deut 9:10; Exod 20 1-17.) It is not specified how many commandments were on each tablet. Perhaps one tablet held the first four commandments which reflects love for God and the remaining six commandments on the second tablet reflecting love for each other. Why did God instruct Moses to come alone? Why weren't there two human witnesses to establish truth? Although Moses was the only human witness, there was the spiritual unseen witness of the Holy Spirit. Moses was with God for forty days. Similarly, Jesus was in the wilderness for forty days, but the Holy Spirit was with him. He was never alone.

Jesus is a Witness

> Rev 1:5—"And from Jesus Christ, who is the faithful witness, and the first begotten of the dead, and the prince of the kings of the earth. Unto him that loved us and washed us from our sins in his own blood."

> Rev 3:14—"... these things saith the Amen, the faithful and true witness, the beginning of the creation of God."

> John 8:12-19—"Then spake Jesus again unto them, saying, 'I am the light of the world, he that followeth me shall not walk in darkness, but shall have the light of life.' The Pharisees therefore said unto him, 'thou bearest record of thyself, thy record is not true.' Jesus answered and said unto them, 'though I bear record of myself, yet my record is true for I know whence I came, and whither I go, but ye cannot tell whence I come, and whither I go. Ye judge after the flesh, I judge no man. And yet if I judge,

my judgment is true, for I am not alone, but I and the Father that sent me. It is also written in your law, that the testimony of two men is true. I am one that bear witness of myself, and the Father that sent me beareth witness of me.' Then said they unto him, 'where is thy Father?' Jesus answered, 'ye neither know me, nor my Father, if ye had known me, ye should have known my Father also.'"

Although Jesus in John 14:6 declared that he was the way, the truth, and the life, he was by no means implying that he was solely and exclusively the truth. He acknowledged the Father as being inclusive in this truth. He spoke as the Father gave him utterance. In the same verse, Jesus proclaimed that, "no man cometh to the Father but by me." In the continued discourse with the disciples, Jesus expounds in John 14.

John 14:7-11—"If ye had known me, ye should have known my Father also and from henceforth ye know him and have seen him. Philip saith unto him, 'Lord, show us the Father, and it sufficeth us.' Jesus saith unto him, 'have I been so long time with you, and yet hast thou not known me, Philip? He that hath seen me hath seen the Father, and how sayest thou then, show us the Father? Believest thou not that I am in the Father, and the Father in me? The words that I speak unto you I speak not of myself, but the Father that dwelleth in me, he doeth the works. Believe me that I am in the Father, and the Father in me, or else believe me for the very works' sake.'"

God the Father is a Witness

John 8:18—"I am one that bear witness of myself, and the Father that sent me beareth witness of me."

John 5:30-31,37—"I can of mine own self do nothing, as I hear, I judge, and my judgment is just because I seek not mine own will but the will of the Father which hath sent me. If I bear witness of myself, my witness is not true. And the Father himself which hath sent me, hath borne witness of me. Ye have neither heard his voice at any time, nor seen his shape."

Holy Spirit is a Witness

> Acts 5:30-32—"The God of our fathers raised up Jesus, whom ye slew and hanged on a tree. Him hath God exalted with his right hand to be a prince and a Savior, for to give repentance to Israel, and forgiveness of sins. And we are his witnesses of these things; and so is also the Holy Ghost, whom God hath given to them that obey him."

Hebrews 10 poignantly summarizes the role of the earthly sanctuary and its sacrifices versus the ministry of Jesus, the eternal sacrifice, and the witness of the Holy Spirit.

> Heb 10:9-16—"Then said he, 'lo, I come to do thy will, O God.' He taketh away the first, that he may establish the second. By the which will we are sanctified through the offering of the body of Jesus Christ once for all. And every priest standeth daily ministering and offering oftentimes the same sacrifices, which can never take away sins, but this man, after he had offered one sacrifice for sins forever, sat down on the right hand of God; from henceforth expecting till his enemies be made his footstool. For by one offering he hath perfected forever them that are sanctified. Whereof the Holy Ghost also is a witness to us, for after that he had said before, this is the covenant that I will make with them after those days, saith the Lord, I will put my laws into their hearts, and in their minds will I write them."

Summary—Key Points From These Scriptures

The Father is a witness. Jesus is a witness. The Holy Spirit is a witness.

- They all bear witness of each other and for each other.
- It requires a minimum of two to be witnesses.
- One witness cannot establish truth, it requires a minimum of two. One to be a witness for the other.
- Judgment cannot be carried out without witnesses; it takes at least two to effectuate judgment.
- If the Godhead was composed of one, then truth could not be established.

- If the Godhead was composed of one, and that one was to be crucified, then there would be no witness nor a Godhead.
- If the Godhead was composed of two, and one was to be crucified, there would be one left, but one cannot establish truth. Two had to remain for truth to exist

The Godhead knew there was to be a sacrifice. Jesus would be crucified, thereby leaving two members of the Godhead—the Father and Holy Spirit, to be witnesses and establish truth. When Jesus was crucified and died and laid in the tomb, the Father and the Holy Spirit were the two witnesses of the Godhead left to maintain truth and be witnesses for three days. When Jesus ascended back to heaven to be with the Father, he sent the omnipresent Holy Spirit (Comforter) to aid Christians in witnessing. At all times there must be two or three to establish truth. *Therefore, the Godhead had to be three!*

Three co-eternal, equal beings, who are witnesses with each other and for each other, at the same time. Not in an evolutionary period or periods of time. Truth is present and immediate—it does not and cannot evolve over time. Truth cannot change, so it cannot evolve. Evolution involves change or metamorphosis. If truth evolved, then it would be subject to external influences at each stage of its evolution. God's word is truth. It cannot change, it cannot be altered, it cannot be compromised, it does not evolve, conform, or change over time. God is Truth. Jesus is truth. The Holy Spirit is truth. When God said, "I AM, that I AM," he was expressing an unchangeable nature in an immediate, consistent, present moment, yet for eternity. He did not say "I AM" that "I will be" nor "I AM" that "I was," but "I AM that I AM" (Exod 3:14.)

> Fun Fact: The root meaning of "am" is Latin for love. God is the "I AM" means God is love. Many language translations for love include: amor (Spanish), amore (Italian), l'amour (French.)

Creation as a Witness of Truth

Creation was immediate—a seven consecutive day creation period, wherein the triune Godhead created specific and unique things on each day and rested on the seventh day. Creation did not evolve over seven epochs of time(s) or centuries as evolutionists ascribe. On the third day of creation God created three types of vegetation; grass, herbs, and trees.

On the fourth day, God created three sources of light; sun, moon, and stars. Vegetation needed sunlight to grow and live, so God created sunlight the following day. It had to be literal days as vegetation needed light to survive. If it was not literal days, how could trees survive for years without sunlight? Evolution would have to hypothesize that sunlight existed before vegetation. This would contradict the biblical narrative. If sunlight was created epochs before vegetation, how would the soil be fertile enough to sustain vegetation? Genesis records that God had not caused it to rain upon the earth but provided a mist that came up from the ground to irrigate the soil (Gen 2:5–6.) On the fifth day, life-form was created; fish and fowl were placed into their habitats. On the sixth day man came alive by the breath of God and placed in a garden home. Creation's timeline reflected nature's truth. The ground was vaporized by mist, which allowed vegetation to take root. The sun empowered life to blossom from this flora. The birds found lodgings in the trees and animals ate of the herbs. Adam and Eve cared for the animals and the animals offered companionship. Eden was the template for sustainable living. God created a scientific and an interdependent ecosystem to sustain all life forms. All existing together and not millions of years apart.

Nature as a Witness

Nature is a profound silent witness declaring that there is an all-wise, omniscient, omnipotent, omnipresent God who created the heaven, the earth, the sea, and all that is within. Nature also declares as a witness that God is faithful and provides for mankind's daily needs.

> Ps 19:1–4—"The heavens declare the glory of God, and the firmament sheweth his handywork. Day unto day uttereth speech, and night unto night sheweth knowledge. There is no speech nor language, where their voice is not heard. Their line is gone out through all the earth, and their words to the end of the world. In them hath he set a tabernacle for the sun, which is as a bridegroom coming out of his chamber, and rejoiceth as a strong man to run a race."

> Job 12:7–10—"But ask now the beasts, and they shall teach thee and the fowls of the air, and they shall tell thee. Or speak to the earth, and it shall teach thee, and the fishes of the sea shall declare unto thee. Who knoweth not in all these that the hand of

the Lord hath wrought this? In whose hand is the soul of every living thing, and the breath of all mankind."

Ps 89:37—"It shall be established forever as the moon, and as a faithful witness in heaven."

Acts 14:17—"Nevertheless he left not himself without witness, in that he did good, and gave us rain from heaven, and fruitful seasons, filling our hearts with food and gladness."

Christians as Witnesses

Before Jesus left this outer court (earth) he emphasized the importance of witnessing. Witnessing is a demonstration of faith. Witnessing, especially in these last days is vitally important, as the proclamation of the gospel will precede the second coming of Christ. Witnessing must also proclaim that the triune Godhead are three co-eternal and co-equal persons, co-existing in perfect truth. For in the mouth of two or three witnesses truth is established. What should witnessing entail?

Luke 24:45–49—"Then opened he their understanding, that they might understand the scriptures, and said unto them, 'thus it is written, and thus it behooved Christ to suffer, and to rise from the dead the third day and that repentance and remission of sins should be preached in his name among all nations, beginning at Jerusalem. And ye are witnesses of these things. And behold, I send the promise of my Father upon you but tarry ye in the city of Jerusalem, until ye be endued with power from on high.'"

Acts 1:8—"But ye shall receive power, after that the Holy Ghost is come upon you and ye shall be witnesses unto me both in Jerusalem, and in all Judaea, and in Samaria, and unto the uttermost part of the earth."

Matt 24:14—"And this gospel of the kingdom shall be preached in all the world for a witness unto all nations, and then shall the end come."

Isa 43:10–12—"Ye are my witnesses, saith the Lord, and my servant whom I have chosen that ye may know and believe me, and understand that I am he, before me there was no God formed, neither shall there be after me. I, even I, am the Lord and beside me there is no savior. I have declared, and have saved, and I have shewed, when there was no strange god among you therefore ye are my witnesses, saith the Lord, that I am God."

Acts 1:22—"Beginning from the baptism of John, unto that same day that he was taken up from us, must one be ordained to be a witness with us of his resurrection."

Acts 2:32—"This Jesus who God raised up, whereof we all are witnesses."

Rom 8:16—"The Spirit itself beareth witness with our spirit, that we are the children of God."

1 John 5:10-11—"He that believeth on the Son of God hath the witness in himself; he that believeth not God hath made him a liar because he believeth not the record that God gave of his Son. And this is the record, that God hath given to us eternal life, and this life is in his Son."

Summary: witnessing should be about:

- Jesus Christ and the gospel, the good news of salvation
- Jesus is one with God who came in the flesh
- There is no other God who should be worshipped but the God who is the Creator
- Jesus Christ died and is risen
- Jesus is the light of the world and reservoir of eternal life
- God is a good God who cares and provides for our needs
- The Holy Spirit is an active witness for the Godhead on earth
- We must be born again—born of the Holy Spirit to be a child of God
- Sinners must repent for the remission of sins
- The second coming of Christ

Witnessing is not just a declaration of faith through personal testimony but is the proclamation of the gospel and salvation through the triune Godhead.

— 8 —

3 Architects, 1 Design
The Godhead's Creation

(light. life. likeness)

These three key elements were essential for creation.

Earth at Creation

Earth is the engineering mastermind of three architects, yet it is one cohesive design. The creation story began with three words, "*let there be*" and three descriptives chronicled earth's terrain; *without form*, *void*, and *dark* (Gen 2:1.)

The earth was without form (had no likeness), void (had no life), and dark (had no light.) Without light, life, and likeness, there could be no creation. It would be an incomplete and unsustainable world. The Godhead then began the creative process by first creating light and then various life forms.

Day 1—"And God *said,* 'let there be *light*' and there was *light*" (Gen 1:3.)

Day 2-6—God *spoke life* into existence—land, trees, grass, vegetation, sun, moon, stars, animals, fish, birds etc. The sun, moon, and stars were secondary sources of *light* (Gen 1:9–25.)

Day 6—God formed man out of the dust (Gen 1:26.)

Light counteracted the darkness. Life counteracted the voidness. But what was created to counter "without form" (formlessness)? To form means to give likeness. Therefore, "without form" means to have no likeness. God formed things with his hands like a potter, as he did when he formed Adam from the dust. Man was made into the image or likeness of God.

> Gen 1:26-27—"Let us make man in our image, after our likeness."

> Gen 2:7—"And the Lord God formed man of the dust of the ground."

In Jeremiah 1:5, God declared that before he formed us in the womb, he knew us and sanctified us. Similarly, God must have had an image in his mind of what the earth was supposed to be, yet when he created the earth, it was created without form (without likeness.) The earth had no form or likeness. Therefore, likeness was required to counter "without form." Man was given the likeness of God but what did God create for the likeness of the earth?

After six days of creation were completed, the earth teaming with light and life, began taking form. God declared that everything was very good (Gen 1:31.) "Thus the heavens and the earth were finished, and all the host of them. And on the seventh day God ended his work which he had made, and he rested on the seventh day from all his work which he had made. And God blessed the seventh day and sanctified it because that in it he had rested from all his work which God created and made" (Gen 2:1-3.)

The seventh day was the sanctified, holy day of rest or Sabbath. The seventh day was specifically made to be the perfect frame that formed and fitted the canvas of God's six-days of creation. It was the finishing touch. Sabbath was God's emblem of form or likeness. It was not just an ordinary day—it was blessed, sanctified, and made holy. It reflected God's holiness and creative power. It reflected God's likeness of holiness.

Sabbath at Creation

The word "Sabbath" is from the Hebrew verb, "*shavat*" which means to rest. The Sabbath was made for all mankind to bring us into the loving conformity to the spiritual likeness of God. The Sabbath bridged physical creation to man's spiritual birth. Six days of natural creation was crowned by the seventh day. The birth of worship was the Sabbath. It was a vital part of the creation story. From Eden to Sinai, God etched the relevance of the Sabbath by placing it prominently in the Ten Commandments written on the tablets of stones given to Moses. The fourth commandment is the only command that begins with the word "remember." It is also the longest and most detailed commandment.

> Exod 20:8-11—"Remember the sabbath day, to keep it holy. Six days shalt thou labor, and do all thy work, but the seventh day is the sabbath of the Lord thy God, in it thou shalt not do any work, thou, nor thy son, nor thy daughter, thy manservant, nor thy maidservant, nor thy cattle, nor thy stranger that is within thy gates, for in six days the Lord made heaven and earth, the sea, and all that in them is, and rested the seventh day, wherefore the Lord blessed the sabbath day, and hallowed it."

From Adam in Eden to Moses in the Old Testament, to Jesus in the New Testament, to us today, the seventh-day Sabbath rest remains unchanged.

> Heb 4:3-4,8-11—"For we which have believed do enter into rest, as he said, 'as I have sworn in my wrath, if they shall enter into my rest,' although the works were finished from the foundation of the world. For he spake in a certain place of the seventh day on this wise, and God did rest the seventh day from all his works. For if Jesus had given them rest, then would he not afterward have spoken of another day. There remaineth therefore a rest to the people of God. For he that is entered into his rest, he also hath ceased from his own works, as God did from his. Let us labor therefore to enter into that rest, lest any man fall after the same example of unbelief."

Observing and keeping the Sabbath is God's creative way of reforming and transforming mankind into his spiritual likeness through his son Jesus Christ. It is part of the process of sealing us to sanctification. It was made for all mankind from the foundation of the world. Adam kept the first Sabbath in Eden with the Godhead from sunset on the sixth day to sunset on the seventh day. Moses was given the written version of the commandments by God on Mount Sinai. It was more detailed as God knew that mankind would forget this sacred day or attempt to change it to another day other than the seventh day. The Sabbath was not made only for the children of Israel but for all mankind hence the reason God engraved it into the Ten Commandments. Jesus, while on earth along with the disciples, kept the Sabbath. Jesus acknowledged that, "the

Sabbath was made for man and not man for the Sabbath, therefore the Son of man is Lord also of the Sabbath" (Mark 2:27–28.) It is embedded in God's law, and it is immutable.

Seventh-day Sabbath—What's in a Name?

S.abba.th and S.eve.nth

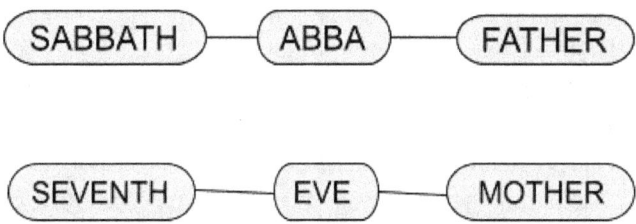

Strategically embedded in the word Sabbath is God's name, "*Abba*" which means Father. It is interesting to note that there are three biblical references to Abba; Mark 14:36, Rom 8:15, and Gal 4:6. God chose to stamp and seal his name in the Sabbath day of rest as a reminder and memorial of himself and his creative power. God created the seventh day and it was the only day that was blessed, sanctified, and made holy. In the word "seventh" is the word "*Eve,*" which means mother of all living (Gen 3:20.) Sabbath is a symbolic union carved out of the week to bring mankind back into harmony with the likeness of God, the Creator of all living.

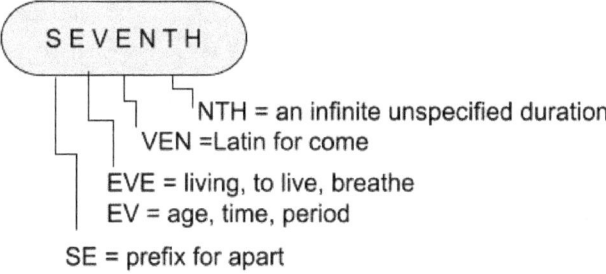

The seventh-day Sabbath is a holy time set apart where God beckons us to come apart and rest from all labor and cares of the world and worship

God the Creator of all living creation. The Sabbath is unchangeable and everlasting.

Fun Facts:

- Sabbath is mentioned three times in the fourth commandment.
- Abba and Eve are both palindromes, they are spelt the same forwards and backwards.
- Creation time—A day equals 1,440 minutes. Six days equals 144 hours. The number 144 perhaps implies an end to something or the beginning of rest. At the end of each day (1,440 minutes), God declared creation "good." At the end of each day there is nightly rest. At the end of the sixth day (144 hours), God declared creation "very good." The end of six days (144 hours) of creation, ushered mankind into spiritual and physical rest from six days of labor. The seventh day Sabbath is the beginning of rest. Another interesting reference to the number 144 is the reference to the wall of the city in the New Jerusalem. It is the heavenly city that will descent to earth. The wall's thickness measures 144 cubits (Rev 21:17.) A wall that acts like a seal around the city. Perhaps the number 144 also implies a seal/to be sealed/sealing. Revelation 14:1–3 refers to 144,000 end-time witnesses who will be sealed with the Father's name in their forehead. This symbolic number represents end-time messengers who will be key witnesses giving the loud cry of the approach of the second coming of Christ. They are also called the "firstfruits unto God and to the Lamb." The second coming of Christ will usher all the redeemed who are sealed with the character of Christ, to enter into eternal rest with God. (Rev 14:4)

Godhead—Light, Life, and Likeness

Deuteronomy 19:15 declares that in the mouth of two or three witnesses the matter is established. At creation God spoke things into existence. Without the spoken word there would be no creation. God had to speak in order to allow the witness of Jesus to be manifested, in order to manifest light and life. It was the word that created the world. The life (breath) was the Holy Spirit. The light was Jesus. The likeness was God. Each member of the Godhead is not confined to these singular attributes, because they are all co-eternal and co-equal; they all share these three attributes within themselves. However, at creation they took on individual forms while working together to accomplish one goal. They did not compete with each other but worked in perfect collaboration and synergy.

Life (Breath)—Holy Spirit

The Hebrew for breath is *ru'ahh* which means wind. The Latin root word *spir* means to breathe. The creation story began in Genesis 1:2, with the movement of the immaterial member of the Godhead upon the face of the waters. "The Spirit of God moved upon the face of the waters." This must have been the Holy Spirit in the form of wind—breathing upon the water.

> Job 27:3—"All the while my breath is in me, and the spirit of God is in my nostrils."
>
> John 20:22—"And when he had said this, he breathed on them, and saith unto them, 'receive ye the Holy Ghost.'"
>
> John 3:8—"The wind bloweth where it listeth, and thou hearest the sound thereof, but canst not tell whence it cometh, and whither it goeth, so is everyone that is born of the Spirit."

Light—Jesus

God created the sun to be the physical light but Jesus, the Son is the spiritual light.

> Luke 2:21,32—"And when eight days were accomplished for the circumcising of the child, his name was called JESUS, which was so named of the angel before he was conceived in the womb. A light to lighten the Gentiles, and the glory of thy people Israel."
>
> John 8:12—"Then spake Jesus again unto them, saying, 'I am the light of the world, he that followeth me shall not walk in darkness, but shall have the light of life.'"
>
> John 9:5—"As long as I am in the world, I am the light of the world."
>
> 2 Cor 4:6—"For God, who commanded the light to shine out of darkness, hath shined in our hearts, to give the light of the knowledge of the glory of God in the face of Jesus Christ."

Likeness (Image)—God

The first two of the ten commandments are the blueprint revealing the connection between the sovereign God and likeness or image. These two commandments are God's declaration and an architectural spiritual design of likeness or image that mankind should pattern their character from.

> Exod 20:2–5—"I am the Lord thy God, which have brought thee out of the land of Egypt, out of the house of bondage. Thou shalt have no other gods before me. Thou shalt not make unto thee any graven *image*, or any *likeness* of anything that is in heaven above, or that is in the earth beneath, or that is in the water under the earth. Thou shalt not bow down thyself to them, nor serve them, for I the Lord thy God am a jealous God, visiting the iniquity of the fathers upon the children unto the third and fourth generation of them that hate me, and shewing mercy unto thousands of them that love me, and keep my commandments."

> Gen 1:26–27—"And God said, 'let us make man in *our image*, after *our likeness* and let them have dominion over the fish of the sea, and over the fowl of the air, and over the cattle, and over all the earth, and over every creeping thing that creepeth upon the earth.' *So, God created man in his own image, in the image of God created he him; male and female created he them*."

Man was created in the likeness of God. If we break the first and second commandments and make images for ourselves, we are usurping God and making ourselves our own god. This is idolatry. God admonishes against self-worship or putting anything in place of the one true God. Likeness or image is reserved only for God. Matthew 22:17–21 captures an encounter between Jesus and the Pharisees regarding giving tribute money unto Caesar.

> "Tell us therefore, what thinkest thou? Is it lawful to give tribute unto Caesar, or not? But Jesus perceived their wickedness, and said, 'why tempt ye me, ye hypocrites? Shew me the tribute money.' And they brought unto him a penny. And he saith unto them, 'whose is this image and superscription?' They say unto him, 'Caesar's.' Then saith he unto them, 'render therefore unto Caesar the things which are Caesar's and unto God the things that are God's.'"

Jesus uses the illustrative sketch of a coin to highlight that we are like the coin. The image on the coin showed who had authority over the land.

Similarly, God imprints his likeness (image) on us. If we put any other image atop or above his image, then we debase or devalue the worth of the coin, i.e., ourselves and give our allegiance over to that image and fall into idolatry and apostasy. If we put any other image above God's image, then we are inherently rendering our worship to that image, i.e., rendering "unto Caesar the things which are Caesar." Sin has marred, tarnished, and replaced the original likeness or image of God. Thus, it was imperative that God should send the son, Jesus (the light) to restore us back to the likeness (image) of God. If we maintain God's image then we belong to God and will render to God our worship, in reflecting his character thereby rendering "unto God the things which are God's."

How Did the Godhead Create the World?

> Gen 1:1–3—"In the beginning God created the heaven and the earth. And the earth was without form, and void, and darkness was upon the face of the deep. And the Spirit of God moved upon the face of the waters. And God said, 'let there be light' and there was light."

God spoke the world into existence over six literal consecutive days (144 hours) and rested and sanctified the seventh day as a memorial of creation. Genesis records that before God began speaking things into existence, he created the heaven and the earth. There is no indication that he spoke the heaven and the empty shell of the earth into existence. Perhaps, he did speak them into existence but Genesis records that they were created instead of spoken into existence. Water was also created before the six-day creation process began. Water must have been created by all three witnesses in heaven because John records that nothing was made without Jesus. Genesis 1:2 records that the Spirit of God moved upon the face of the waters. How was the Spirit of God able to move over the waters? As noted, breath was expelled from the nostrils of God or from the mouth of God. The word "spirit" comes from the Latin "*spiritus*" which means to breathe. Therefore, the Holy Spirit was the breath at creation. Jesus was the voice at creation. When God spoke, the unseen Jesus, who was not yet made into flesh, was God's voice. God is a Spirit. Jesus at creation was also in spirit form. Jesus was the Word that became flesh. He came to earth much like a spokesperson for the Godhead. The voice of Jesus has creative life-giving power. It brought light from darkness; it brought life from voidness; it called Lazarus from the tomb, and it will summon the dead from dusty graves at the second coming. The unified creative force of the triune God—breathing, speaking, and forming. All three architects created and executed this divine master plan.

> Questions to ponder: When God created the earth, why was it important to speak things into existence? Could he not have thought them into existence or pointed a finger and manifested them physically?

Creation Stories—Light, Life, Likeness

We started off this book discussing the seed, tree, and fruit analogies and the parallelism to the Holy Spirit, God, and Jesus. We can also draw parallels to the seed being the Holy Spirit, hence life. The fruit parallels Jesus, hence, the light. The tree parallels God, hence, likeness. When a seed is planted it must be watered. A watered seed releases life, which takes on a physical likeness of a tree with limbs and leaves; bringing to light the birth of a fruit in the fullness of time. This is the embodiment of the creation story of plants. Similarly, a sperm and an egg releases life in a womb of water, which takes on a physical likeness of a human with limbs and organs; bringing to light the birth of another offspring in the fullness of time. This is the creation story of human birth. Similarly, the earth standing out of water and in water (2 Pet 3:5), at the Creator's word and hands brought forth life. This life took on spiritual likeness with the Sabbath and physical likeness of trees, animals, and humans. In the fullness of time, Jesus, the "firstfruit" and the light, came into the world. This is the creation story of earth.

A plant needs light to survive; humans need sunlight to survive; the earth needs sunlight to survive. A plant needs sustained life (air) to survive; humans need sustained breath (oxygen) to survive; the earth needs sustained gaseous elements to survive which includes oxygen. Plants, humans, and the earth could not exist without likeness, which is the framework that supports its unique identity and existence. The creation of a tree; the creation of a human; the creation of the world embodies life, light, and likeness.

Sustaining Spiritual Light, Life, and Likeness

The apostle John describes the light (Jesus) coming into earth as a light coming into a dark world giving the world the opportunity to come out of spiritual darkness into marvelous spiritual light. Jesus is also the life—the living Word.

> John 1:1-5, 9—"In the beginning was the Word, and the Word was with God, and the Word was God. The same was in the beginning with God. All things were made by him, and without him was not anything made that was made. In him was life, and the life was the light of men. And the light shineth in darkness and the darkness comprehended it not. That was the true Light, which lighteth every man that cometh into the world."

John also describes mankind receiving the likeness of God; a spiritual birth by accepting the fullness of the Christ. A spiritual adoption by modeling Christ's character, who is the image of God. If we model Christ, we inherently adopt the likeness of God.

> John 1:12-17—"But as many as received him, to them gave he power to become the sons of God, even to them that believe on his name, which were born, not of blood, nor of the will of the flesh, nor of the will of man, but of God. And the Word was made flesh, and dwelt among us, and we beheld his glory, the glory as of the only begotten of the Father full of grace and truth. John bare witness of him, and cried, saying, 'this was he of whom I spake, he that cometh after me is preferred before me, for he was before me. And of his fulness have all we received, and grace for grace. For the law was given by Moses, but grace and truth came by Jesus Christ.'"

John describes the Holy Spirit akin to water in the form of baptism. Jesus came to baptize with the Holy Spirit to take away sins thus imparting eternal life.

> John 1:26,29-34—"John answered them, saying, 'I baptize with water but there standeth one among you, whom ye know not.' The next day John seeth Jesus coming unto him, and saith, 'behold the Lamb of God, which taketh away the sin of the world. This is he of whom I said, after me cometh a man which is preferred before me, for he was before me. And I knew him not but that he should be made manifest to Israel, therefore, am I come baptizing with water.' And John bare record, saying, 'I saw the

Spirit descending from heaven like a dove, and it abode upon him. And I knew him not but he that sent me to baptize with water, the same said unto me, upon whom thou shalt see the Spirit descending, and remaining on him, the same is he which baptizeth with the Holy Ghost. And I saw, and bare record that this is the Son of God.'"

Sustained spiritual growth is achieved by being connected to God the Father, the son Jesus Christ, and the indwelling Holy Spirit—the three creative forces of life, light, and likeness.

— 9 —

3 Lies, 1 Truth

Fall of Man

(Immortality. Illumination. Idolatry)

Light, life, and likeness were essential for the creation of the world. Likewise, they were and are essential in the recreation of the fallen human race.

> Gen 1:26—"And God said, let us make man in our image, after our likeness, and let them have dominion over the fish of the sea, and over the fowl of the air, and over the cattle, and over all the earth, and over every creeping thing that creepeth upon the earth."
>
> Gen 2:7—"And the Lord God formed man of the dust of the ground, and breathed into his nostrils the breath of life, and man became a living soul."

God made man in his own image or likeness. God gave man dominion over the creatures. This supremacy reflected the likeness of God, in that God has power and dominion over the world. The likeness of God also means the character of God. Man was to reflect the character of God by pursuing holiness, righteousness, and perfection. Man was to reflect the likeness of God by procreating and multiplying to populate the earth. Man was also to care for creation which is reflective of God's loving, and caring nature. A physical stature was given to man (torso, head, limbs, eyes etc.), which is a physical likeness of Jesus, who became flesh and lived in human form.

The creation story of mankind clearly identified the following:

- God gave man breath—life
- God gave man image/character/dominion—likeness
- God gave man a garb of light at creation but after sin, God gave Jesus—light

After Adam and Eve ate of the forbidden fruit, God provided Jesus as the plan for man's salvation.

> Gen 3:15—"And I will put enmity between thee and the woman, and between thy seed and her seed, it shall bruise thy head, and thou shalt bruise his heel."

This proclamation made by God was "addressed to the serpent [and] applied directly to Satan himself, pointing forward to his ultimate defeat and destruction."[1] Jesus would defeat and destroy Satan, but Jesus would be bruised for our iniquities. This marvelous plan of redemption and salvation was laid out from the creation of the world.

The Fall of Man—Three Lies

In the midst of God's beautiful creation story, the archenemy, Satan lurked. He could not copy God's creative power of giving life, so he sought to counteract it with spiritually deadly lies spoken to Eve. The devil in the form of a serpent told Eve three lies to counteract God's true light, life, and likeness. These three lies caused the fall of man from grace and gave sin the entrance way into the world. These lies will play great prominence in these last days, so it is important to avoid these repeated deceptions.

> Gen 2:16-17—"And the Lord God commanded the man, saying, 'of every tree of the garden thou mayest freely eat but of the tree of the knowledge of good and evil, thou shalt not eat of it, for in the day that thou eatest thereof thou shalt surely die.'"

God commanded the first parents to not eat of the tree of knowledge of good and evil, otherwise they would "surely die." However, the serpent counteracted what God had told them.

1. White, *Patriarchs and Prophets*, 58.

> Gen 3:1–5—"Now the serpent was more subtle than any beast of the field which the Lord God had made. And he said unto the woman, 'yea, hath God said, ye shall not eat of every tree of the garden?' And the woman said unto the serpent, 'we may eat of the fruit of the trees of the garden but of the fruit of the tree which is in the midst of the garden, God hath said, ye shall not eat of it, neither shall ye touch it, lest ye die.' And the serpent said unto the woman, *'ye shall not surely die, for God doth know that in the day ye eat thereof, then your eyes shall be opened, and ye shall be as gods, knowing good and evil.'"*

"Ye shall not surely die," "Your eyes shall be opened," and "Ye shall be as gods knowing good and evil." With these three lies, the devil sought to contradict God's three fundamental creational truths—life, light, and likeness. These truths, although literal in the creation story, had spiritual undercurrents.

Lie #1—"You Shall Not Surely Die."

This lie was the first sin and lie told in the garden and on planet earth. The serpent was contradicting the elements of life—both physical and spiritual. The immortality of the soul was the first lie. God created man by breathing in him the breath of life. God's breath is eternal, but man's body is temporal. We cease to live once the breath departs. There is a physical limit to man's lifespan and existence, but the serpent contradicted this by fallaciously implying that there was no limit. This lie has permeated into many religions. Many believe that the deceased live on in the spirit realm and offer prayers to dead saints or relics. Immortality and spiritualism are still present-day deceptions. Adam and Eve also began to die spiritually once they partook of the forbidden tree. They became spiritually separated from God, because the wages of sin is the beginning of spiritual death (Rom 6:23.) The Godhead is the only source of eternal life and sin causes separation from this source of eternal life.

> Questions to ponder: Why would Cain have needed to kill Abel if Abel was immortal? Why do we have homicides if murderers knew that victims would return as spirits to incriminate them?

> Job 7:9–10—"As the cloud is consumed and vanisheth away, so he that goeth down to the grave shall come up no more. He shall return no more to his house, neither shall his place know him anymore."

> Eccl 9:5—"For the living know that they shall die but the dead know not anything, neither have they anymore a reward, for the memory of them is forgotten."

God's word is clear, the dead cease from living. The soul is not immortal and does not live on in the spirit realm, nor does dead loved ones visit in spirit form nor in dreams. If such strange apparitions appear, these are deceptive demons appearing as loved ones. Many seek out spirit mediums to connect them to deceased loved ones, not knowing that the source of this deception is Satan and fallen angels appearing as their loved ones. Immortality of the soul and the state of the dead will be deceptive lies used again by Satan in these last days.

Lie #2—"Your Eyes Shall be Opened."

The serpent espoused this lie to contradict the element of light. Eyes are associated with light; to be enlightened and to see things beyond the natural realms; to be illuminated.

> Matt 6:22—"The light of the body is the eye; if therefore thine eye be single, thy whole body shall be full of light."

> Acts 26:18—"To open their eyes, and to turn them from darkness to light, and from the power of Satan unto God, that they may receive forgiveness of sins, and inheritance among them which are sanctified by faith that is in me."

God created light to separate darkness. In spiritual parallelism, Jesus is the only true light for mankind, separating us from sin and Satan. God wants our eyes opened to discern the wiles and deception of the devil. The devil's lies deceived Eve and by extension mankind, into thinking that there was an alternate light. Eve was also deceived into thinking that her eyes would be opened to see things beyond the physical realms—perhaps to see spiritual things. This deception has led many to seek out occult theologies in pursuit of secret inner knowledge and illumination of an "all-seeing eye," dangerously placing themselves in spiritual darkness. Only God has the power to open the eyes to see spiritually manifested things become real. Our eyes should be opened only to spiritually see the will and purpose of God for our lives.

> Gen 3:7—"And the eyes of them both were opened, and they knew that they were naked, and they sewed fig leaves together, and made themselves aprons."

After they ate the fruit, their eyes were opened but only to the physical reality that they were naked. The first parents were deceived. They only saw their true sinful state, nakedness, and shame. They were now separated from God. They were no longer clothed by God's pure light.

> Gen 21:19 (story of Hagar)—"And God opened her eyes, and she saw a well of water."

> Num 22:31—"Then the Lord opened the eyes of Balaam, and he saw the angel of the Lord standing in the way, and his sword drawn in his hand, and he bowed down his head, and fell flat on his face."

> 2 Kgs 6:17—"And Elisha prayed, and said, 'Lord, I pray thee, open his eyes, that he may see.' And the Lord opened the eyes of the young man and he saw and behold the mountain was full of horses and chariots of fire roundabout Elisha."

> Luke 24:30-31—"And it came to pass, as he sat at meat with them, he took bread, and blessed it, and brake, and gave to them. And their eyes were opened, and they knew him, and he vanished out of their sight."

The deception of illumination, of being enlightened with inner knowledge of the spirit world, has given birth to astrology, secret societies, seances, and spirit mediums just to name a few. This search for forbidden knowledge has deceptively led many to seek light from spiritual darkness.

Lie #3—"Ye Shall be as Gods, Knowing Good and Evil."

The serpent was contradicting the element of likeness. Mankind was made in the image (likeness) of God but was not created to be gods or to be like gods—making ourselves idols and demi-gods. The Creator is the only God, and we are the creations. Making a likeness of God is idolatry or trying to be like God is self-worship, which is the breaking of the first and second commandments.

> Exod 20:3-4—"Thou shalt have no other gods before me. Thou shalt not make unto thee any graven image, or any likeness of

anything that is in heaven above, or that is in the earth beneath, or that is in the water under the earth."

The knowledge of good and evil resided in that tree and God commanded Adam not to eat of it lest he would die. God intended the first parents to have eternal life and not death. God wanted to protect them and all mankind from evil and from the mere knowledge of evil. After eating the fruit, they became aware of evil, and this was the entrance way to sin that has contaminated the planet.

> Amos 5:14—"Seek good, and not evil, that ye may live and so the Lord, the God of hosts, shall be with you, as ye have spoken."
>
> 3 John 11—"Beloved, follow not that which is evil, but that which is good. He that doeth good is of God but he that doeth evil hath not seen God."
>
> Ps 37:27—"Depart from evil and do good; and dwell for evermore."

These verses reveal God's desire to protect mankind from the knowledge of evil. Eve was tempted by the thought of being like God and was deceived. Eating the fruit did not make her like God. This deceptive lie is still being spewed out in the form of self-exaltation, false worship, prideful boasting, and idolatry. Man was created in the likeness of God to reflect his character, to be obedient and submissive to his will. Mankind was not created to make themselves idols—attempting to usurp the authority and likeness of God.

The three lies by Satan are summarized in 1 John 2:16, "for all that is in the world, the lust of the flesh, and the lust of the eyes, and the pride of life, is not of the Father, but is of the world."

> Questions to ponder: How can a created being be a god or think they can become like the God that created him. If they are created beings doesn't this make them automatically inferior?

Jesus the Savior

> Gen 3:15—"And I will put enmity between thee and the woman, and between thy seed and her seed, it shall bruise thy head, and thou shalt bruise his heel."

From the foundation of the world, God had a plan of salvation for the fallen race and the woman (the church.) To counter the three lies told by Satan, God sent the only begotten son, Jesus to be the truth, the Savior, and the light of the world to pay the penalty for sin. Jesus would deal a deadly blow to the serpent by crushing its head, but Christ would be nailed to the cross by his hands and feet (heel) in AD 31. The heart of a climbing snake is close to its head, so it was fitting that the prophecy pointed to the crushing of its head which would render a deadly blow to the heart. Jesus was bruised for our iniquities. The crushing of the serpent's head foreshadows the end of time when all sins will be transferred back to the devil who is the originator of sin. Light, life, and likeness were not only essential for the creation of the world but are vital for the spiritual recreation of fallen man. God wants to take the darkness, voidness, and formlessness of the frail human existence and give light, life, and likeness, which ultimately is Jesus Christ!

The creation story is profoundly beautiful. God did not create or started with a perfect, beautiful world. He took it in its imperfect state and transformed it to his perfect likeness. Likewise, we are not perfect beings, but God wants to take us in our imperfect state and make us perfect in his likeness. The human condition is void (emptiness), without form (no identity), and dark (prone to evil) without the Savior. We must see ourselves as void, without form, and dark, seeking for God to fill us, form us, and flood us with light. The Spirit of God will move once we acknowledge our emptiness. God is a creative force. He cannot create something or someone who is full (self-righteous) or complete (self-sufficient.) He takes our nothingness and makes it complete—makes it come to life! He makes all things new again! This is the creative genius of a personal hands-on intimate loving God who uniquely designed us in his heart before we came into physical being. God wants to touch us, fill us, and breathe life into us.

> 2 Cor 5:17–21—"Therefore if any man be in Christ, he is a new creature, old things are passed away, behold, all things are become new. And all things are of God, who hath reconciled us to himself by Jesus Christ, and hath given to us the ministry of reconciliation; to wit, that God was in Christ, reconciling the world unto himself, not imputing their trespasses unto them, and hath committed unto us the word of reconciliation. Now then we are ambassadors for Christ, as though God did beseech you by us, we pray you in Christ's stead, be ye reconciled to God.

> For he hath made him to be sin for us, who knew no sin, that we might be made the righteousness of God in him."

Jesus, heaven's ambassador, sent on an extraordinary mission to save planet earth from sin reconciling us to the Father. Christ is the likeness of the Father. Likewise, Christians must be the likeness of Christ to be reconciled to God.

Three Stages of Salvation

There are three stages of salvation; justification, sanctification, and glorification. Justification is the act of being made just with God, in right standing, through acceptance of the merits of the sacrifice of Jesus. When the sinner accepts Christ, the Savior's light immediately shines into the darkened heart. This mirrors the creation story when God said, "let there be light," to immediately dispel the darkness of the earth. Sanctification is the daily on-going imparting of the Holy Spirit allowing transformation of character unto holiness. This mirrors the creation story. The first parents, Adam and Eve were placed in the garden of Eden; they were to dress it and keep it and maintain obedience to all of God's command including what they could or could not eat. They were to care for the animals. They were in a daily commune with God. This was God's way of daily developing their character. Glorification is the completion of the character—Christians reflecting the perfect righteousness of Christ. It is the finished work. It is the removal of sin and being in a state of readiness or worthiness for heaven. This mirrors the creation story. When God had finished the six days of creating all life forms, he declared it to be, not just good but very good; his declaration of perfection and completion. God created the seventh day as the finishing cap stone, that was blessed and sanctified (made holy.) Glorification is the finishing of the work. When Jesus was crucified, his last words were, "it is finished." Before ascending to heaven, Jesus prayed the prayer of glorification to the Father, "I have glorified thee on the earth, I have finished the work which thou gavest me to do" (John 17:4.) The salvation of mankind rests solely upon the merits of the sacrifice of Jesus.

> 2 Thess 1:12—"That the name of our Lord Jesus Christ may be glorified in you, and ye in him, according to the grace of our God and the Lord Jesus Christ."

Eph 4:21—"If so, be that ye have heard him, and have been taught by him, as the truth is in Jesus."

John 14:6—"Jesus saith unto him, 'I am the way, the truth, and the life, no man cometh unto the Father, but by me.'"

Jesus is the source of truth. Jesus is the only way to the Father. He is the example, template, and pattern. Eternal life is the acceptance of the light of Jesus and being transformed in his likeness and character. This is the recreation of man. To counter the lies of immortality, illumination, and idolatry, Jesus became the embodiment of life, light, and likeness—the great plan of salvation.

— 10 —

3 Temptations, 1 Escape
Deception and Restoration

(light. life. likeness)

Adam and Eve were deceived. Deception will be the primary tool used by Satan in these end-times. When Jesus was asked by the disciples what were the signs of the end of the world, Jesus gave deception as the first sign.

> Matt 24:3-5—"And as he sat upon the mount of Olives, the disciples came unto him privately, saying, 'tell us, when shall these things be and what shall be the sign of thy coming, and of the end of the world?' And Jesus answered and said unto them, 'take heed that no man deceive you. For many shall come in my name, saying, I am Christ and shall deceive many.'"

Jesus was describing the deception of light—false christs appearing as angels of light. Deception is the withholding of truth; being presented with lies in an attempt to mislead. The prefix "de" means from and "cept" has a Latin root meaning "taken." Deception is to be taken or led away from truth.

Three Foundations of Deceit

> 1 John 2:15-16—"Love not the world, neither the things that are in the world. If any man love the world, the love of the Father is not in him. For all that is in the world, the lust of the flesh, and the lust of the eyes, and the pride of life, is not of the Father, but is of the world."

In the previous chapter we looked at the three lies told by Satan. These three lies have three foundations or roots of deceit—lust of the flesh, lust of the eyes, and the pride of life. These deceptions were the source of the lies used to tempt Eve and to tempt Jesus in the wilderness and will be used even more forcefully in these end-times.

Lust of the Flesh

> Gen 3:1,6—"Now the serpent was more subtle than any beast of the field which the Lord God had made. And he said unto the woman, 'yea, hath God said, ye shall not eat of every tree of the garden?' And when *the woman saw that the tree was good for food*, and that it was pleasant to the eyes, and a tree to be desired to make one wise, she took of the fruit thereof, and did eat, and gave also unto her husband with her, and he did eat."

> Matt 4:1-4—"Then was Jesus led up of the Spirit into the wilderness to be tempted of the devil. And when he had fasted forty days and forty nights, he was afterward hungered. And when the tempter came to him, he said, '*if thou be the Son of God, command that these stones be made bread*.' But he answered and said, 'it is written, man shall not live by bread alone, but by every word that proceedeth out of the mouth of God.'"

> Rev 13:17—"And that *no man might buy or sell*, save he that had the mark, or the name of the beast, or the number of his name."

Eve was tempted with a fruit. Jesus was tempted with bread. Last days Christians will be tempted with the withholding of access to food and basic necessities unless they accept the mark of the beast. God's people will also be faced with the temptation of appetite. Tempted into eating unhealthy foods versus the food that God gave as the original diet—fruits, nuts, grains, and a plant-based diet. Jesus admonished that we must not live by the flesh but by the word; for the flesh profiteth nothing (Matt 4:4; John 6:63.)

Lust of the Eyes

Gen 3:4–6—"And the serpent said unto the woman, 'ye shall not surely die, for God doth know that in the day ye eat thereof, then your eyes shall be opened, and ye shall be as gods, knowing good and evil.' And when the woman saw that the tree was good for food, and that *it was pleasant to the eyes . . .*"

Matt 4:8–10—"Again, the devil taketh him up into an exceeding high mountain, *and sheweth him all the kingdoms of the world, and the glory of them*; and saith unto him, 'all these things will I give thee if thou wilt fall down and worship me.' Then saith Jesus unto him, 'get thee hence, Satan, for it is written, thou shalt worship the Lord thy God, and him only shalt thou serve.'"

Rev 18:2–3—"And he cried mightily with a strong voice, saying, 'Babylon the great is fallen, is fallen, and is become the habitation of devils, and the hold of every foul spirit, and a cage of every unclean and hateful bird. For all nations have drunk of the wine of the wrath of her fornication, and the *kings of the earth have committed fornication with her, and the merchants of the earth are waxed rich through the abundance of her delicacies.*'"

Mark 4:19—"And the cares of this world, and the deceitfulness of riches, and the lusts of other things entering in, choke the word, and it becometh unfruitful."

Mark 10:24—"And the disciples were astonished at his words. But Jesus answereth again, and saith unto them, 'children, how hard is it for them that trust in riches to enter into the kingdom of God!'"

Eve was tempted with the eye pleasing allurement of the fruit and the offer of enlightenment. Jesus was tempted with the eye pleasing allurement of wealth, fame, power, and pleasantries. End-time Christians and the world alike will be tempted and coerced into giving their allegiance to the beast power (Babylon), in exchange for jobs, financial security, wealth, social freedoms, trade agreements etc. Jesus warned against putting our trust in riches; our trust must be in God alone.

Pride of Life

Pride is defined as a high or inordinate opinion of one's own dignity, importance, merit, or superiority.[1]

> Gen 3:4–6—"And the serpent said unto the woman, 'ye shall not surely die, for God doth know that in the day ye eat thereof, then your eyes shall be opened, and *ye shall be as gods, knowing good and evil.*' And when the woman saw that the tree was good for food, and that it was pleasant to the eyes, and a tree to be desired *to make one wise*, she took of the fruit thereof, and did eat, and gave also unto her husband with her and he did eat."

> Matt 4:5–7—"Then the devil taketh him up into the holy city, and setteth him on a pinnacle of the temple, and saith unto him, 'if thou be the Son of God, *cast thyself down, for it is written, he shall give his angels charge concerning thee* and in their hands they shall bear thee up, lest at any time thou dash thy foot against a stone.' Jesus said unto him, 'it is written again, thou shalt not tempt the Lord thy God.'"

> 2 Tim 3:1–2—"This know also, that in the last days perilous times shall come. For men shall be lovers of their own selves, covetous, boasters, *proud*, blasphemers, disobedient to parents, unthankful, unholy . . ."

> 2 Pet 3:3–4—"Knowing this first, that there shall come in the last days scoffers, walking after their own lusts, and saying, 'where is the promise of his coming, for since the fathers fell asleep, all things continue as they were from the beginning of the creation.'"

Eve was tempted with thoughts of being like God, superior, and wise. Jesus was tempted to provokingly test God's power, presence, and faithfulness, by showing-off and jumping from a pinnacle. Last day Christians and the world alike will be tempted to become more proud, boastful, and self-seeking. Scoffers and even some apostate Christians will be tempted to question God's promises. Jesus countered these three deceptive temptations by using Scripture, by repeating, "it is written . . ." Jesus also highlighted the spiritual solutions to deceptions.

---

1. Dictionary.com, s.v, "pride."

Lust of the Flesh Versus True Life

How did Jesus overcome the temptation of lust of the flesh?

> Matt 4:4—"But he answered and said, 'it is written, man shall not live by bread alone, but by every word that proceedeth out of the mouth of God.'"

> Deut 8:3—"And he humbled thee, and suffered thee to hunger, and fed thee with manna, which thou knewest not, neither did thy fathers know, that he might make thee know that man doth not live by bread only, but by every word that proceedeth out of the mouth of the Lord doth man live."

Lust of the flesh is the deception and temptation of satisfying and sustaining physical life, but Jesus points to the real spiritual source of life and that is the word of God. Jesus fasted forty days and forty nights, sustained only by the word. Christians must also be sustained by the spiritual word of God.

Lust of the Eyes Versus True Light

How did Jesus overcome the temptation of lust of the eyes?

> Matt 4:10—"Then saith Jesus unto him, 'get thee hence, Satan, for it is written, thou shalt worship the Lord thy God, and him only shalt thou serve.'"

> Deut 6:13-14—"Thou shalt fear the Lord thy God, and serve him, and shalt swear by his name. Ye shall not go after other gods, of the gods of the people which are roundabout you."

> Acts 26:18—"To open their eyes, and to turn them from darkness to light, and from the power of Satan unto God, that they may receive forgiveness of sins, and inheritance among them which are sanctified by faith that is in me."

Lust of the eyes is the deception and temptation of satisfying and sustaining emotional life through temporal means. The drive for self-importance, wealth, power, and fame is often driven by the need to fill an emotional void. However, the true source of light is the Godhead. God promises to supply all needs according to his riches in glory (Phil 4:19.)

Pride of Life Versus True Likeness

How did Jesus overcome the temptation of pride and self-exaltation?

> Matt 4:7—"Jesus said unto him, 'it is written again, thou shalt not tempt the Lord thy God.'"

> Deut 6:16—"Ye shall not tempt the Lord your God, as ye tempted him in Massah."

Jesus countered this temptation by quoting Moses. The children of Israel chided against Moses, blaming him for bringing them into the wilderness to die of thirst.

> Exod 17:2-7—"Wherefore the people did chide with Moses, and said, 'give us water that we may drink.' And Moses said unto them, 'why chide ye with me, wherefore do ye tempt the Lord?' And the people thirsted there for water, and the people murmured against Moses, and said, 'wherefore is this that thou hast brought us up out of Egypt, to kill us and our children and our cattle with thirst?' And Moses cried unto the Lord, saying, 'what shall I do unto this people, they be almost ready to stone me.' And the Lord said unto Moses, 'go on before the people, and take with thee of the elders of Israel, and thy rod, wherewith thou smotest the river, take in thine hand, and go. Behold, I will stand before thee there upon the rock in Horeb, and thou shalt smite the rock, and there shall come water out of it, that the people may drink.' And Moses did so in the sight of the elders of Israel. And he called the name of the place Massah, and Meribah, because of the chiding of the children of Israel, and because they tempted the Lord, saying, is the Lord among us, or not?"

> Ps 78:56-58—"Yet they tempted and provoked the most high God and kept not his testimonies. But turned back and dealt unfaithfully like their fathers; they were turned aside like a deceitful bow. For they provoked him to anger with their high places and moved him to jealousy with their graven images."

Pride is to have a self-deceptive presumptuous confidence or a haughty self-exalting spirit. The children of Israel rebelled against God with graven images thus allowing pride to envelope their hearts. They made their own graven image thus replacing the true likeness of God. Pride is the deception and temptation of satisfying and sustaining spiritual life by being like God or replacing the true God with man-made gods. Man-made gods are not only graven images but can be self, ideas, thoughts, religious traditions etc. It was this prideful spirit that caused the Israelites to tempt God. They doubted his presence and his promise to take care of their needs. They were going ahead of God, demanding that their immediate needs be met, demanding that God prove himself, instead of humbly trusting and waiting on him to supply their spiritual and physical needs. In heaven, Lucifer wanted to be like God, and it was pride or self-exaltation that caused Lucifer, along with one third of the angels to be cast out of heaven. This attempt to usurp God's authority is now being played out on planet earth. The devil tempted Jesus to jump from a high elevated pinnacle to prove that God was with him; provoking God to act by sending angels to save him. This is the same mindset of self-elevation that Lucifer was projecting—this is an attribute of pride. Removing pride requires the return to the true likeness of God, to the complete obedience to the commandments and a life of patient humility.

The three temptations were rooted in three areas of deceit. The three areas of deceit targeted the three areas of the human experience—physical, emotional, and spiritual. These three areas of the human existence and experience that the devil targeted were the body, mind, and soul. In all three temptations, Jesus pointed to God and the word as the only way of escape from temptations. "It is written" was the tri-fold rebuke. We are reminded in 1 Corinthians 10:13, "there hath no temptation taken you, but such as is common to man, but God is faithful, who will not suffer you to be tempted above that ye are able but will with the temptation also make a way to escape, that ye may be able to bear it."

> Interesting Fact: Massah has a contemporary meaning and was a word used by slaves to describe their bossy plantation masters. It is also used today to describe someone who is stubborn.

Deception of Light

The core tenets of the Godhead are light, life, and likeness. In these last days, Satan will counter these tenets with deceptions. Deception of light will involve false lights—false messiahs, false miracles, and a false second coming. "And the serpent said unto the woman, 'ye shall not surely die, for God doth know that in the day ye eat thereof, then your eyes shall be opened, and ye shall be as gods, knowing good and evil'" (Gen 3:4–5.) This serpentine deceptive language will again deceive many. Eyes are associated with light—to be enlightened. The eye is the organ of sight, to see.

In the Old Testament, a seer was a prophet of light. They received supernatural divine insight from God, prophetic messages, and was anointed with the spirit of discernment (1 Sam 9:9.) Many seers/prophets in those days spoke out against idolatry and spiritual wickedness. Their message of repentance was often rejected by rebellious nations who sought after false light and false seers/prophets. The book of Isaiah records, "that this is a rebellious people, lying children, children that will not hear the law of the Lord, which say to the seers, see not, and to the prophets, prophesy not unto us right things, speak unto us smooth things, prophesy deceits" (Isa 30:9–10.)

The devil deceived Eve by telling her that her eyes would be opened—that she would be enlightened. She became enchanted with the thoughts of receiving supernatural insight into the spirit realm and receiving power to know all things, to see into the future, which was the prerogative of God alone. From Genesis to the seers/prophets of old, to these end-times, this same deception is being perpetrated. Many false light bearers are amongst us.

> 2 Cor 11:14–15—"And no marvel, for Satan himself is transformed into an angel of light. Therefore, it is no great thing if his ministers also be transformed as the ministers of righteousness, whose end shall be according to their works."

> Isa 8:19–20—"And when they shall say unto you, seek unto them that have familiar spirits, and unto wizards that peep, and that mutter should not a people seek unto their God, for the living to the dead? To the law and to the testimony, if they speak not according to this word, it is because there is no light in them."

Satanic forces will more forcefully emerge; counterfeit light claiming to be the Messiah and will perform false miracles. There are presently many false messiahs, teachers, apostles, and preachers, but as we near the return of Christ, there will be many more. Isaiah 8:20 gives the litmus test that reveals a false prophet—they will not speak according to the Word of God (Scripture/Bible.) Jesus warned that there will be an increase in false light towards the end of earth's history (Matt 24:3–5.) These false light bearers will deceive many by performing false miracles, professing that spiritual fire is falling from heaven. This will lure many flocking to false revivals seeking instantaneous miracles.

> Rev 16:14—"For they are the spirits of devils, working miracles, which go forth unto the kings of the earth and of the whole

world, to gather them to the battle of that great day of God Almighty."

Rev 13:13-14—"And he doeth great wonders, so that he maketh fire come down from heaven on the earth in the sight of men, and deceiveth them that dwell on the earth by the means of those miracles which he had power to do in the sight of the beast, saying to them that dwell on the earth, that they should make an image to the beast, which had the wound by a sword, and did live."

Satan will perform deceptive miracles involving fire (light) coming down from heaven in the sight (eyes) of men. Satan will also perform a false counterfeit second coming and will attempt to deceive many using some element of a grand light show. The deceiver will attempt to perform a false second coming of Christ by unleashing a false messiah upon the earth. We know that in the presence of the true God there is lightning, and the second coming will indeed be a spectacular event as described in these verses.

Zech 9:14—"And the Lord shall be seen over them, and his arrow shall go forth as the lightning, and the Lord God shall blow the trumpet, and shall go with whirlwinds of the south."

Matt 24:27,30-31—"For as the lightning cometh out of the east, and shineth even unto the west, so shall also the coming of the Son of man be. And then shall appear the sign of the Son of man in heaven and then shall all the tribes of the earth mourn, and they shall see the Son of man coming in the clouds of heaven with power and great glory. And he shall send his angels with a great sound of a trumpet, and they shall gather together his elect from the four winds, from one end of heaven to the other."

Rev 1:7—"Behold, he cometh with clouds and every eye shall see him, and they also which pierced him, and all kindreds of the earth shall wail because of him."

The second coming of Christ, the true Messiah will be visible and audible to all. It will not be a secret because every eye shall bear witness. Loud blowing of trumpets, spectacular lightning, tens of thousands of angels; an exhibition of all power and great glory. How will we decipher the true Messiah's coming versus the false messiah? There are many authentic signs and attributes of Jesus' second coming, but one of the most significant and clear signs is that the dead in Christ will be raised from the dead.

Deception of Life

Deception of life involves false appearances of the dead. "And the serpent said unto the woman, ye shall not surely die" (Gen 3:4.) The Godhead is the only reservoir for life. Satan cannot create, sustain nor resurrect life, so his only recourse in creating a deception for life is to marshal demons to impersonate the dead.

> 1 Thess 4:16-17—"For the Lord himself shall descend from heaven with a shout, with the voice of the archangel, and with the trump of God and the dead in Christ shall rise first. Then we which are alive and remain shall be caught up together with them in the clouds, to meet the Lord in the air: and so shall we ever be with the Lord."

> John 5:25—"Verily, verily, I say unto you, the hour is coming, and now is, when the dead shall hear the voice of the Son of God and they that hear shall live."

> John 11:25—"Jesus said unto her, 'I am the resurrection, and the life, he that believeth in me, though he were dead, yet shall he live."

> John 1:4—"In him was life, and the life was the light of men."

These verses highlight two key elements—light and life of the Messiah, who is the only true light of the world. Jesus is the resurrection and the life. It will not be the loud climactic, apocalyptic, and boisterous trumpet noise that will wake the dead. It will be the voice of Christ that will wake up the dead. The Godhead is the architect of life and is the only one that can resurrect life. Humans give birth to the life that God formed in the womb; the spark of life (breath) comes only from God. Satan cannot give life or resurrect life, therefore one clear indicator of a false second coming is that there will be no resurrection of the dead.

State of the Dead and Spiritualism

> "I saw that the saints must have a thorough understanding of present truth, which they will be obliged to maintain from the Scriptures. They must understand the state of the dead; for the spirits of devils will yet appear to them, professing to be beloved relatives or friends, who will declare to them unscriptural doctrines. They will do all in their power to excite sympathy and

will work miracles before them to confirm what they declare. The people of God must be prepared to withstand these spirits with the Bible truth that the dead know not anything, and that they who thus appear are the spirits of devils."[2]

There will be an increase in spiritual apparitions of dead loved ones, but these are merely demonic spirits seeking to deceive. The Word of God clearly states that the dead will not live again until Christ returns to resurrect them, and the voice of the Son of God calls them from dusty graves. The resurrection of the righteous Christians will be the clear distinction between the true second coming of Christ versus the false deceptive second coming perpetrated by Satan.

Deception of Likeness

"Ye shall be as gods, knowing good and evil" (Gen 3:5.) This deceptive lie of being like God or having God's likeness will involve false worship, false god, and the enforcement of a false sabbath. The book of Revelation, Chapter 13, points to two beast kingdoms that will play prominent roles in this world-wide deception. The first beast kingdom receives power from Satan (Rev 13:4.) The second beast kingdom gives its allegiance to the first beast and forces everyone to worship the image or likeness of the first beast. This will be through legislation and laws mandating worship on a false sabbath.

> Rev 13:14-15—"And deceiveth them that dwell on the earth by the means of those miracles which he had power to do in the sight of the beast, saying to them that dwell on the earth, that they should make an image to the beast, which had the wound by a sword, and did live. And he had power to give life unto the image of the beast, that the image of the beast should both speak, and cause that as many as would not worship the image of the beast should be killed."

It was self-exaltation or pride that cost Lucifer and one third of the angels their place in heaven. Lucifer wanted to be like God. He coveted the worship that was given to God and sought to usurp God. He was cast out of heaven to earth where he continues his agenda through human agents. The culmination of these deceptions will see the enforcement of worship of a false image or likeness, in defiance of God's true commandment.

2. White, *Early Writings*, 262.

However, God has a true remnant church that will stand faithful to the commandments. This will be explored in more detail in Chapter 15.

Restoration

Deceptive lies led to the downfall of man. Deception is not merely lies but they are lies clothed with the intent to deceive. The deceiver sought to beguile Eve by baiting her with half-truths; a subtle lure to disarm her faith in God and made her entertain thoughts of doubt. Three deceptive lies plunged planet earth into the dark bowels of sin, separating man from God. A separation that has denied direct physical contact with God. Sinful man could no longer be in the direct presence of a sinless God. God's plan of restoration was to send Jesus to restore us back to the light, life, and likeness of the Father.

The apostle Paul wrote to the church at Colosse of the restoration of fallen man back to the Father. It's a message to us today.

> Col 1:12-15,20-22—"Giving thanks unto the Father, which hath made us meet to be partakers of the inheritance of the saints in light. Who hath delivered us from the power of darkness, and hath translated us into the kingdom of his dear Son. In whom we have redemption through his blood, even the forgiveness of sins. Who is the image of the invisible God, the firstborn of every creature. And, having made peace through the blood of his cross, by him to reconcile all things unto himself; by him, I say, whether they be things in earth, or things in heaven. And you, that were sometime alienated and enemies in your mind by wicked works, yet now hath he reconciled in the body of his flesh through death, to present you holy and unblameable and unreproveable in his sight."

> Col 2:4,8-9,18—3:1-4—"And this I say, lest any man should beguile you with enticing words. Beware lest any man spoil you through philosophy and vain deceit, after the tradition of men, after the rudiments of the world, and not after Christ. For in him dwelleth all the fulness of the Godhead bodily. Let no man beguile you of your reward in a voluntary humility and worshipping of angels, intruding into those things which he hath not seen, vainly puffed up by his fleshly mind. If ye then be risen with Christ, seek those things which are above, where Christ sitteth on the right hand of God. Set your affection on things above, not on things on the earth. For ye are dead, and your life

is hid with Christ in God. When Christ, who is our life, shall appear, then shall ye also appear with him in glory."

Summary

- The construct of the triune Godhead is built upon three core tenets—light, life, and likeness
- The construct of the earth was built upon—light, life, and likeness
- Three lies of Satan led to man's downfall—"you will not surely die," "your eyes will be opened," "you shall be as gods knowing good and evil"
- The three deceptive lies and the three temptations are built upon three pillars—lust of the flesh, lust of the eyes, and the pride of life These will also be the sources of deception in these last days
- The three lies and their core pillars seek to counter God's core tenets of light, life, and likeness
- Deception led to the fall of man, but through Jesus Christ, mankind received restoration

Immortality	Illumination	Idolatry
Life versus death	Light versus darkness	Likeness versus diverseness
"Ye shall not surely die"	"Your eyes shall be opened"	"Ye shall be as gods, knowing good and evil"
Lust of the flesh	Lust of the eyes	Pride of life
Physical	Emotional	Spiritual
Body	Mind	Soul

Rom 8:6–9—"For to be carnally minded is death, but to be spiritually minded is life and peace. Because the carnal mind is enmity against God, for it is not subject to the law of God, neither indeed can be. So, then they that are in the flesh cannot please God. But ye are not in the flesh, but in the Spirit, if so be that the Spirit of God dwell in you. Now if any man have not the Spirit of Christ, he is none of his."

— 11 —

3 Heads, 1 Tail
The Archenemy of the Godhead

(Darkness. Death. Diverseness)

The battle of the ages began with the conflict between the triune Godhead and the archenemy Satan, the tail. Head signifies honor, while tail alludes to someone who is a liar and deceiver (Isa 9:15.) The three core tenets of the Godhead are light, life and likeness. The archenemy of the Godhead, therefore, must be the three polar opposites; darkness, death, and diverseness. What separates or divides these polar opposites from the tenets of the triune Godhead? It began in Genesis.

Darkness

Gen 1:1-4—"In the beginning God created the heaven and the earth. And the earth was without form, and void, and darkness was upon the face of the deep. And the Spirit of God moved upon the face of the waters. And God said, 'let there be light, and there was light.' And God saw the light, that it was good, and *God divided the light from the darkness.*"

God, who is all light, entered the darkness and immediately light and darkness were divided. God's presence was now the divider between light and darkness.

light ←GOD→ darkness

Death

The first mention of death in the creation story was in God's warning to Adam not to eat of the forbidden fruit lest he would surely die.

> Gen 2:15-17—"And the Lord God took the man and put him into the garden of Eden to dress it and to keep it. And the Lord *God commanded* the man, saying, 'of every tree of the garden thou mayest freely eat, but of the tree of the knowledge of good and evil, thou shalt not eat of it, *for in the day that thou eatest thereof thou shalt surely die*.'"

life ←law→ death

God commanded Adam, thereby giving him a law. God's commandment is a law. Keeping the commandment (law) meant life, however, breaking it meant death. The law or commandment of God, therefore, is the divider between life and death—both physical and spiritual life and death.

Diverseness

After the serpent (Satan) deceived Eve into eating the forbidden fruit, God came down to investigate.

> Gen 3:13-15—"And the Lord God said unto the woman, 'what is this that thou hast done?' And the woman said, 'the serpent beguiled me, and I did eat.' And the Lord God said unto the serpent, 'because thou hast done this, thou art cursed above all cattle, and above every beast of the field; upon thy belly shalt thou go, and dust shalt thou eat all the days of thy life. And I will put *enmity between thee and the woman,* and between thy

seed and her seed; it shall bruise thy head, and thou shalt bruise his heel.'"

woman's seed (likeness of God) ←enmity→ serpent's seed (diverseness)

Adam and Eve were created in the image or likeness of God (Gen 1:26.) Woman also represents God's church and those who would become followers of Christ. The serpent and its seed are the polar opposite of the likeness of God. The serpent and its seed are different or diverse. Diverse is also the word used to describe the antichrist beast power in Daniel's vision (Dan 7:7,24.) Enmity means enemy, malice, opposition, hostile feeling, or internal conflict. There was to be hatred and division between the woman and the serpent. The woman (church) would abhor anything that resembled the serpentine image and similarly the serpent would hate the woman because she reflected Christ. Enmity became the divider between likeness and diverseness.

Summary

- God separates us from darkness versus light
- Law (commandment) separates us from death versus life
- Enmity separates diverseness (image of serpent/Satan) versus likeness (image of God)

The three foundational tenets of the Godhead; light, life, and likeness and the archenemy; darkness, death and diverseness are evident in the creation story. These tenets were also evident in the exodus journey of the children of Israel as they fled Egypt and will also play a pivotal role for end-time Christians (spiritual Israel) who are called to flee spiritual apostate Babylon.

Children of Israel—Light Versus Darkness

For four hundred years, the children of Israel were slaves in Egypt. They were finally released from the bondage of Pharaoh and began their exodus journey through the wilderness to the promised land. During their journey, God's loving and caring presence was with them tangibly. A pillar of cloud by day to protect them from the heat and to lead their way and a pillar of fire by night for warmth against the cool night air.

> Exod 13:20-22—"And they took their journey from Succoth, and encamped in Etham, in the edge of the wilderness. And the Lord went before them by day in a pillar of a cloud, to lead them the way, and by night in a pillar of fire, to give them light, to go by day and night. He took not away the pillar of the cloud by day, nor the pillar of fire by night, from before the people."

In a moment of regret, Pharaoh and his army pursued them in an attempt to bring them back into captivity. The children of Israel were now boxed in by the approaching army and the impassable Red Sea ahead.

> Exod 14:10-20—"And when Pharaoh drew nigh, the children of Israel lifted up their eyes, and behold, the Egyptians marched after them, and they were sore afraid, and the children of Israel cried out unto the Lord. And they said unto Moses, 'because there were no graves in Egypt, hast thou taken us away to die in the wilderness, wherefore hast thou dealt thus with us, to carry us forth out of Egypt? Is not this the word that we did tell thee in Egypt, saying, let us alone, that we may serve the Egyptians. For it had been better for us to serve the Egyptians, than that we should die in the wilderness.' And Moses said unto the people 'fear ye not, stand still, and see the salvation of the Lord, which he will shew to you today, for the Egyptians whom ye have seen today, ye shall see them again no more forever. The Lord shall fight for you, and ye shall hold your peace.' And the Lord said unto Moses, 'wherefore criest thou unto me, speak unto the children of Israel, that they go forward. But lift thou up thy rod, and stretch out thine hand over the sea, and divide it and the children of Israel shall go on dry ground through the midst of the sea. And I, behold, I will harden the hearts of the Egyptians, and they shall follow them, and I will get me honor upon Pharaoh, and upon all his host, upon his chariots, and upon his horsemen. And the Egyptians shall know that I am the Lord, when I have gotten me honor upon Pharaoh, upon his chariots, and upon his horsemen.' And the angel of God, which went before the camp of Israel, removed and went behind them, *and the pillar of the cloud went from before their face, and stood behind them. And it came between the camp of the Egyptians and the camp of Israel; and it was a cloud and darkness to them, but it gave light by night to these, so that the one came not near the other all the night.*"

As Pharaoh and his army approached the Israelites, God's presence, the pillar of cloud, moved from before them and went behind them. God separated the children of Israel from the Egyptians. The children of Israel were still enveloped by light, but the Egyptians saw darkness! God divided the light (children of Israel) from the darkness (the Egyptians.)

Children of Israel—Life Versus Death

The Israelites faced the Red Sea, a life-or-death crossroad. God instructed Moses to lift up his rod. The rod had no inherent power within itself; it was the power of God that parted the Red Sea. Rod symbolizes power; it also means correction or a supporter of life. Although the children of Israel had murmured and complained against Moses, and some even desired to go back to Egypt they knew that the decision between life or death required obedience.

> Exod 14:16, 21-22—"But lift thou up thy rod, and stretch out thine hand over the sea, and divide it and the children of Israel shall go on dry ground through the midst of the sea. And Moses stretched out his hand over the sea and the Lord caused the sea to go back by a strong east wind all that night, and made the sea dry land, and the waters were divided. And the children of Israel went into the midst of the sea upon the dry ground and the waters were a wall unto them on their right hand, and on their left."

The Red Sea parted, and they crossed over on dry land. The Egyptians however, continued to pursue them. After the Israelites had safely crossed, God instructed Moses to again stretch forth his hand over the sea. The sea engulfed Pharoah and his army.

> Exod 14:29-30—"But the children of Israel walked upon dry land in the midst of the sea and the waters were a wall unto them on their right hand, and on their left. Thus, the Lord saved Israel that day out of the hand of the Egyptians, and Israel saw the Egyptians dead upon the seashore."

Life was given to the children of Israel and death to the Egyptians. It was obedience to God's commands that saved the Israelites. Conversely, it was rebellion or disobedience against God that caused the death of the Egyptians. The law (commands) separated life from death.

Children of Israel—Likeness Versus Diverseness

Enmity separates likeness from diverseness. This animosity was quite evident between Pharaoh and the Egyptians and the Israelites. From creation, enmity has been a dividing wedge between God's people and those who align themselves with the archenemy, Satan. The same holds true for end-time spiritual Israel.

> Exod 14:4-5,8—"And I will harden Pharaoh's heart, that he shall follow after them and I will be honored upon Pharaoh, and upon all his host, that the Egyptians may know that I am the Lord. And they did so. And it was told the king of Egypt that the people fled and the heart of Pharaoh and of his servants was turned against the people, and they said, 'why have we done this, that we have let Israel go from serving us?' And the Lord hardened the heart of Pharaoh king of Egypt, and he pursued after the children of Israel, and the children of Israel went out with a high hand."

> Ps 89:13,18—"Thou hast a mighty arm, strong is thy hand, and high is thy right hand. For the Lord is our defense and the Holy One of Israel is our king."

There is a spiritual warfare that stirs the archenemy, Satan, to seek to mar the likeness of God. The children of Israel reflected the likeness of God. They chose to be obedient and to keep God's commandments. Pharaoh and his army were instruments of Satan; stirred by enmity, they sought to recapture the Israelites and bring them back into slavery. The irreconcilable dichotomy of likeness and diverseness converged on the shores of the Red Sea, however, the mighty intervening hand of God brought the Israelites to safety.

Modern-Day Spiritual Israel—Light Versus Darkness

Ancient Israel and the exodus movement was a type pointing us to today's end-time antitypical Christians (spiritual Israel.) The children of Israel were led by God out of the bondage of Egypt, likewise today's spiritual Israel is being called out of the bondage of spiritual Babylon and its false worship systems. The exodus story though literal has deep spiritual meanings. Both Egypt and Babylon symbolized sin, false worship, idolatry, rebellion, apostasy etc.

> Rev 12:1-4—"And there appeared a great wonder in heaven, a woman clothed with the sun, and the moon under her feet, and upon her head a crown of twelve stars. And she being with child cried, travailing in birth, and pained to be delivered. And there appeared another wonder in heaven, and behold a great red dragon, having seven heads and ten horns, and seven crowns upon his heads. And his tail drew the third part of the stars of heaven, and did cast them to the earth, and the dragon stood before the woman which was ready to be delivered, for to devour her child as soon as it was born."

From creation in the garden of Eden, to the Old Testament book of Moses (Exodus) to the New Testament account of John in Revelation, the conflict between light and darkness is evident. The woman described in Revelation is God's church. She is clothed in the light of the sun, moon, and stars. On the other hand, the archenemy, the dragon, Satan has no source of light and hence is in darkness. In the exodus movement, God separated his people from the archenemy by standing between them as the pillar of cloud. Today, spiritual Israel has the son, Jesus Christ.

> Rev 12:7-11—"And there was war in heaven, Michael and his angels fought against the dragon, and the dragon fought and his angels, and prevailed not, neither was their place found anymore in heaven. And the great dragon was cast out, that old serpent, called the Devil, and Satan, which deceiveth the whole world, he was cast out into the earth, and his angels were cast out with him. And I heard a loud voice saying in heaven, 'now is come salvation, and strength, and the kingdom of our God, and the power of his Christ, for the accuser of our brethren is cast down, which accused them before our God day and night. And they overcame him by the blood of the Lamb, and by the word of their testimony, and they loved not their lives unto the death.'"

God fought against the Egyptians. Jesus (Michael) fought against the dragon. Pharaoh, his chariots, and captain represents Satan, the beast power, false prophets, atheism, and the host of those who align with them. The modern-day chariot being used is the vehicle of propagating the agenda of the archenemy, Satan. However, the Godhead fights for those who align themselves with the true light. Jesus is the divider between spiritual Israel (children of light), and modern-day apostate Babylon (children of darkness.) He is their salvation and strength. Overcoming darkness requires the spiritual covering of the blood of the Lamb, accepting the sacrifice of Jesus.

> 2 Cor 4:6—"For God, who commanded the light to shine out of darkness, hath shined in our hearts, to give the light of the knowledge of the glory of God in the face of Jesus Christ."
>
> John 8:12—"Then spake Jesus again unto them, saying, 'I am the light of the world he that followeth me shall not walk in darkness, but shall have the light of life.'"
>
> John 3:19—"And this is the condemnation, that light is come into the world, and men loved darkness rather than light, because their deeds were evil."

In heaven, Jesus as Michael fought against the archenemy, the dragon. The dragon (Satan) was cast out of heaven into earth. The cosmic battle between light and darkness has been playing out on this planet from the foundation of the earth. Christ came to be the light of the world, to separate mankind from spiritual darkness.

Modern-Day Spiritual Israel—Life Versus Death

In the creation story God placed the tree of knowledge of good and evil in the midst (middle) of the garden and commanded Adam and Eve not to eat of it lest they would surely die (Gen 2:16–17—3:3.) This command (law) was the divider separating life from death. In the exodus story God parted the Red Sea allowing the children of Israel to walk in the midst of the sea upon dry land (Exod 14:22.) It was dry land that separated the waters on the left from waters on the right. God told Moses to speak unto the children of Israel that they go forward. This command given to Moses and the separation of the Red Sea was the pivotal decision between life or death for the Israelites. Choosing to obey God's command and walk upon the dry ground in the middle of two walls of water saved the Israelites from their archenemy, the approaching Egyptian army. These two literal accounts have deep spiritual meanings for modern-day spiritual Israel.

God's commands are laws. The law separates life from death. God gave Adam a verbal law. Moses and the children of Israel were given both a verbal command to go forth and cross the Red Sea and also the written law on tablets of stone at Mount Sinai. For modern-day spiritual Israel these same verbal and written commands are just as binding. These laws are now written in the heart through Christ who is the embodiment and fulfillment of God's law.

> Rom 10:4—"For Christ is the end of the law for righteousness to everyone that believeth."
>
> Matt 5:17—"Think not that I am come to destroy the law, or the prophets; I am not come to destroy, but to fulfill."

The prophecy foretelling the coming Messiah revealed that he would be "cut off " or killed in the middle of the prophetic week (Dan 9:26-27.) Jesus was crucified three and a half years after he began his earthly ministry. He was crucified in the midst (middle) of two thieves; one on the right and one on the left (Mark 15:27.) The symbolism of "midst" is poignant as it points to the centrality of God's law. There is no deviation to the left or the right. For the Israelites the way to salvation was the narrow way of dry land. For modern-day Israelites the narrow way is through Jesus who declared himself to be the way (John 14:6.)

The law separates life from death. Jesus was the embodiment of God's law in the flesh. The choice between life or death is in choosing to be obedient to God's law and in accepting the fulfillment of the law, through Jesus Christ.

Modern-Day Spiritual Israel—
Likeness Versus Diverseness

Mankind was created in the likeness of God. Anything opposing this image is different or diverse from the true image of God. In Eden, God placed enmity between the seed of the woman (likeness of God) and the seed of the serpent (likeness of Satan.) This animosity or hatred has festered into spiritual warfare and the battle for the human soul is still at stake.

> Rev 12:13-17—"And when the dragon saw that he was cast unto the earth, he persecuted the woman which brought forth the man child. And to the woman were given two wings of a great eagle, that she might fly into the wilderness, into her place, where she is nourished for a time, and times, and half a time, from the face of the serpent. And the serpent cast out of his mouth water as a flood after the woman, that he might cause her to be carried away of the flood. And the earth helped the woman, and the earth opened her mouth, and swallowed up the flood which the dragon cast out of his mouth. And the dragon was wroth with the woman and went to make war with the remnant of her seed, which keep the commandments of God, and have the testimony of Jesus Christ."

> Rev 13:7—"And it was given unto him to make war with the saints, and to overcome them and power was given him over all kindreds, and tongues, and nations."

This polarizing division of enmity can never be reconciled. This spiritual warfare compels everyone to make a clear, concise, and unwavering choice—to choose to be obedient to God or by default to be children of disobedience and becoming the seeds of the serpent. The climax of this enmity was nowhere more evident than at the cross. The Savior was crucified. The ultimate climax of the bruising of the serpent's head will be at the end of the world when all sin will be transferred back to the originator of sin, Satan, the enemy of mankind. However, there are daily blows to the serpent's head when a sinner turns from sin and disobedience. The rebellious mindset of disobedience is cast off and they become new creatures in Christ.

> Eph 2:15–16—"Having abolished in his flesh the enmity, even the law of commandments contained in ordinances; for to make in himself of twain one new man, so making peace. And that he might reconcile both unto God in one body by the cross, having slain the enmity thereby."
>
> 2 Cor 11:2–3—"For I am jealous over you with godly jealousy, for I have espoused you to one husband, that I may present you as a chaste virgin to Christ. But I fear lest by any means, as the serpent beguiled Eve through his subtlety, so your minds should be corrupted from the simplicity that is in Christ."
>
> Phil 2:5—"Let this mind be in you, which was also in Christ Jesus."

Jesus came to reveal the true image of God, thus empowering us from deceptively adopting the image of the archenemy. The seed of the woman/church (Christians) must reflect God's likeness found in Jesus Christ.

Parallels—Eden, Exodus, and End-Time Spiritual Israel

There are many parallel themes that can be drawn between Eden, exodus, and end-time spiritual Israel, but we will highlight a few key ones.

Truth Versus Lies

Truth versus lies will play a pivotal role in end-time deceptions. The fall of man began when the serpent told Eve three lies. Jesus warned the disciples that deception will be one of the first signs of the end of the world. These deceptions will take the form of false Christs and false prophets (Matt 24:4,24.) Truth is the only antidote for lies. What is truth?

> Ps 85:11—"Truth shall spring out of the earth and righteousness shall look down from heaven."

> John 14:6—"Jesus saith unto him, 'I am the way, the truth, and the life, no man cometh unto the Father, but by me.'"

> John 17:17—"Sanctify them through thy truth, thy word is truth."

> Ps 119:151—"Thou art near, O Lord; and all thy commandments are truth."

These are the three core foundations of truth: Jesus, the word, and the commandments. The children of Israel walked upon dry land (earth), the bedrock that brought them to salvation. Modern-day spiritual Israel will only obtain salvation through the truth which is found in these three tenets. The archenemy of the Israelites, the Egyptian army was consumed in the flood of waters which represented the wrath of God. In the prophetic book of Revelation, the serpent cast out of his mouth "water as a flood" against the woman (God's remnant seed.)

> Rev 12:15-17—"And the serpent cast out of his mouth water as a flood after the woman, that he might cause her to be carried away of the flood. And the earth helped the woman, and the earth opened her mouth and swallowed up the flood which the dragon cast out of his mouth. And the dragon was wroth with the woman and went to make war with the remnant of her seed, which keep the commandments of God, and have the testimony of Jesus Christ."

> Rev 12:6,14—"And the woman fled into the wilderness, where she hath a place prepared of God, that they should feed her there a thousand two hundred and threescore days. And to the woman were given two wings of a great eagle, that she might fly into the wilderness, into her place, where she is nourished for a time, and times, and half a time, from the face of the serpent."

Water represents the word (Prov 18:4; Eph 5:26.) Pharoah and his army pursued the children of Israel into the wilderness. God overthrew the Egyptians with literal water (flood) but modern-day spiritual Israel is being chased by the serpent with a flood of water in its mouth. The woman is helped by God and fled into the wilderness for "a time, times, and half a time" or 1260 days or 1260 years in prophetic time. The Bible uses the one day equals one year principle (Num 14:34; Ezek 4:6.) The earth helped the woman and swallowed up the flood that spewed from the mouth of the serpent. This flood of water spewed from the serpent's mouth are words that are untruths and lies spoken by ungodly men (2 Sam 22:5.) The earth represents the truth that counters and neutralizes the lies (flood.)

History records that for a period of 1260 years the papal Roman Empire persecuted Christians during a period known as the Dark Ages (AD 538 to AD 1798.) During this time the Bible was taken away and replaced with papal dogmas and traditions. The true light (Word of God) was replaced with spiritual darkness. Millions of Christians were martyred and those who managed to escape hid in desolate places, e.g., the Waldensians who hid in alpine mountains, valleys, and in the wilderness. It was also during the Dark Ages, that the sixteenth-century Protestant Reformation was born, when Martin Luther, an Augustine monk, nailed his Ninety-five Theses to the door of the Castle Church in Wittenberg. His theses challenged the unbiblical dogmas and traditions of the papal Roman Catholic Church. Many Protestants fled from Europe to America thereby fulfilling this prophecy that the earth helped the woman. America was a beacon of hope and religious freedom away from tyranny of the persecutions they had faced. In these pivotal last days of earth's history, the serpent will again persecute the woman (God's remnant church.) The remnant church is true to God's commandments and has the testimony of Jesus. The testimony of Jesus is the spirit of prophecy (Rev 19:10.) To counter the lies and deception of the archenemy, Revelation admonishes that modern-day Israel must expose and flee from false doctrines, traditions, and teachings.

> Isa 8:20—"To the law and to the testimony, if they speak not according to this word, it is because there is no light in them."

The litmus test to revealing false prophets and false religions will be God's laws, commandments, and words. Any doctrine or religion that goes against God's laws or commandments is in spiritual darkness.

Modern-day spiritual Israel must stay true to God's laws, commands, and word and depart from spiritual Egypt and Babylon which are false prophets, false doctrine, and false religious institutions.

Egypt and Babylon

> Exod 14:28-31—"And the waters returned, and covered the chariots, and the horsemen, and all the host of Pharaoh that came into the sea after them; there remained not so much as one of them. But the children of Israel walked upon dry land in the midst of the sea, and the waters were a wall unto them on their right hand, and on their left. Thus, the Lord saved Israel that day out of the hand of the Egyptians, and Israel saw the Egyptians dead upon the seashore. And Israel saw that great work which the Lord did upon the Egyptians, and the people feared the Lord, and believed the Lord, and his servant Moses."

> Rev 12:3-4—"And there appeared another wonder in heaven, and behold a great red dragon, having seven heads and ten horns, and seven crowns upon his heads. And his tail drew the third part of the stars of heaven and did cast them to the earth and the dragon stood before the woman which was ready to be delivered, for to devour her child as soon as it was born."

> Rev 13:1-2—"And I stood upon the sand of the sea, and saw a beast rise up out of the sea, having seven heads and ten horns, and upon his horns ten crowns, and upon his heads the name of blasphemy. And the beast which I saw was like unto a leopard, and his feet were as the feet of a bear, and his mouth as the mouth of a lion and the dragon gave him his power, and his seat, and great authority."

Pharoah and his army parallel the dragon and his army (the beast power, false prophets, and the fallen angels.) The Egyptian army drowned in the Red Sea, and in Revelation, we see a beast emerging from the sea. Literal Egypt, the type, has given rise to spiritual Babylon, the antitype. Egypt represents the spirit of idolatry, atheism, and sin (Isa 19:3; Ezek 30:13-16) and Babylon represents false worship. The children of Israel fled Egypt and today spiritual Israel is commanded to flee Babylon.

> Rev 18:1-4—"And after these things I saw another angel come down from heaven, having great power, and the earth was lightened with his glory. And he cried mightily with a strong voice,

saying, 'Babylon the great is fallen, is fallen, and is become the habitation of devils, and the hold of every foul spirit, and a cage of every unclean and hateful bird. For all nations have drunk of the wine of the wrath of her fornication, and the kings of the earth have committed fornication with her, and the merchants of the earth are waxed rich through the abundance of her delicacies.' And I heard another voice from heaven, saying, 'come out of her, my people, that ye be not partakers of her sins, and that ye receive not of her plagues.'"

Red Apple, Red Sea, and Red Dragon

Red is generally a symbol of conflict, danger, warning, or sacrifice. Red conjures up an imagery of anger. A red flag raised in battle is a signal to fight. Red stop signs bring traffic to a halt; red ink is used in journal entries to signal financial deficit; the color red is used for the highest and most severe level of terrorist threat; a red card is used in sports to eject players; red sky at morning is a forecast of bad weather. Biblical and spiritual references include; sin as red as scarlet/crimson (Isa 1:18); blood shed as a sacrifice for sin (Matt 26:28); man on red horse given power to take peace from the earth and kill (Rev 6:4); a woman (church) riding a scarlet (red) beast symbolizing a sinful apostate adulterous false church (Rev 17:3.) Another profound set of symbolism of red are the parallels of the red apple, Red Sea, and red dragon. These were all spiritual obstacles and impediments for God's people.

Garden of Eden—Test of Obedience

Gen 3:2–3,6,9,11—"And the woman said unto the serpent, 'we may eat of the fruit of the trees of the garden, but of the fruit of the tree which is in the midst of the garden, God hath said, ye shall not eat of it, neither shall ye touch it, lest ye die.' And when the woman saw that the tree was good for food, and that it was pleasant to the eyes, and a tree to be desired to make one wise, she took of the fruit thereof, and did eat, and gave also unto her husband with her, and he did eat. And the Lord God called unto Adam, and said unto him, 'where art thou?' And he said, 'who told thee that thou wast naked? Hast thou eaten of the tree, whereof I commanded thee that thou shouldest not eat?'"

3 Heads, 1 Tail

Wilderness of Egypt—Test of Faith

Exod 13:18—"But God led the people about, through the way of the wilderness of the Red Sea and the children of Israel went up harnessed out of the land of Egypt."

Heb 11:29—"By faith they passed through the Red Sea as by dry land, which the Egyptians assaying to do were drowned."

Wilderness of Earth—Test of Obedience, Faith, and Patience

Rev 12:3,17—14:12—"And there appeared another wonder in heaven, and behold a great red dragon, having seven heads and ten horns, and seven crowns upon his heads. And the dragon was wroth with the woman and went to make war with the remnant of her seed, which keep the commandments of God, and have the testimony of Jesus Christ. Here is the patience of the saints, here are they that keep the commandments of God, and the faith of Jesus."

The creation story in Eden does not tell us what kind of fruit Eve ate. There is no proof that it was an apple. For the purpose of parallelism, we will conjecture that it was a red apple. The fruit was a test of obedience. Being obedient to God's law meant eternal life, on the other hand, disobedience meant spiritual and physical death. Death was and still is the archenemy of life. The exodus story in Egypt was a test of faith. The Red Sea was impassable, but not impossible for God to make a way of salvation for the faithful. The end-time Christians are now faced with the red dragon. This dragon is Satan masked in a cloak of a religio-political garb, the beast power, false religions, and false prophets. They will soon be unmasked with the revival of religious persecution against those who refuse to accept the mark of the beast. Those who will persevere are those who are obedient to God's laws and commandments, having the faith of Jesus, and enduring patiently till the end.

Salvation

The plan of salvation from the creation of the world to the exodus journey, to the current end-times of earth's history has never changed. The

Godhead always had a plan to save mankind. The plan was the Savior, Jesus Christ.

> Gen 3:15—"And I will put enmity between thee and the woman, and between thy seed and her seed; it shall bruise thy head, and thou shalt bruise his heel."

> Exod 14:13-14—"And Moses said unto the people, 'fear ye not, stand still, and see the salvation of the Lord, which he will shew to you today, for the Egyptians whom ye have seen today, ye shall see them again no more forever. The Lord shall fight for you, and ye shall hold your peace.'"

> Rev 12:9-10—"And the great dragon was cast out, that old serpent, called the devil, and Satan, which deceiveth the whole world, he was cast out into the earth, and his angels were cast out with him. And I heard a loud voice saying in heaven, 'now is come salvation, and strength, and the kingdom of our God, and the power of his Christ, for the accuser of our brethren is cast down, which accused them before our God day and night.'"

> 1 Pet 1:19-21—"But with the precious blood of Christ, as of a lamb without blemish and without spot. Who verily was foreordained before the foundation of the world but was manifest in these last times for you. Who by him do believe in God, that raised him up from the dead, and gave him glory, that your faith and hope might be in God."

The epic spiritual battle of all ages, the archenemy of the soul, has pitted light versus darkness, life versus death, and the likeness of God versus the diverseness of Satan. Spiritual warfare raging unto the mental terrain of the human consciousness. But victory has been won, through the blood of the Lord Jesus Christ, heaven's ambassador of the Godhead.

— 12 —

3 Rooms, 1 Way in
The Godhead in the Sanctuary

(Outer Court. Holy Place. Most Holy Place)

In the chapter on Judgment, we discussed the sanctuary. The sanctuary was the portable tent that God commanded Moses to construct while the children of Israel journeyed from Egypt to the promised land of Canaan. God commanded Moses on Mount Sinai to make this earthly replica after the blueprint of the heavenly sanctuary so that he would be in their midst, to dwell and abide.

> Exod 25:8—"And let them make me a sanctuary, that I may dwell among them."

> Heb 8:5—"Who serve unto the example and shadow of heavenly things, as Moses was admonished of God when he was about to make the tabernacle; for, see, saith he, that thou make all things according to the pattern shewed to thee in the mount."

The sanctuary was also God's blueprint for salvation, not just for the Israelites in the wilderness but for us today. David in Psalms proclaimed, "thy way, O God is in the sanctuary, who is so great a God as our God" (Ps 77:13.) Thirdly, it was a place for God's people to atone for their sins. If anyone sinned they were required to bring a sacrifice to the sanctuary and the High Priest would offer the blood of that animal for the sins that were committed. The sacrifice could be a bullock, lamb, goat, or bird depending on what the sinner could afford. This sacrificial sanctuary service was an object lesson to teach the consequence of sin, and to act as a deterrent against committing sin.

> Lev 4:1–6—"And the Lord spake unto Moses, saying, 'speak unto the children of Israel, saying, if a soul shall sin through ignorance against any of the commandments of the Lord concerning things which ought not to be done, and shall do against any of them; if the priest that is anointed do sin according to the sin of the people, then let him bring for his sin which he hath sinned a young bullock without blemish unto the Lord for a sin offering. And he shall bring the bullock unto the door of the tabernacle of the congregation before the Lord, and shall lay his hand upon the bullock's head, and kill the bullock before the Lord. And the priest that is anointed shall take of the bullock's blood and bring it to the tabernacle of the congregation. And the priest shall dip his finger in the blood, and sprinkle of the blood seven times before the Lord, before the vail of the sanctuary.'"

Q: Why was blood necessary?

> A: Rom 6:23—"For the wages of sin is death."

> A: Lev 17:11—"For the life of the flesh is in the blood, and I have given it to you upon the altar to make an atonement for your souls, for it is the blood that maketh an atonement for the soul."

> A: Heb 9:22—"And almost all things are by the law purged with blood, and without shedding of blood is no remission."

"The broken law of God demanded the life of the transgressor. The blood, representing the forfeited life of the sinner, whose guilt the victim bore, was carried by the priest into the holy place and sprinkled before the veil, behind which was the ark containing the law that the sinner had transgressed. By this ceremony the sin was, through the blood, transferred in figure to the sanctuary. Such was the work that went on, day by day, throughout the year. The sins of Israel were thus transferred to the sanctuary, and a special work became necessary for their removal. God commanded that an atonement be made for each of the sacred apartments. "He shall make an atonement for the holy place, because of the uncleanness of the children of Israel and because of their transgressions in all their sins."[1]

The accumulation of blood that soaked and stained the veil had to be cleansed from the sin it represented. How was this done? How was the sanctuary cleansed? Once a year on the holy Day of Atonement, on the tenth day of the seventh month, an unblemished lamb was sacrificed for the sins of the people. This foreshadowed the coming of the Messiah, Jesus, who became the sacrificial Lamb for the world. This holiest of days required that the High Priest alone was to enter the Most Holy Place which was the holiest apartment of the sanctuary. He was to atone for the sins of himself, his household, and the people. To begin this solemn ceremony, the High Priest would first offer his bullock for his own sin sacrifice and that of his household. Then he would present two goat offerings at the entrance of the tabernacle. Lots were cast, one for the Lord and the other for the scapegoat. The goat upon which the Lord's lot fell was sacrificed. The scapegoat was kept alive but only to be released into the wilderness. The blood from the Lord's goat, which represented the sin offering for the people, was taken into the Most Holy Place. After sprinkling the blood upon the mercy seat, the High Priest returned to the outer court to the scapegoat. The High Priest laid both hands upon its head and confessed all the iniquities and trespasses of the people. The goat was then led away into the wilderness, away from the camp, thereby symbolically, cleansing the sanctuary and separating them from sin.

The sanctuary had three compartments or rooms; outer court, Holy Place, and Most Holy Place. It represented three stages of salvation; justification, sanctification, and glorification. It encompassed the three phases of judgment; investigative, sentencing, and executive. Each compartment of the sanctuary was strategically built with specific furniture and emblems which were symbolic witnesses of the triune Godhead. Each and every aspect symbolized and reflected God the Father, Jesus the Lamb/the coming Messiah, and the unseen Holy Spirit. The sanctuary was the visual reminder that worship and sacrifice were to be given only to the one true and living God.

---

1. White, *The Great Controversy*, 418.

Outer Court

The outer court was the first compartment. It was the open courtyard where sinners brought their sacrifice to the priest. The outer court in a crude sense was symbolic of a courtroom, where the judge, prosecutor, defense lawyer, defendants, and witnesses converged seeking spiritual justice or pardon. There were two visible pieces of furniture; the altar of burnt offering, and the lavar. The apostle John described the third key element to be the presence of the Holy Spirit, the unseen witness. "And there are three that bear witness in earth, the spirit, and the water, and the blood, and these three agree in one" (1 John 5:8.) The blood was from the animal sacrifice, it was sprinkled upon the altar of burnt offering, water was from the lavar, and thirdly, the presence of the unseen Holy Spirit. The outer court pointed to the coming Messiah. The blood represented Jesus Christ, the sacrificial Lamb of God who would shed his blood on the "altar" of Calvary. The water symbolically represented physical baptism which declared union to Christ and acceptance of his death, burial, and resurrection. The spirit represented the Holy Spirit and the acceptance of the spiritual baptism of faith. The outer court was also symbolic of the earth.

Eastern Entrance Gate

There was only one way into the sanctuary, and this was through the entrance gate. It was thirty feet wide or twenty cubits. Unlike the white linen exterior surrounding the sanctuary, the curtains of the gate were linen panels of three colors; red, blue, and scarlet. The gate represented Jesus. He is the only way to the Father.

> John 14:6—"Jesus answered, "I am the way and the truth and the life. No one comes to the Father except through me."

> Matt 7:13-14—"Enter ye in at the strait gate, for wide is the gate, and broad is the way, that leadeth to destruction, and many there be which go in there at. Because strait is the gate, and narrow is the way, which leadeth unto life, and few there be that find it."

The entrance gate was on the eastern side. This was symbolic and significant, as the east is the dwelling place of God (Ezek 10:19—11:1.) The garden of Eden was placed in the east and the tree of life was also in the east (Gen 2:8—3:24.) The tribe of Judah encamped on the east side. They were given this most prominent position as it was prophesied by their father Jacob, whose name God later changed to Israel. "Judah, thou art he whom thy brethren shall praise, thy hand shall be in the neck of thine enemies, thy father's children shall bow down before thee. Judah is a lion's whelp from the prey, my son, thou art gone up; he stooped down, he couched as a lion, and as an old lion, who shall rouse him up? The scepter shall not depart from Judah, nor a lawgiver from between his feet, until Shiloh come, and unto him shall the gathering of the people be" (Gen 49:8–10.) Judah symbolically represented God. God has all power and authority as the lawgiver and in whose hand is the scepter of righteousness and judgment. Judah also represented the coming Messiah, the Lion of the tribe of Judah (Rev 5:5), and the Shiloh, which means prince of peace (Isa 9:6.) The east is where Jesus will make his appearance at the second coming (Matt 24:27.)

> Fun Fact: There are thirty-one references to Shiloh in the Bible (KJV.) There are three references with "lion" and "Judah" together in the same verse.

The Hebrew word for east is *mizrach*, which originates from *zarach* which means to shine. East literally means, "towards the sun." The sun rises in the east. Many churches were, and still are built with the main entrances to the east, as was the case in Rome. Throughout the centuries however, pagan worship of the sun evolved. This was and still is idolatrous and is an abomination to God, as described by the prophet Ezekiel (Ezek 8:16–18.) It was from pagan worship that the celebration of Easter evolved. The word east is embedded in Easter. Today, millions celebrate Easter unaware of its pagan roots of sun worship. Sun worship in the form of legislation enforcing Sunday worship will play a prominent role in these last days as the mark of the beast is unveiled. This will be discussed in more detail in Chapter 15.

Altar of Burnt Offering

ALTAR OF INCENSE.   ALTAR OF BURNT-OFFERING.   LAVER.

The altar of burnt offering was the altar upon which animal sacrifices were made to atone for sins. It was overlaid with bronze and was 5 cubits long x 5 cubits wide x 3 cubits high or 7.5 ft x 7.5 ft x 4.5 ft (Exod 27:1.) The blood of the sacrifice was sprinkled upon the altar by the priest. It was made of shittim wood (acacia), which was a thorny tree. This foreshadowed the crown of thorns Jesus was to wear. Acacia is said to be resistant to decay. This foreshadowed that the body of the buried Christ would not suffer decay (Ps 16:10.) The animals being sacrificed were male without defects. The sinner was required to place their hands upon the head of the sin offering (Lev 1:3-4.) This paralleled Jesus, who was the perfect sacrifice, for he knew no sin. The weight of sin was placed upon him, during the intense night in the garden of Gethsemane. He sweated drops of blood (Luke 22:44.) The lamb was killed in the outer court, likewise Jesus was crucified on earth (the outer court.) Jesus left the glory of heaven (akin to the Holy and Most Holy Place) and came to earth (outer court) to be the sacrificial Lamb for the sins of all mankind.

Laver

The laver was made of brass and used by the priests to cleanse themselves after performing sacrifices upon the altar (Exod 30:18.) Upon entering or exiting the Holy Place, they were required to wash their hands and feet. The priests had to be physically and spiritually clean before they approached the presence of the Holy God. The laver in parallelism symbolized baptism.

> Fun Fact: Wash in various languages—lavage (French), lavaggio (Italian), lava (Latin), lavar (Portuguese and Spanish.) A lavatory is a modern term for basin or washroom.

Blood, Water, and the Holy Spirit

Blood and water represented by the altar and laver were two prominent and symbolic emblems. The third prominent element at work in the outer court was the Holy Spirit. The Holy Spirit was the unseen witness.

> 1 John 5:5-8—"Who is he that overcometh the world, but he that believeth that Jesus is the Son of God? This is he that came by water and blood, even Jesus Christ, not by water only, but by water and blood. And it is the Spirit that beareth witness because the Spirit is truth. For there are three that bear record in heaven, the Father, the Word, and the Holy Ghost, and these three are one. And there are three that bear witness in earth, the Spirit, and the water, and the blood and these three agree in one."

The ritual of offering sacrifices no doubt was pointing to the coming Messiah, Jesus Christ who was to take away the sins of the world by shedding his blood. When he was pierced on the cross, water and blood gushed from his side, a silent witness that indeed he was and is the Messiah, the Lamb of God.

> John 19:34-35—"But one of the soldiers with a spear pierced his side, and forewith came there out blood and water. And he that saw it bear record, and his record is true, and he knoweth that he saith true, that ye might believe."

Another example of the water and blood witness is with Pilate, the Roman governor. Pilate, before handing Jesus over to the people to be crucified, washed his hands in water and declared that he was "innocent of the blood of this just person" (Matt 27:24.) This imagery of Pilate washing his hands conjures images of the priest washing his hands after shedding the innocent blood of the animal sacrifice.

Water and blood, in both a literal and symbolic manner, was present at the Last Supper. In preparation for the Last Supper, Jesus instructed the disciples to seek out and follow a man who would be bearing a pitcher of water (Mark 14:13.) The man would lead them to the guest chamber (upper room.) During the Last Supper, Jesus washed their feet with water, and they partook of the emblems of bread and unfermented wine representing his blood. There were three key emblems; water, bread, and wine. These three emblems are still used during communion services as a witness of the sacrifice of Jesus, who is the substitute for sin. Symbolically, the water represents baptism (spiritual cleansing); the bread represents Jesus who was the bread who came down from heaven and also the Word (Bible/Scripture/spiritual sustenance); the wine represents spiritual redemption through the blood (Mark 14:22–24.) The wine also represents the Holy Spirit (Eph 5:18.) Parallels to Christ can be drawn from the man with the pitcher of water that led the disciples to the upper room. Jesus is our spiritual High Priest who has the water of life (John 4:14) and leads mankind to the upper room wherein dwells the Father. He is the only way to eternal salvation for those who choose to follow him into the heavenly sanctuary.

> Fun Facts: Water is somewhat of a trinity; made of one oxygen and two hydrogen atoms (H_2O.) It takes on three forms; solid, liquid, and gas. It is the only common substance to exist as a solid, liquid, and gas in normal terrestrial conditions. All known forms of life depend on water.

Outer Court—Justification

What is justification? It is God declaring the unrighteous to be righteous. How does the outer court apply to us today? Symbolically, the outer courtyard is the arena of the great exchange. The transaction of grace, where the sinner trades sin and spiritual death for eternal life. The lavar is the symbol of the watery grave of baptism where the sinner dies to self and comes up in Christ with a renewed life. This is justification. The altar of burnt offering symbolically represents Christ's death; the ultimate sacrifice so that the sinner can live. The courtyard is also symbolically the arena of death. The sinner dies to sin and Christ died for the sinner. Sin is covered by blood and the sinner is justified. Justification requires three things of the sinner; to confess, to repent, and to be baptized.

> Rom 6:4—"Therefore we are buried with him by baptism into death, that like as Christ was raised up from the dead by the glory of the Father, even so we also should walk in newness of life."

The lavar is also a symbol for the daily washing in the word—daily reading of the Scriptures (Eph 5:26.)

Outer Court—Judgment (Executive)

What does it mean to execute judgment? It means to carry out the punishment. In the sanctuary, it was in the outer court that the sacrifice was slain, which is a literal form of execution. The guilty sinner brought their animal sacrifice and confessed their sins on the head of the sacrifice. The sacrifice was executed and the blood was brought into the inner room (Holy Place) by the priest. The animal's flesh was subsequently consumed by fire on the altar of burnt offering. The sacrifice died a literal death, and the sinner was to die to sin spiritually and to die to the flesh, figuratively. Jesus Christ was the sacrificial Lamb. He was executed on a Roman cross. He ascended to heaven and brought his own precious blood to the Holy Place to atone and pay the penalty of death for all. The altar of burnt offering is the altar upon which we must die to self; we burn away the fleshly desires, lusts, and temptations. We alter the old nature through the power of the Holy Spirit and become new creatures in Christ.

> Heb 10:10-12,15-19—"By the which will we are sanctified through the offering of the body of Jesus Christ once for all. And every priest standeth daily ministering and offering oftentimes the same sacrifices, which can never take away sins. But this man, after he had offered one sacrifice for sins forever, sat down on the right hand of God, whereof the Holy Ghost also is a witness to us; for after that he had said before, this is the covenant that I will make with them after those days, saith the Lord, I will put my laws into their hearts, and in their minds will I write them, and their sins and iniquities will I remember no more. Now where remission of these is, there is no more offering for sin. Having therefore, brethren, boldness to enter into the holiest by the blood of Jesus."

> Heb 9:12-15—"Neither by the blood of goats and calves, but by his own blood he entered in once into the holy place, having obtained eternal redemption for us. For if the blood of bulls and of goats, and the ashes of a heifer sprinkling the unclean, sanctifieth to the purifying of the flesh, how much more shall the blood of Christ, who through the eternal Spirit offered himself without spot to God, purge your conscience from dead works to serve the living God? And for this cause he is the mediator of the new

testament, that by means of death, for the redemption of the transgressions that were under the first testament, they which are called might receive the promise of eternal inheritance."

On the annual Day of Atonement (cleansing of sin from the sanctuary), after the High Priest came out of the Most Holy Place to the outer court, he took the sins and placed them upon the head of the scapegoat. Judgment was executed upon the originator of sin. The scapegoat represented Satan. The scapegoat was then taken away by a fit man into the wilderness (Lev 16:21.) There is a common theme of one being driven away or removed during the executive phase. Adam and Eve were driven out of Eden. Cain was driven from the presence of the Lord. Scapegoat driven out to the wilderness. Sin results in separation from God. It was in the outer court, i.e., earth, that the precious Lamb of God, Jesus was slain. Jesus felt the agony of separation from the Father. Three hours of darkness shrouded the land and at the ninth hour Jesus cried out, "Eli, Eli, lama sabachthani, that is to say, my God, my God, why hast thou forsaken me?" (Matt 27:45-46.) His bruised body was taken from the cross to the tomb. He rose from the dead and was subsequently taken up ceremoniously to heaven in a cloud of angels to reunite with the Father (Acts 1:9.)

The earthly sanctuary was a replica of the heavenly sanctuary. The earthly sanctuary was a type or pattern, and the heavenly sanctuary is the anti-type or real. As will be fully explored in the next segment, the investigative phase of judgment in heaven began in the Most Holy Place in 1844 and is still ongoing. After Jesus completes this investigative judgment, he will move to the Holy Place to begin the sentencing phase and then the final phase of executive judgment will be carried out in the outer court (earth) immediately before the second coming. The executive judgment of earth will be the final punishment upon this planet. True and just judgment cannot be carried out unless there are witnesses. In any halls of justice, witnesses are called to take the stand.

> Jude 1:14-16—"And Enoch also, the seventh from Adam, prophesied of these, saying, behold, the Lord cometh with ten thousands of his saints, to execute judgment upon all, and to convince all that are ungodly among them of all their ungodly deeds which they have ungodly committed, and of all their hard speeches which ungodly sinners have spoken against him. These are murmurers, complainers, walking after their own lusts, and

their mouth speaketh great swelling words, having men's persons in admiration because of advantage."

The book of Revelation, chapters 15 to 18, outlines specific events that will take place as the executive judgment is carried out upon earth. These will be the seven last plagues. While on earth, Jesus declared that he did not come to judge. Rightfully so, as he had come to pay the penalty for sin and to save mankind from judgment if they did not repent from their sins. However, at the second coming he will be coming with punitive executive judgment.

> John 12:47-48—"And if any man hear my words, and believe not, I judge him not, for I came not to judge the world, but to save the world. He that rejects me, and receives not my words, has one that judges him; the word that I have spoken, the same shall judge him in the last day."

Blood and water as we saw earlier were two tangible witnesses in the outer court. If the outer court represents earth, how will blood and water play out in the final executive phase of judgment? Preceding the second coming there will be seven last plagues poured out. The second and third plagues will turn water to blood.

> Rev 16:3-4—"And the second angel poured out his vial upon the sea and it became as the blood of a dead man: and every living soul died in the sea. And the third angel poured out his vial upon the rivers and fountains of waters and they became blood."

In ancient Egypt the first plague was water turning to blood. Christians in these last days will be faced with the water and the blood experience—the water through baptism, i.e., testing of our faith and the blood, i.e., tribulation and persecution. Our water experience must be mixed with blood. Testing of faith intersecting with persecution—like the water and blood gushing from the pierced side of the Savior. But the beautiful promise is that we will overcome by the outpouring of the Holy Spirit, by the blood of Jesus and by witnessing, giving our testimony. "And they overcame him by the blood of the Lamb, and by the word of their testimony, and they loved not their lives unto the death" (Rev 12:11.)

Holy Place

The Holy Place was the second compartment of the sanctuary. It held three sacred objects (furniture); golden lampstand, altar of incense, and the table of showbread.

Golden Lampstand

> Exod 25:31–33—"And thou shalt make a candlestick of pure gold, of beaten work shall the candlestick be made, his shaft, and his branches, his bowls, his knops, and his flowers, shall be of the same. And six branches shall come out of the sides of it; three branches of the candlestick out of the one side, and three branches of the candlestick out of the other side. Three bowls made like unto almonds, with a knop and a flower in one branch, and three bowls made like almonds in the other branch, with a knop and a flower; so in the six branches that come out of the candlestick."

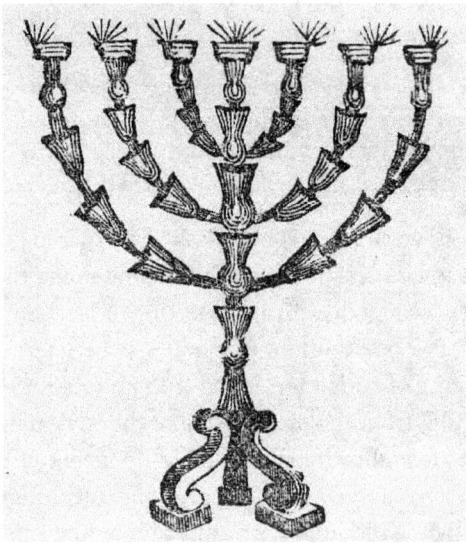

It provided light for the priests as they worked in the Holy Place. It was to remain lit continually and was fueled by olive oil. It had seven branches—one horizontal center column with six branches, three on each side of the center column. It had the likeness of a tree. Tree symbolizes life (Gen 2:9; Deut 20:19.) In essence, it was three tripods. Each tripod had three lamps, giving the same amount of light. Symbolically in harmony with the triune Godhead, all three connected to carry out one function and one purpose. There was no specified measurement noted in Scripture, but Moses was told by God to make it out of one talent of gold, which was about seventy-five pounds. It was located on the south side opposite the table of showbread. The branches would most likely be pointing or directed towards east to west. The lampstand (light) also symbolically pointed to Jesus, who described himself as the light of the world (John 8:12.) Olive oil is highly significant and symbolic. It was from the Mount of Olive that Jesus ascended to heaven (Acts 1:11–12.) It will be this same mount upon which Christ will return as prophesied by Zechariah. "And his feet shall stand in that day upon the mount of Olives, which is before Jerusalem on the east, and the mount of Olives shall cleave in the midst thereof toward the east and toward the west, and there shall be a very great valley, and half of the mountain shall remove toward the north, and half of it toward the south" (Zech 14:4.) Profoundly, this prophecy pointed out the significance of east to west. Jesus corroborated this prophecy, by telling the disciples that his return will be as, "the lightning cometh out of the east, and shineth even unto the west, so shall also the coming of the Son of man be" (Matt 24:27.) The top of the branches of the lampstand had bowls fashioned after the shape of almonds. There were ornate knobs fashioned after the almond blossom and flower. Almond is from the Hebrew root word *shakeid* which means to watch or wake. This is fitting as almonds are oval shaped like the eyes. In the heavenly sanctuary there are seven lamps of fire which represent the seven Spirits of God (Rev 4:5.) The slain Lamb (Jesus) in Revelation is described as having seven eyes which represent the seven Spirits of God sent out throughout the earth (Rev 5:6.) The Almighty God watching over all mankind. It is interesting to note that the first three letters of Almighty and almond begin with the same three letters. The oil (lamp) represented the Holy Spirit (1 Sam 16:13; Matt 25:1–13.) The lampstand embodied the watchful presence of the triune Godhead. The lampstand with its center shaft and engrafted branches also reminds us that Jesus is the vine and Christians are the branches (John 15:5.) Ever connected—daily trimming their lamps; drawing sustenance from the Holy Spirit; allowing their light to shine for the glory of God.

    Fun Fact: The almond tree is between 4–10m (13–33 feet.)

Table of Showbread

Exod 25:23—"Thou shalt also make a table of shittim wood, two cubits shall be the length thereof, and a cubit the breadth thereof, and a cubit and a half the height thereof."

TABLE OF SHEW BREAD.

The measurement was 36 inches long x 18 inches wide x 27 inches high. All multiples of three. It held twelve loaves represented by the twelve tribes of Israel and by extension the twelve apostles. "And thou shalt take fine flour and bake twelve cakes thereof two tenth deals shall be in one cake. And thou shalt set them in two rows, six on a row, upon the pure table before the Lord. And thou shalt put pure frankincense upon each row, that it may be on the bread for a memorial, even an offering made by fire unto the Lord" (Lev 24:5–7.) The bread was baked with fine unleavened flour and remained for one week, and on the seventh-day Sabbath, the priest removed it, and ate it in the Holy Place and replaced it with fresh bread. It was also called the bread of the presence and was to be a reminder of how God fed the Israelites in the wilderness. He is the giver of life and the daily bread (John 6:35.) The unleavened bread also symbolized Jesus, the bread that came down from heaven and giveth life to the world (John 6:32–35.) The bread is also likened to the word of God

(Matt 4:4; Deut 8:3.) When Satan tempted Jesus to turn stone to bread, he overcame temptation by quoting scripture. Today, Christians partake in holy communion ceremonies with the serving of bread which represents the body of Christ and the gift of spiritual life. Sustaining this spiritual life requires daily reading the Bible and meditating upon the word of God.

Altar of Incense

> Exod 30:1–2,8–9—"And thou shalt make an altar to burn incense upon, of shittim wood shalt thou make it. A cubit shall be the length thereof, and a cubit the breadth thereof, foursquare shall it be, and two cubits shall be the height thereof; the horns thereof shall be of the same. And when Aaron lighteth the lamps at even, he shall burn incense upon it, a perpetual incense before the Lord throughout your generations. Ye shall offer no strange incense thereon, nor burnt sacrifice, nor meat offering, neither shall ye pour drink offering thereon."

The burning of incense served several functions. The practical function was to cover and envelope the odor that emanated from the sacrifices. It also symbolically represented the prayers of God's people (Rev 5:8.)

The incense produced an aroma pleasing to the Lord. It measured 1 cubit length x 1 cubit width x 2 cubit height (1.5 ft x1.5 ft x 3 ft.) It was also made of shittim (acacia) wood and was placed strategically before the veil, separating the Ark of Testimony, where the presence of God dwelt. The incense was to burn continually day and night. Three sweet spices were combined with frankincense; stacte, onycha, and galbanum (Exod 30:34.)

Stacte in Hebrew is *nataph* which means drops—"oozing out in drops." In Latin, stacte refers to the bleeding of the tree. Stacte is likened to myrrh because of the gum resin that oozes slowly in drops or tears from a tree, like the acacia tree. Myrrh in Aramaic means bitter. The color has a reddish-brown hue. This imagery conjures up striking parallelism to Jesus in the garden of Gethsemane. He agonized in prayer and oozed drops of blood which mingled with his sweat. He asked the Father to let this cup pass, but it was this bitter cup of sin he had to drink to pay the penalty for sin. Interesting to note that at Jesus' birth, gifts of frankincense and myrrh were given. Myrrh was also offered while he was on the cross, but he refused it. Onycha was the Greek word chosen to replace the original Hebrew word *shecheleth* when the Old Testament was translated to Greek. Shecheleth in Hebrew translation means to roar like a lion. Shecheleth is related to the Syriac *shehelta* which is translated as a tear, distillation, or exudation. Onycha has potentially double meanings, it either originated from the claw (fingernail) of a mollusk (shellfish) or from a plant. God would not incorporate any unclean animal into the holy sanctuary, so it is more plausible that onycha was a plant-based spice. Galbanum is a gum resin which occurs in small, round, semi-translucent tears or in brownish yellow masses. It has a pleasant aromatic odor and a bitter taste. All these descriptions draw parallels to Christ who is described as the Lion of the tribe of Judah and yet was the Savior who was a man of sorrows and drank the bitter cup of sin.

The incense represented prayer. As Jesus connected daily with the Father via prayer, we too must connect with the Godhead daily in prayer. God labors with us in our triumph and in our bitter pains and trials.

Holy Place—Sanctification

What is sanctification? Sanctification is to be divinely consecrated—set apart for God's holy use. The Holy Place had bread, which represented the word of God and Jesus; the lamp was the light which also represented the word of God and Jesus; the oil represented the Holy Spirit, and incense represented prayer. Sanctification begins with three foundational tenets; *the word* (table of showbread), *the Holy Spirit* (lampstand with oil), and *prayer* (altar of incense.) Sanctification is a lifetime process and not an immediate or instantaneous transformation. It requires the infilling of the Holy Spirit, daily reading, studying of the word, and being doers of the word, and being constant in prayer (commune with God.)

> John 17:17—"Sanctify them through thy truth; thy word is truth."
>
> Eph 5:26—"That he might sanctify and cleanse it with the washing of water by the word."

As in the outer court, the Holy Spirit is the active invisible agent in the Holy Place, aiding in the sanctification of the sinner.

Q: What are some specific things God made holy or sanctified?

- Sabbath, the seventh day of the week (Exod 20:8—31:13)
- The Levites/priests—they were anointed with oil. The literal oil played a key role in the sanctification process. Spiritually, Christians must be anointed (filled) with the holy oil—the Holy Spirit (Exod 28:41—29:7,21,29; Lev 8:12,30)
- The Tabernacle and furnishings—places of worship should be sanctified; a sanctuary where there is reverence for God (Lev 8:10)

Anointing with oil played a key role in sanctification in some of these examples. Jesus was anointed with oil before the crucifixion. How was this part of his sanctification? Jesus was fully man, yet fully divine. He was God in the flesh. He was always holy and sinless. However, before the crucifixion Jesus prayed for God to glorify him. Glorification is the next stage following sanctification. He lamented that the disciples did not anoint his head with oil, but that Mary had anointed his feet with oil (Luke 7:46; John 12:3.) Pouring oil over the head was a common rite of passage given to a priest, king, or an inaugurated ruler (1 Sam 10:1—16:13; 1 Kgs 1:39; 2 Kgs 9:3.) Anointing Jesus' feet foreshadowed death (John 12:7.) Oil was poured on Jesus' feet and not on his head as he was not sent to be an earthly king. However, this simple act of being anointed on the feet was a form of sanctification. Jesus was already holy, but he took on human flesh to be an example. Before the crucifixion Jesus gave a heartfelt prayer in the presence of the disciples.

> John 17:1,5,17,19—"These words spake Jesus and lifted up his eyes to heaven and said, 'Father the hour is come; glorify thy son, that thy son also may glorify thee. And now, O Father, glorify thou me with thine own self with the glory which I had with thee before the world was. Sanctify them through thy truth; thy word is truth. And for their sakes I sanctify myself, that they also might be sanctified through the truth.'"

Jesus was glorified in heaven with the Father, but on earth he was not yet, "re-glorified," but was in the sanctification stage after being anointed. It is in this prayer that Jesus asked the Father to sanctify the disciples through the truth (word.) Christ was showing the disciples by his example, the roadmap to sanctification and glorification. Although the disciples had been with Jesus for three and a half years, their own sanctification phase was not revealed until he was about to depart for heaven. Sanctification is not an instantaneous change after baptism but is a lifelong process as the Christian grows in Christ, in the word, in spending time daily in prayer, and being anointed with the Holy Spirit. When we are anointed, God pours out the oil of the Holy Spirit, transforming first our minds. "Let this mind be in you, which was also in Christ Jesus" (Phil 2:5.) The Hebrew word for oil is *shemen or shamen* which means to be fat (beaten oil.) The parent root for this word is *shem* which is usually translated as name but in Hebrew means character. Like the seed, it is the Holy Spirit that enables growth—"to be fat." This growth nurtures the development of the character. Sanctification is the junction in the road of the Christian journey, wherein the character of Christ is developed by the daily infilling of the Holy Spirit.

Jesus spent the last night before the crucifixion in the garden of *Gethsemane* amongst a grove of olive trees. Gethsemane in Hebrew is *gat shemanim* which means oil press (beaten oil.) Oil is extracted by being pressed. The weight of sin was upon Jesus; he was pressed down. The sanctification journey will see Christians pressed by the cares of the world, which aids in the perfection of character. We must endure the Gethsemane experience. Olive trees take a long time to grow and mature, approximately three years. Similarly, it takes time for Christians to grow and mature.

Holy Place—Judgment (Sentencing)

To sentence means to declare or pronounce punishment. Sentencing is the second phase of judgment. The first phase, the investigative phase, began in the Most Holy Place in heaven in 1844 (refer to Appendix.) Christ is still in the Most Holy Place as our mediator and intercessor. When the Godhead completes this investigative phase, probation for the earth will end and Christ will move from the Most Holy Place to the Holy Place to declare sentencing. In the book of Revelation, John in vision was shown the heavenly sanctuary. He was shown seven angels with the seven last plagues.

> Rev 22:11-15—"He that is unjust, let him be unjust still, and he which is filthy, let him be filthy still, and he that is righteous, let him be righteous still, and he that is holy, let him be holy still. And behold, I come quickly, and my reward is with me, to give every man according as his work shall be. I am Alpha and Omega, the beginning and the end, the first and the last. Blessed are they that do his commandments, that they may have right to the tree of life and may enter in through the gates into the city. For without are dogs, and sorcerers, and whoremongers, and murderers, and idolaters, and whosoever loveth and maketh a lie."

> Rev 16:1—"And I heard a great voice out of the temple saying to the seven angels, 'go your ways, and pour out the vials of the wrath of God upon the earth.'"

The heavenly gavel falls, and judgment is pronounced. The angels are given the vials of God's punishment and wrath that will be poured out upon earth.

The Veil

> Exod 26:31-33—"And thou shalt make a veil of blue, and purple, and scarlet, and fine twined linen of cunning work, with cherubims shall it be made. And thou shalt hang it upon four pillars of shittim wood overlaid with gold; their hooks shall be of gold, upon the four sockets of silver. And thou shalt hang up the veil under the taches, that thou mayest bring in thither within the veil the ark of the testimony, and the veil shall divide unto you between the holy place and the most holy."

Separating the Holy Place from the Most Holy Place was a veil or curtain made of fine linen. It shielded the presence of God, the Shekinah Glory from the view of sinful man. The veil was a protection for the children of Israel. No sinner can see God's face and live as God told Moses. "And he said, 'thou canst not see my face, for there shall no man see me, and live" (Exod 33:20.) On the holy Day of Atonement, the High Priest was allowed to go beyond the veil into the Most Holy Place, only after he had gone through the purification process. The veil (curtain) was suspended on four pillars of acacia wood. It had three colors; blue, purple, and scarlet and was embroidered with figures of cherubims. These were also the colors of the robe worn by the High Priest (Exod 28:4-6.) The veil was beautifully laced and steeped with symbolism. It represented the coming Messiah who would be earth's intercessor. Christ was to suffer and hang on a wooden cross suspended between heaven and earth. Christ stands between God and the sinner.

> Heb 10:19-21—"Having therefore, brethren, boldness to enter into the holiest by the blood of Jesus, by a new and living way, which he hath consecrated for us, through the veil, that is to say, his flesh, and having a high priest over the house of God."

> Rev 19:7-8—"Let us be glad and rejoice, and give honor to him, for the marriage of the Lamb is come, and his wife hath made herself ready. And to her was granted that she should be arrayed in fine linen, clean and white, for the fine linen is the righteousness of saints."

The twined linen material represented Jesus' righteousness. The saints must be clothed with the righteousness of Christ to enter the presence of God. To be twined is to be interwoven or twisted together, derived from twain. To be clothed with the righteousness of Christ means to abide in Christ, as a branch is intertwined into the vine (John 15:4-6.)

> Fun Fact: There were three things made specifically of twined linen. The curtains surrounding the sanctuary, the veil, and the priest's clothes.

When Jesus was crucified, the veil in the temple was torn from top to bottom, signifying the end of ceremonial animal sacrifices. No human hands could have done this, it was torn by God himself (Mark 15:38-39.) Jesus was taken from the cross and wrapped in linen (Mark 15:46.) The sacrificial Lamb of God paid the penalty for sin, giving the sinner direct access to God, allowing all to come boldly before the throne of grace. There is no longer a need for human intercessors, priests, or pastors—all have direct access to God through Jesus Christ the Son!

> Heb 4:14-16—"Seeing then that we have a great high priest, that is passed into the heavens, Jesus the Son of God, let us hold fast

our profession. For we have not a high priest which cannot be touched with the feeling of our infirmities; but was in all points tempted like as we are, yet without sin. Let us therefore come boldly unto the throne of grace, that we may obtain mercy, and find grace to help in time of need."

Colors

Blue, purple, and scarlet (red) were the three colors primarily used in the sanctuary. There were three things made with these three colors; the veil, the curtains at the entrance of the tent, and the priest's robe.

- Blue symbolizes divinity because it is the color of the sky and sea. It is also the color of God's glory and throne (Exod 24:10; Ezek 1:26—10:1.) It is also royalty (Esth 8:15.)
- Blue is the symbol of Jesus, the sacrificial Lamb and also the symbol of the dispersal of evil.
- Scripture states that, "the blueness of a wound cleanseth away evil, so do stripes the inward parts of the belly" (Prov 20:30.) Jesus was inflicted with stripes from the Roman whip, but we are healed and redeemed from sin by his sacrifice (Isa 53:5; 1 Pet 2:24.)
- Blue (azure) was the color of Judah's camp in the wilderness encampment in Mount Sinai. Judah's camp also had the emblem of the lion (Gen 49:9.) When Jacob blessed his son Judah, he was to be the ruler and lawgiver (Gen 49:10.) This is fitting because Jesus is described as the Lion of the tribe of Judah, the fulfillment of the law of God (Rev 5:5.)
- Purple symbolizes royalty and wealth.
- Purple was a symbol of Jesus, the sacrificial Lamb. During the mock trial, Roman soldiers clothed him in a purple robe (John 19:2.)
- Scarlet symbolizes power, importance, and influence.
- Scarlet symbolizes the shed blood of Jesus, the sacrificial Lamb. He bore the corporate sin of humanity to reconcile us back to God (Heb 10:9; Isa 1:18.)
- Scarlet was the color of Reuben's camp. It is interesting to note that it was Reuben and Judah that averted the slaying of Joseph their brother when the brothers had conspired to kill him and instead

sold him into slavery (Gen 37:22–27.) It was Joseph who in turn saved his whole family during the famine. Joseph is a "type" of Christ in terms of the sacrifice made to save many despite being separated from his father and was condemned to die. God's protective hand took Joseph from the pit of sure death and took Jesus from the death tomb.

> Fun facts: Ancient Egyptian cultures believed that blue could protect them against evil. Blue dye was also used to color the cloth to wrap the mummies. Blue LED light is used in wound healing as it has antimicrobial properties. Mixing blue and red gives purple.

In the apocalyptic and prophetic book of Revelation, the false church is identified as the harlot woman who is decked out in two of these colors—purple and scarlet (Rev 17:4.) This false church is a counterfeit to God's true church. It is decked out with wealth of gold and precious stones, which is symbolic of purple. This false church also has global influence and power symbolized by the color red. However, blue is missing. Blue symbolizes divinity, therefore, this false church (institution) does not have the divinity of God, nor does it reflect the truth as sanctioned in God's word. False church, worship and religion will be discussed in more detail in Chapter 15.

Shittim (Acacia) Wood

The veil was hung on four pillars of shittim (acacia) wood. Shittim in Hebrew means thorn. The veil symbolized the flesh of Christ and foreshadowed the cross upon which Jesus would be crucified with a crown of thorns on his head (Mark 15:17.) Acacia wood is commonly known as wattle, which means interwoven. It is a thorny tree with twisted branches and gum resin exuding from the bark. Gum resin invokes images of Jesus sweating drops of blood in the final hours in the garden of Gethsemane, and on the cross, water and blood gushing from his pierced side (Luke 22:44; John 19:34.) Acacia is known to be rot-resistant; a perfect symbolism to Jesus, whose body did not see any corruption in the tomb (Ps 16:10; Acts 2:31.)

> Fun Fact: It is believed to be amongst the burning shittim bush that God appeared to Moses.

Most Holy Place

The Most Holy Place was the third compartment of the tabernacle. It was a perfect cube; 10 cubits length x 10 cubits width x 10 cubits height (15 ft x 15ft x 15ft.) It was also called the Holy of Holies. This was the sacred room where the presence of God dwelt. It is profoundly fitting that this was the third compartment, and it was a perfect cube. Three represents the triunity of the Godhead and ten being God's number, symbolizing perfection, completeness, and holiness. The veil (curtain) separated the Holy Place from the Most Holy Place. The High Priest was the only one allowed in this sacred room, and this was once a year on the solemn Day of Atonement.

Ark of the Covenant

The Most Holy Place held the Ark of the Covenant (also known as the Ark of the Testimony)—the golden chest which held the presence of God. It measured 2.5 cubits length x 1.5 cubits breath x 1.5 cubits height (3.75 ft x 2.25 ft x 2.25 ft.) The presence of God within the Ark was so sacred that when the Ark was transported from place to place, the children of Israel were instructed to walk about two thousand cubits (three thousand feet) behind it (Josh 3:3–4.) This was for their own protection, as sinful man would be consumed by the presence of a holy sinless God—the Shekinah Glory. The golden Ark held three things; the Ten Commandments on tablets of stone, Aaron's rod, and manna.

Co.ven.ant—What's in a Name?

(co = with, together) + (ven = come) + (ant = suffix that means one that performs an action or being in a state or condition.) Covenant is the action of coming together in a binding relational agreement with God.

Mercy Seat

The Mercy Seat was the lid covering the Ark. There were two golden cherubims at each end of the Mercy Seat. They faced each other and their wings formed an arch over the seat. Their gaze was downward in a reverential awe towards the seat and ark which held the law of God.[2] The Mercy seat symbolized that God's justice and judgment is tempered with loving mercy. In the real heavenly sanctuary, it is before the mercy seat that Christ is now pleading his blood on the sinner's behalf.

Aaron's Rod

Some of the Israelites murmured against Moses and Aaron during the exodus journey. They questioned Moses' authority and by extension they questioned God's choice of choosing Moses and Aaron to be their leaders. God was displeased with their murmurings and told Moses to command each of the twelve tribes to bring forth a rod. The man's rod that budded would be the man God would choose to be the priest of the sanctuary. Aaron's rod that budded was to serve as a witness and reminder of the rebellious nature of murmuring and doubting (Num 17:1–13.) Murmuring reflected their lack of faith in God and was a reminder that God was the one who chose Aaron to be the High Priest.

2. White, *Life Sketches*, 95.

Manna

Manna was the coriander seed-like wafer that rained down from heaven to feed the children of Israel for forty years (Exod 16:14-15.) During the long exodus journey, their taste buds grew disenchanted with God's daily servings of this nameless meal. It was dubbed, "what is this?" They lamented for the rich delicacies they enjoyed in Egypt (Num 11:1-6.) They complained against God, Moses, and Aaron. This unbelieving spirit caused them to question and doubt. Manna was placed in the Ark to bear witness of God's unfailing provisions and faithfulness.

Commandments on Tables of Stones

The Ten Commandments were given to Moses on Mount Sinai during the pilgrimage from Egypt towards the promised land of Canaan (Exod 19:20-25—20:1-20.) This journey is symbolic of renouncing sin and heading towards the promise of a place God has gone to prepare for us in heaven. The commandments were written by the hand of God on two tablets of stones. They were a blueprint of God's character that the children of Israel needed to emulate, as a covenant of obedience (Deut 4:13-20.) The commandments were not just for Moses and the children of Israel, it was for all mankind. From the creation of the world, God instilled these same moral indices upon earth's first family. Adam and Eve were instructed verbally of what was required of them. Cain and Abel, the first brothers, were also instructed by God. Whether verbal commands or written commands, they emanate from the same unchanging God. We are spiritual Israel and the commandments are as binding today as they were in the days of Adam, Eve, Cain, Abel, Moses, and the children of Israel. God's commands are to be written in our hearts and minds (Heb 10:16.)

Obedience, Faith, Patience

The three emblems placed inside the Ark (the Ten Commandments, manna, and Aaron's rod), embodied obedience, faith, and patience. The test of obedience, faith, and patience are three key areas upon which Christians will be tested. The end-time prophetic book of Revelation declares, "here is the patience of the saints, here are they that keep the commandments of God, and the faith of Jesus" (Rev 14:12.) Having the faith of Jesus means an unwavering trust in God that he will provide for our daily spiritual and physical needs. Patience is to not get weary while awaiting the return of Christ, especially during the approaching time of trouble. Jesus warned that the elect will go through the tribulation. In Matt 24:3, the disciples asked Jesus to tell them of the sign of the end of the world. In the lengthy discourse he conveyed, "for in those days shall be affliction, such as was not from the beginning of the creation which God created unto this time, neither shall be. And except that the Lord had shortened those days, no flesh should be saved, but for the elect's sake, whom he hath chosen, he hath shortened the days" (Mark 13:19–20.) The calming reassurance that Jesus gave to the disciples must be the mantra for end-time Christians—"but he that shall endure unto the end, the same shall be saved" (Matt 24:13.) Obedience means keeping the letter and the spirit of all ten commandments and not accepting man-made religious traditions or compromises. The fourth commandment, Sabbath, will be a paramount test—the true Sabbath (sunset Friday to sunset Saturday) versus the altered day of rest (Sunday), which was changed on March 7, AD 321 by the pagan Roman Empire.

The Ten Commandments

The Ten commandments are God's covenant laws of love. Christ himself declared, "if ye keep my commandments, ye shall abide in my love, even as I have kept my Father's commandments, and abide in his love" (John 15:10.) The commandments embody the triunity of the Godhead and the profound number three. The first four commandments reflect mankind's love for God—agape love. We will first examine the first three commandments:

> "I am the Lord thy God, which have brought thee out of the land of Egypt, out of the house of bondage.
>
> 1. Thou shalt have no other gods before me.
>
> 2. Thou shalt not make unto thee any graven image, or any likeness of anything that is in heaven above, or that is in the earth beneath, or that is in the water under the earth. Thou shalt not bow down thyself to them, nor serve them, for I the Lord thy God am a jealous God, visiting the iniquity of the fathers upon the children unto the third and fourth generation of them that hate me, and shewing

mercy unto thousands of them that love me, and keep my commandments.

3. Thou shalt not take the name of the Lord thy God in vain, for the Lord will not hold him guiltless that taketh his name in vain" (Exod 20:2–7.)

Alludes to *name*—"The Lord thy God" is mentioned three times; once in the introduction before the first commandment, once in the second, and once in the third. God's name is holy and must not be taken in vain.

Alludes to *creation*—three realms; the heaven, earth, and sea/water.

Alludes to *worship*—only the one true God should be worshipped. God is the only living God. Any other gods or relics are called graven images. The word graven infers a grave, which implies dead gods and dead works. The Greek word for graven is *charagma* which means stamp or mark. A graven image is an idol, a false god, or a mark of false worship.

The first three commandments address *who to worship*—the Lord thy God. Now, we will look at the fourth commandment.

4. "Remember the Sabbath day, to keep it holy. Six days shalt thou labor and do all thy work. But the seventh day is the Sabbath of the Lord thy God, in it thou shalt not do any work, thou, nor thy son, nor thy daughter, thy manservant, nor thy maidservant, nor thy cattle, nor thy stranger that is within thy gates; for in six days the Lord made heaven and earth, the sea, and all that in them is, and rested the seventh day, wherefore the Lord blessed the sabbath day, and hallowed it."

Alludes to *name*—"The Lord" is noted three times; once as "the Lord thy God," and twice as "the Lord."

Alludes to *creation*—three realms; heaven, earth, and sea.

Alludes to *worship*—God ordained the observance of the seventh-day, Sabbath as the day of worship. It is described in three words; blessed, hallowed, and holy.

Alludes to the seal of God—three key components comprise a seal. His name is Lord. His title is Creator. His territory is heaven, earth, and sea.

The fourth commandment addresses *who to worship, why we worship, and when to worship*. The Lord God is to be worshipped because he is the Creator. The seventh-day Sabbath is God's holy day of worship. The Sabbath was the seal placed upon the creation week. It was the only day of the week to be given a name by God. The other days at creation were known numerically as the first day, second day, third day, fourth day, fifth day and sixth day. The first mention of the name Sabbath was in Exod 16:23, when God admonished the Israelites in the wilderness to gather twice as much manna on the sixth day, in preparation for the approaching seventh-day Sabbath of rest. They were to rest and not gather anything on the Sabbath as it was to be kept holy. It is interesting to note there are three commandments that refer to worship—first, second, and fourth. The last six commandments reflect mankind's love for each other which is phileo love.

5. Honor thy father and thy mother, that thy days may be long upon the land which the Lord thy God giveth thee.
6. Thou shalt not kill.
7. Thou shalt not commit adultery.
8. Thou shalt not steal.
9. Thou shalt not bear false witness against thy neighbor.
10. Thou shalt not covet thy neighbor's house, thou shalt not covet thy neighbor's wife, nor his manservant, nor his maidservant, nor his ox, nor his ass, nor anything that is thy neighbor's.

Religions over the centuries have distorted, changed, or abrogated God's holy commandments. God cannot change therefore the commandments cannot change. Mankind was given these moral foundational tenets to develop the character and mold them into the holy character of the Creator.

Character and the Seal of God

Rev 7:2–3—"And I saw another angel ascending from the east, having the seal of the living God and he cried with a loud voice to the four angels, to whom it was given to hurt the earth and the sea. Saying, 'hurt not the earth, neither the sea, nor the trees, till we have sealed the servants of our God in their foreheads.'"

Rev 9:3–4—"And there came out of the smoke locusts upon the earth and unto them was given power, as the scorpions of the earth have power. And it was commanded them that they should not hurt the grass of the earth, neither any green thing, neither any tree, but only those men which have not the seal of God in their foreheads."

Rev 14:1—"And I looked, and, lo, a Lamb stood on the mount Zion, and with him a hundred forty and four thousand, having his Father's name written in their foreheads."

What is the name of God written in the forehead? What is the seal of God? Having the name of God in the forehead is reflecting God's character—a spiritual marriage covenant. The church is described as the bride of Christ. A bride takes on the name of her husband which is a marriage seal or covenant. A married couple becomes one flesh (Mark 10:8.) The name and character of God is embodied in the commandments and in Jesus Christ. A seal has three primary components; name, title, and territory. Embedded in the fourth commandment is God's seal. God identifies his name three times as the Lord. He identifies his title as Creator when he proclaimed, "the Lord made." He identifies his territory as heaven, earth, and sea. The seal of God is the Sabbath commandment.

commandments ↔ character of God ↔ name of God ↔ image of God ↔ seal of God = Sabbath.

Satan has always sought to distort the character of God. In these last days of earth's history, Satan and the forces of evil will attempt to counterfeit God's image, name, and seal (mark.) This false trinity consists of the dragon (Satan), the beast (false church), and the false prophets (false religions) (Rev 16:13.) This false trinity will elevate creation over the Creator. This alliance will seek to force and coerce mankind into breaking God's commandment by enforcing worship on a false sabbath. Christians must stay steadfast to God's blueprint of his character which is the unchangeable commandments.

Most Holy Place—Glorification

Once a year on the Day of Atonement, the High Priest entered the Most Holy Place. On this holiest of days, on the tenth day of the seventh month, God required that the sanctuary and the people be cleansed of sin. The priest was to cleanse (wash) himself and put on the holy garments before approaching the presence of the Shekinah Glory. A lamb was sacrificed and the blood was sprinkled upon the mercy seat. This symbolized transgression against God's commands but tempered with mercy. Glory means honor, respect, and reverence. We show honor, respect, and reverence to God when we reflect or embody God's character (image), his name, and his seal. Glorification is the final stage of the salvific process.

While on earth, Jesus was fully divine and was his own embodiment of glory, which he had with the Father from creation. He temporarily suspended his glory to come to a sinful world to reflect the Father and to live out God's character for our example. As Jesus was about to leave earth to return to heaven to reunite with the Father, he spoke about glorification to the disciples.

> John 17:1,4-6—"These words spake Jesus, and lifted up his eyes to heaven, and said, 'Father, the hour is come, glorify thy Son, that thy Son also may glorify thee. I have glorified thee on the earth, I have finished the work which thou gavest me to do. And now, O Father, glorify thou me with thine own self with the glory which I had with thee before the world was. I have manifested thy name unto the men which thou gavest me out of the world; thine they were, and thou gavest them me, and they have kept thy word.'"

Glorification is fully reflecting God's character, obeying his commandments, and manifesting and honoring his name. It is therefore fitting that the Ten Commandments were placed inside the Ark of the Covenant in the Most Holy Place. Glory is connected to name and character. Moses on mount Sinai asked God to reveal his glory.

> Exod 33:18-19—34:5-6—"And he said, 'I beseech thee, shew me thy glory.' And he said, 'I will make all my goodness pass before thee, and I will proclaim the name of the Lord before thee and will be gracious to whom I will be gracious and will shew mercy on whom I will shew mercy.' And the Lord descended in the cloud, and stood with him there, and proclaimed the name of the Lord. And the Lord passed by before him, and proclaimed, 'the Lord, the Lord God, merciful, and gracious, longsuffering, and abundant in goodness and truth.'"

Characteristics of God's name—goodness, graciousness, merciful, longsuffering, truthful. The Hebrew word for name is *shem*, which means breath; the same word used in Gen 2:7, when God breathed the breath of life into man at creation. It not only reflects physical life but also means character. At creation man was given the character of God with this breath. God is often called *Hashem* in Judaism, meaning "The Name."

Glorification is reflecting God's name and character. His character is reflected in the Ten Commandments.

Most Holy Place—Judgment

The investigative phase of judgment was in the Most Holy Place. On the Day of Atonement while the High Priest was making atonement for the sins of the people, they were required to afflict their souls. This was to be a solemn time of deep internal introspection and reconnection with God. If the earthly sanctuary was a replica of the heavenly sanctuary, then the heavenly sanctuary must also reflect this phase of judgment. Daniel 12:1-2 takes us through the time when Jesus will leave the Most Holy Place (Michael stands up) and passes through the Holy Place where earth is sentenced, and the time of great trouble is pronounced. The seven last plagues will be poured out upon earth. Then Jesus returns to earth (outer court) to execute judgment and resurrect the dead. This mirrors any modern-day courtroom. The Most Holy Place is akin to a judge's private chamber; a place to review cases, the evidence, and deliberates. After the judge leaves the chamber, he or she returns to the courtroom to announce the verdict and execute the sentence. Christ is soon to exit the Most Holy Place and return to earth to execute judgment. The world is now in a solemn time of probation—time of spiritual internal introspection.

Has the Investigative Judgment Begun in Heaven?

The investigative judgment in heaven began in 1844 in the Most Holy Place. After the crucifixion in AD 31, Jesus ascended from earth and went into the Holy Place in heaven (Heb 9:24.) On October 22, 1844, Jesus moved from the Holy Place to the Most Holy Place to begin the investigative judgment. The prophetic revelation was given by inspiration of the Holy Spirit to a group of Bible truth-seeking Christians from various denominations in the 1800s (Refer to the Appendix.) The church that was birthed out of this prophetic encounter was the Seventh-day Adventist Church. Though disappointed that Jesus did not return to earth in 1844, they were shown that the cleansing of the sanctuary meant that Jesus moved from the Holy Place to the Most Holy Place to begin the investigative phase of judgment in the heavenly sanctuary (Dan 8:14.) The Godhead convened in the Most Holy Place to begin the solemn task of pre-advent investigative judgment. The threefold Godhead is the judge, jury, defense, and witness for mankind in this anti-typical Day of Atonement. Jesus is our High Priest interceding on our behalf (Heb 4:14.)

Who is Being Judged in the Pre-Advent Investigative Judgment?

> 1 Pet 4:17—"For the time is come that judgment must begin at the house of God, and if it first begin at us, what shall the end of them that obey not the gospel of God?"

This pre-advent judgment began with the judgment of the dead. First for those who died professing the faith of Christ and then for those who died not professing the faith of Christ.

> Rev 6:9-11—20:12—"And when he had opened the fifth seal, I saw under the altar the souls of them that were slain for the word of God, and for the testimony which they held. And they cried with a loud voice, saying, 'how long, O Lord, holy and true, dost thou not judge and avenge our blood on them that dwell on the earth?' And white robes were given unto every one of them, and it was said unto them, that they should rest yet for a little season, until their fellow servants also and their brethren, that should be killed as they were, should be fulfilled. And I saw the dead, both small and great, stand before God, and the books were opened, which is the book of life, and the dead were judged out of those things which were written in the books, according to their works."

The righteous dead are judged first. They receive white robes, which is symbolic and not literal. They are deemed worthy and will continue to rest until Jesus returns to resurrect them and reward them literally. After the pre-advent judgment of the dead, the judgment of the living will begin. It is not known when this will begin. The investigative judgment of the living precedes the second coming of Christ. Many are misguided in thinking that when Christ returns there will be a second chance to repent. Whilst the Godhead tarries, all should daily seek repentance, for we do not know when our names and character will be called into judgment.

— 13 —

3 Traits, 1 Personality
Christian Character

(Seed. Tree. Fruit)

Jesus came to earth to reflect the character of God. He is our example. The character of Christ must be perfected in us through the workings of the Holy Spirit in a completely surrendered life fueled by his love.

Jesus used parables and analogies of plants, trees, fruits, and seeds to portray Christians, the kingdom of heaven, and the Christian journey.

Christians as Seeds

Matt 13:24-27,36-38 (parable of wheat and tares)—"Another parable put he forth unto them, saying, 'the kingdom of heaven is likened unto a man which sowed good seed in his field. But while men slept, his enemy came and sowed tares among the wheat, and went his way. But when the blade was sprung up, and brought forth fruit, then appeared the tares also. So, the servants of the householder came and said unto him, 'sir, didst not thou sow good seed in thy field, from whence then hath it tares?' Then Jesus sent the multitude away, and went into the house, and his disciples came unto him, saying, 'declare unto us the parable of the tares of the field.' He answered and said unto them, 'he that soweth the good seed is the Son of man, the field is the world, *the good seed are the children of the kingdom*, but the tares are the children of the wicked one."

Jesus likens true Christians (children of the kingdom), as good seeds that grew and brought forth fruit. The tares however, brought forth no fruit. This will be a character or personality flaw that differentiates true Christians from false. What are the fruits that true Christians must bear? We will look at this in more detail in the next segment.

False Christians—Tare Character

The tare (*lolium temulentum*) is typically known as darnel or poison darnel. The plant stem can grow up to one meter tall (three feet), with inflorescence, i.e., the complete flower head in the ears and has purple grain. The roots are shallow. Darnel usually grows in the same production zones as wheat. It bears a close resemblance to wheat until the ear appears. The similarity between these two plants is so great that in some regions, darnel is referred to as false wheat. The spikelets are oriented edgeways to the stem and have only a single glume (leaf-like structure), while those of wheat are oriented with the flat side to the stem and have two glumes. Wheat will appear brown when ripe, whereas darnel is black. The French word for darnel is *ivraie* and from Latin *ebriacus*, which means intoxicated. The botanical name, *lolium temulentum*, is from Latin *temulent*, "drunken," though this sometimes is said to be "from the heavy seed heads lolling over under their own weight."[1] Lolium is from the Greek word for craft, deceit, or treacherous.[2] In some parts of continental Europe the seeds of darnel have the reputation of causing intoxication in men, beasts, and birds. The effects being sometimes so violent as to produce convulsions. In Scotland the name of *Sleepies*, is applied to darnel, from the seeds causing narcotic effects.[3] It has similar inebriating properties like beer. The grains can be poisonous.

1. Findwords.info, s.v., "darnell."
2. Herbiguide.com.au, s.v., "darnell."
3. Findwords.info, s.v., "darnell."

Spiritual Interpretations and Analogies of Tares (Darnel)

The darnel has purple grain before it ripens and becomes black. The woman (false church) is identified in Rev 17:4 as being arrayed in purple. The darnel can grow up to three feet, which implies that it appears to be Christian-like or a true church, but it is a false trinity and a counterfeit. It looks like wheat until the ears appear which means it goes undetected until the harvest. It is a perfect camouflage amongst God true Christians. It has shallow roots which reveals a superficial shallow Christian experience.

Jesus ended the parable by saying, "who hath ears to hear let him hear." A stark warning against deception. It has one glume (leaf-like structure), whilst the wheat has two. It takes a minimum of two to establish truth, not one. This false church or false Christian will not speak the truth but will speak lies, false doctrines, and practice deception. This false church does not preach or teach the full component of the Word of God (Bible.) Wheat appears brown when ripe, while the darnel appears black. There is no light in these false Christians and false churches. The tare character does not have the light of Christ's character. The Latin translation for darnel is *ebriacus* which means inebriated, intoxicated, or drunk. Revelation 17:2 and 18:3 points to a false church, "with whom the kings of the earth have committed fornication, and the inhabitants of the earth have been made drunk with the wine of her fornication." This false church will lure many from the true God and pollute the word of God with "wine," which is false traditions, rituals, doctrines, crafts, and deceptions. The darnel is loaded over with its own weight; this alludes to self-exalting, prideful Christians, and false churches espousing false doctrines. Self-exaltation is a characteristic of the devil who sought to exalt himself above God leading to his expulsion from heaven. The man of sin is described in 2 Thess 2:3-4 as the "son of perdition who opposeth and exalteth himself above all that is called God, or that is worshipped, so that he as God sitteth in the temple of God, shewing himself that he is God." Embedded in this simple yet powerful parable, Jesus was drawing parallels to true Christians (wheat seed) versus false Christians (tares/darnel), and the true church versus the false church.

True Christian—Wheat Character

Wheat kernel is a type of fruit. It consists of three parts; endosperm, bran, and germ. Wheat florets contain three stamens, i.e., the pollen producing reproductive organ of a flower. Two to three grains are produced by the flowers. The flower is not very showy as they have no petals. There are two root types in wheat; the seminal roots or primary roots which appear at germination and the adventitious roots, also known as nodal or crown root. Adventitious roots usually grow as a means of survival, e.g., in response to stressors such as floods, low oxygen environment, nutrient distress, and wounding. Wheat is primarily harvested for flour. Wheat in Latin is *triticum*.

Spiritual Interpretations and Analogies of Wheat

Wheat kernels bring forth fruit. Spiritual fruit is a requirement and sign of a productive and connected Christian life. Jesus admonishes that every branch that does not bear fruit will be cast out (John 15:2.) The flower is not showy which alludes to the quiet and humble nature of true Christians (1 Pet 3:4; Matt 18:4.) Wheat is harvested and made into flour. Flour was an integral part of the sanctuary services. It was used to make the unleavened bread and was placed on the table of showbread in the Holy Place. In the wheat and tare parable, Jesus noted that the wheat will be brought into the barn, whilst the tares will be gathered and burned (Matt 13:30.) The spiritual application of this, is that Christians, like wheat will be brought into God's spiritual and literal presence, however tares have no place in heaven. The adventitious or crown roots are revealed in times of stress. A strong spiritual connection to God is oftentimes more clearly revealed in times of extreme external stressors. Adventitious means "coming from another source and not inherent or innate."[4] In adverse situations true Christians will develop stronger spiritual roots by connecting and grafting themselves closer to the Godhead. This encompasses daily reading of the word, praying, worshipping of God etc.

> Matt 13:6,21,41—"And when the sun was up, they were scorched, and because they had no root, they withered away. Yet hath he not root in himself, but dureth for a while, for when tribulation or persecution ariseth because of the word, by and by he is offended. The Son of man shall send forth his angels, and they shall gather out of his kingdom all things that offend, and them which do iniquity."

---

4. Merriam-Webster.com, s.v., "adventitious."

Tares are those that offend and do iniquity. To offend means to be a stumbling block, to cause to stumble, to sin, or snare. A true Christian must not offend, or be easily offended, and must not practice iniquity (sin.)

Wheat in Latin is *triticum*. Here we see a reference to *tri* which means having three, and *cum* which means with or together. The wheat also has other references to three, e.g., the threefold kernel structure and three productive organs. The spiritual application of this infers that Christians will embrace the triunity of the Godhead. Acceptance of the trifold Godhead is to accept God the Father, Jesus the Son, and the Holy Spirit. To deny one member of the Godhead is to reject all three (1 John 2:22–23.) In the mouth of two or three witnesses every word and truth is established. Triticum originated from the Latin words tero and tritus. Tero means to rub or wear out. Daniel 7:25 points out the false church which will "wear out" the true church.

> Dan 7:25—"And he shall speak great words against the most High and shall wear out the saints of the most High, and think to change times and laws, and they shall be given into his hand until a time and times and the dividing of time."

Persecution during the Dark Ages resulted in millions of Christians killed for their faith. Persecution will again arise against God's true remnant church (Rev 12:17—13:15.) An attribute of a true Christian is one who is willing to suffer persecution for the word of God (Rev 12:11; 2 Tim 3:12.)

In the parable of sower which we will discuss shortly, Jesus says that a Christian who receives the word with a stony heart will not endure persecution. Another analogy of Christians as wheat seed is someone that dies spiritually to self to become spiritually fruitful, a total surrender to the will of God.

> John 12:24—"Verily, verily, I say unto you, except a corn of wheat fall into the ground and die, it abideth alone, but if it dies, it bringeth forth much fruit."

Christians as Fruits

The parable of the sower found in the gospels of Matthew 13, Mark 4, and Luke 8.

Matt 13:3–8,10–11,18–23—"And he spake many things unto them in parables, saying, 'behold, a sower went forth to sow. And when he sowed, some seeds fell by the wayside, and the fowls came and devoured them up. Some fell upon stony places, where they had not much earth and forthwith they sprung up, because they had no deepness of earth, and when the sun was up, they were scorched, and because they had no root, they withered away. And some fell among thorns, and the thorns sprung up, and choked them. But other fell into good ground, and brought forth fruit, some a hundredfold, some sixtyfold, some thirtyfold.' And the disciples came, and said unto him, 'why speakest thou unto them in parables?'

He answered and said unto them, 'because it is given unto you to know the mysteries of the kingdom of heaven, but to them it is not given. Hear ye therefore the parable of the sower. When any one heareth the word of the kingdom, and understandeth it not, then cometh the wicked one, and catcheth away that which was sown in his heart. This is he which received seed by the wayside. But he that received the seed into stony places, the same is he that heareth the word, and anon with joy receiveth it, yet hath he not root in himself, but dureth for a while; for when tribulation or persecution ariseth because of the word, by and by he is offended. He also that received seed among the thorns is he that heareth the word, and the care of this world, and the deceitfulness of riches, choke the word, and he becometh unfruitful. But he that received seed into the good ground is he that heareth the word, and understandeth it, which also beareth fruit, and bringeth forth, some an hundredfold, some sixty, some thirty.'"

The seed is the word of God. To bear fruit, the heart must be fertilized and watered daily scripture by the aid of the Holy Spirit. A Christian is one with "good ground" which is a receptive heart, who reads and hears the word, understands it and bears fruit which means to apply the word in character development.

Are All Christians Expected to Bear Fruit?

John 15:2—"Every branch in me that beareth not fruit he taketh away, and every branch that beareth fruit, he purgeth it, that it may bring forth more fruit."

> Matt 21:19,43—"And when he saw a fig tree in the way, he came to it, and found nothing thereon, but leaves only, and said unto it, 'let no fruit grow on thee henceforward forever.' And presently the fig tree withered away. 'Therefore, say I unto you, the kingdom of God shall be taken from you, and given to a nation bringing forth the fruits thereof.'"
>
> Mark 4:29—"But when the fruit is brought forth, immediately he putteth in the sickle, because the harvest is come."
>
> Luke 3:9-11—"And now also the ax is laid unto the root of the trees, every tree therefore which bringeth not forth good fruit is hewn down and cast into the fire. And the people asked him, saying, 'what shall we do then?' He answereth and saith unto them, 'he that hath two coats, let him impart to him that hath none, and he that hath meat, let him do likewise.'"

Christ expects good fruits for a ripe harvest. Having only leaves and no fruit is having a form of godliness but denying the power thereof. Fruitful traits are developed with the aid of the Holy Spirit taking root in fertile hearts, bringing to fruition, the character of Christ.

What Kinds of Spiritual Fruits are Christians to Bear?

> Gal 5:22-25—"But the fruit of the Spirit is love, joy, peace, longsuffering, gentleness, goodness, faith, meekness, temperance; against such there is no law. And they that are Christ's have crucified the flesh with the affections and lusts. If we live in the Spirit, let us also walk in the Spirit."

Good character reveals that Christ dwells within. Christians should exhibit:

- The fruits of the Spirit
- A good and obedient heart
- Positive attitude, thoughts, and talk
- Love for each other in words and deeds

Why is Bearing Fruit Important?

> John 4:36—"And he that reapeth receiveth wages, and gathereth fruit unto life eternal, that both he that soweth and he that reapeth may rejoice together."

> John 15:8—"Herein is my Father glorified, that ye bear much fruit, so shall ye be my disciples."

Bearing fruit glorifies God. Spiritual fruit, which is character, is the only asset that will be taken to heaven. Character is eternal. Christ is coming back to reap fruits.

How Do You Bear Fruit?

Bearing fruit requires abiding in Christ (John 15:4-7) and dying to self (John 12:23-25.) Abiding in Christ requires obedience to the commandments (John 15:10.) The commandments are to love God and to love others (1 John 5:2-3; John 15:12.) Keeping all of God's commandments includes the Ten Commandments, the command to love each other, moral commands, health commands, relational commands, etc.

Christians as Trees

> Matt 12:33—"Either make the tree good, and his fruit good or else make the tree corrupt, and his fruit corrupt, for the tree is known by his fruit."

A Christian likened to a tree will be known by their fruit, i.e., character. A Christ-like character is an indicator of a true Christian.

> Mark 4:30-32—"And he said, 'whereunto shall we liken the kingdom of God, or with what comparison shall we compare it? It is like a grain of mustard seed, which, when it is sown in the earth, is less than all the seeds that be in the earth. But when it is sown, it groweth up, and becometh greater than all herbs, and shooteth out great branches, so that the fowls of the air may lodge under the shadow of it.'"

Christians are like trees with great branches. The kingdom of God is built up when love is demonstrated. Using the branches of blessings received from God to bless others is a demonstration of this love.

> Jer 17:7-8—"Blessed is the man that trusteth in the Lord, and whose hope the Lord is. For he shall be as a tree planted by the waters, and that spreadeth out her roots by the river, and shall not see when heat cometh, but her leaf shall be green, and shall not be careful in the year of drought, neither shall cease from yielding fruit."

Christians are like trees planted by the water—connected to God; imbuing sustaining strength from him.

> Mark 4:26-29—"And he said, 'so is the kingdom of God, as if a man should cast seed into the ground, and should sleep, and rise night and day, and the seed should spring and grow up, he knoweth not how. For the earth bringeth forth fruit of herself; first the blade, then the ear, after that the full corn in the ear. But when the fruit is brought forth, immediately he putteth in the sickle, because the harvest is come.'"

Jesus uses three stages to chronicle the growth of corn; blade, ear, and corn. The growth process of corn can take sixty to a hundred days depending on the soil and temperature. Like corn, the Christian growth is in stages. Bearing fruit (character of Christ) is a lifetime process; it does not materialize overnight. Sanctification is a lifetime process of daily connecting with the triune Godhead.

> Fun facts: Corn or maize is often 3m (10ft) in height; though some strains can grow up to 13m (43ft.) A leaf blade is generally 9cm (3.5in) in width and 120cm (3ft 11in) in length. The ear is the spiked part of the corn that contains the kernels. Ears develop above a few of the leaves in the midsection of the plant, between the stem and leaf sheath, elongating by around 3 mm (1/8 in) per day, to a length of 18 cm (7 in) with 60 cm (24 in) being the maximum alleged in the subspecies. An ear commonly holds 600 kernels (individual fruits).[5]

Quite a few references to three!

---

5. Wikipedia.org, s.v., "maize."

Key Requirements for Christian Development

Story of the fig tree—Mark 11:12-14,20-26—"And on the morrow, when they were come from Bethany, he was hungry, and seeing a fig tree afar off having leaves, he came, if haply he might find anything thereon, and when he came to it, he found nothing but leaves, for the time of figs was not yet. And Jesus answered and said unto it, 'no man eat fruit of thee hereafter forever.' And his disciples heard it. And in the morning, as they passed by, they saw the fig tree dried up from the roots. And Peter calling to remembrance saith unto him, 'Master, behold, the fig tree which thou cursedst is withered away.' And Jesus answering saith unto them, 'have faith in God, for verily I say unto you, that whosoever shall say unto this mountain, be thou removed, and be thou cast into the sea, and shall not doubt in his heart, but shall believe that those things which he saith shall come to pass, he shall have whatsoever he saith. Therefore, I say unto you, what things soever ye desire, when ye pray, believe that ye receive them, and ye shall have them. And when ye stand praying, forgive, if ye have ought against any, that your Father also which is in heaven may forgive you your trespasses. But if ye do not forgive, neither will your Father which is in heaven forgive your trespasses.'"

The story of the fig tree was an object lesson for the disciples. Jesus used the unfruitful fig tree to highlight two vitally important requirements for Christian development—faith and forgiveness. One cannot bear fruit without faith and forgiveness. The unfruitful fig tree is likened to a Christian who is faithless and unforgiving. The fig tree was cursed although seemingly, it was not yet the time or season for figs (verse 13.) How can figs grow out of season, was perhaps what perplexed the minds of the disciples. Jesus was teaching the disciples that faith is not based on what you see but is in the power of the unseen God. We must see things from the vantage point of God's lens. We must not believe in our unbelief. Unbelief becomes real if we have no faith. This false reality then becomes fear. Fear is the absence of faith. Perhaps the disciples did not believe that the fig tree could bear figs out of season. However, the Godhead is not confined to time or seasons. Time and seasons may be realities to man but imaginary to an infinite and everlasting God. The Christian who is fully connected to Christ is expected to bear fruit in all seasons—in season and out of season, all year round.

Faith

Faith is to proclaim, *"that although I do not see it; it is there!"* *"I do not see it, but it is there!"* We do not see how the seed becomes a tree, but it is there! The tree is in the seed. We do not see how a bare tree will bear fruit, but it is there! The fruit is incubated in the tree. Faith is believing without seeing. The disciples did not see the fig, but it was there. Jesus saw and knew the potential of the fig tree.

Q: How do you unleash this faith?

A: Prayer.

> Mark 11:24—"Therefore I say unto you, what things soever ye desire, when ye pray, believe that ye receive them, and ye shall have them."
>
> 1 Thess 3:10—"Night and day praying exceedingly that we might see your face and might perfect that which is lacking in your faith."

Faith is the substance of things hoped for, the evidence of things not seen (Heb 11:1.)

Sarah bore a child though barren, and the book of Hebrews declares that "through faith also Sarah herself received strength to conceive seed and was delivered of a child when she was past age, because she *judged him faithful* who had promised" (Heb 11:11.) Sarah could not self-will herself into conceiving a child. Similarly, we cannot self-will ourselves to be healed or for God to answer a prayer. We must believe that he is faithful in his word and in his desire to heal, bless, or answer a particular request, according to his will. It is the faithfulness of God and of Jesus that we must believe in—this is faith. The foundation of faith is to first believe and accept that God is faithful. This is the basis of faith. We have faith because we know he is faithful. We have faith because Jesus is obedient to the Father. We must remove ourselves from the equation as the source and originator of faith and look only unto Jesus who is the author and finisher of our faith (Heb 12:2.)

Faith and the Fig Tree—Having the Faith of Jesus

> Rev 14:12—"Here is the patience of the saints, here are they that keep the commandments of God, and the faith of Jesus."

After developing faith *in* Jesus, we must further develop the faith *of* Jesus. This will be paramount as we approach the coming tribulation. Jesus approached the fig tree seeking fruit. This was the faith of Jesus. Jesus' faith was to approach the fig tree in faith hoping and expecting to find figs, although it was not the season for figs. Jesus approached the tree knowing he was hungry, expecting to be fed, expecting to see ripe figs and expecting to find enough figs to feed not just himself but others. Faith is to believe without seeing. Believe anyhow! Approach or step out anyhow! Expect, anyhow! To approach is to act on and act out your faith in God. The disciples had faith in Jesus, but the faith of Jesus is in acting out—moving, stepping out when you cannot see the outcome. Though the evidence says one thing, i.e., it is not the season for figs, yet God says otherwise. The Godhead is not confined to seasons, time, or circumstances.

Jesus is indeed the author and finisher of our faith if we allow him to write the outcome of our faith. We must step out in faith, step aside from our doubts and hesitations. Christians must bear fruit in all seasons, through the power of Christ dwelling in them. Developing the faith of Jesus is to have faith in God. After the disciples saw that the fig tree was cursed and dried up, Jesus beseeched them to have faith in God. He explained that by believing in God and in his power and not doubting, they too can develop the faith of Jesus.

> Fun Fact and Health Nugget: God revealed to Isaiah that he would heal King Hezekiah of his tumor by applying figs to the tumor (2 Kgs 20:5–7.) After he was healed God also instructed King Hezekiah to go into the house of the Lord on the third day.

Forgiving

Christians must be forgiving in order for God to forgive them of their own trespasses.

> Mark 11:25-26—"And when ye stand praying, forgive, if ye have ought against any that your Father also which is in heaven may forgive you your trespasses. But if ye do not forgive, neither will your Father which is in heaven forgive your trespasses."

Love

Trees cannot bear fruit unless the seeds are planted in a fertile, nutrient-dense soil. The soil is likened to the receptive heart. What is the nutrient in the soil? The key nutrient for spiritual growth is love.

> John 15:4,7,10,12—"Abide in me, and I in you. As the branch cannot bear fruit of itself, except it abides in the vine; no more can ye, except ye abide in me. If ye abide in me, and my words abide in you, ye shall ask what ye will, and it shall be done unto you. If ye keep my commandments, ye shall abide in my love, even as I have kept my Father's commandments, and abide in his love. This is my commandment, that ye love one another, as I have loved you."

Abiding in Christ—the Sanctuary Message

John chapter 15 was one of Jesus' most profound farewell messages imparted to the disciples, and by extension to us today. He highlighted three key requirements needed to bear fruit.

Abiding in Christ (bearing fruit) = abiding in the word + keeping the commandments + loving others.

To abide means to abode, dwell, or live. Sanctuary is also an adobe or dwelling place. Abiding in Christ means to spiritually live in him; to rest in his spiritual shelter—his sanctuary, which is his word, his commandments, and his love. Jesus obediently kept the Father's words and commandments and perfectly reflected God's love. Jesus is our example.

> John 15:7,9,10,15—"If ye abide in me, and my words abide in you, ye shall ask what ye will, and it shall be done unto you. As the Father hath loved me, so have I loved you, continue ye in my love. If ye keep my commandments, ye shall abide in my love, even as I have kept my Father's commandments, and abide in his love. Henceforth I call you not servants, for the servant knoweth not what his lord doeth, but I have called you friends, for all things that I have heard of my Father I have made known unto you."

Abiding in His Word

Reading the Bible, meditating upon Scripture, and obeying the word is to abide in Christ. The word is likened to bread and Jesus likens himself as the bread from heaven.

> John 6:33-35—"For the bread of God is he which cometh down from heaven, and giveth life unto the world. Then said they unto him, 'Lord, evermore give us this bread.' And Jesus said unto them, 'I am the bread of life, he that cometh to me shall never hunger, and he that believeth on me shall never thirst.'"

> Matt 4:4—"But he answered and said, 'it is written, man shall not live by bread alone, but by every word that proceedeth out of the mouth of God.'"

In the earthly sanctuary, the physical bread was found in the Holy Place on the Table of Showbread. The sanctuary pointed to the coming Messiah. Christ became flesh; the living bread (word) and dwelt among us. As Jesus was about to embark on his ascension to heaven, he reminded the disciples to keep his word which was the emblem of the bread in the sanctuary.

Keeping His Commandments

Abiding is to keep the commandment of love which is an embodiment of the Ten Commandments which is God's moral law.

> John 14:15—"If ye love me, keep my commandments."

> 1 John 5:2-3—"By this we know that we love the children of God, when we love God, and keep his commandments. For this is the love of God, that we keep his commandments, and his commandments are not grievous."

In the heart of the sanctuary, the Ten Commandments written on tables of stone were found in the Ark of the Covenant in the Most Holy Place. In the new covenant, these same commandments of God's moral laws are written within the heart.

> Jer 31:33; Heb 8:10—"But this shall be the covenant that I will make with the house of Israel, after those days, saith the Lord, 'I will put my law in their inward parts, and write it in their hearts, and will be their God, and they shall be my people.'"

Prov 3:1—"My son, forget not my law, but let thine heart keep my commandments."

Love for Others

Christians must have authentic love for others and a self-sacrificing love like Christ.

> John 13:34-35—"A new commandment I give unto you, that ye love one another, as I have loved you, that ye also love one another. By this shall all men know that ye are my disciples, if ye have love one to another."

> 1 John 4:7—"Beloved, let us love one another, for love is of God, and everyone that loveth is born of God, and knoweth God."

In Jesus' passionate farewell message to the disciples, he highlights the pinnacle of his love in the foreshadowing of the imminent crucifixion.

> John 15:12-13—"This is my commandment, that ye love one another, as I have loved you. Greater love hath no man than this, that a man lay down his life for his friends."

It was in the outer court of the sanctuary that the sacrificial lamb was slain. The lamb pointed to Jesus who would be the sacrifice for sin. He came to this anti-typical outer court (earth), to pay the penalty for sin in the greatest act of love the world has ever witnessed.

> 1 Pet 1:18-19—"Forasmuch as ye know that ye were not redeemed with corruptible things, as silver and gold, from your vain conversation received by tradition from your father, but with the precious blood of Christ, as of a lamb without blemish and without spot."

> Fun Fact: There are thirty-three references to the word lamb in the New Testament (KJV Bible.)

Christian Character

Jesus' farewell message before ascending to heaven embodied the sanctuary message. Psalms 77:13 declares, "thy way, O God, is in the sanctuary; who is so great a God as our God?" The Christian way (journey) must spiritually go via the principles of the sanctuary. The way to heaven is through the sanctuary. The High Priest entered the Most Holy Place and brought with him the warm blood of the sacrificial lamb. Christians can only enter the sacred halls of heaven but by the blood of Jesus and bring the ripe fruit of their character, which must reflect Christ. No one can work their way into heaven because we are not saved by works. Cain brought the works of his hand, the fruits of his labor and it was rejected by God. We are saved by grace; like Abel who brought the blood of an animal sacrifice. Entry to heaven is only by the merits of Christ abiding in us. Only the High Priest was allowed into the Most Holy Place. Likewise, the only entrance into heaven is by abiding in the true vine (Christ); spiritually drawing from his sap (his blood) and producing the fruitful character of Christ. "Early rain produces conversion. Latter rain develops Christlike character."[6]

> "He will cause to come down for you the rain, the former rain, and the latter rain. In the east the former rain falls at the sowing time. It is necessary in order that the seed may germinate. Under the influence of the fertilizing showers the tender shoot springs up. The latter rain, falling near the close of the season, ripens the grain and prepares it for the sickle. The Lord employs these operations of nature to represent the work of the Holy Spirit (See Zech 10:1; Hos 6:3; Joel 2:23, 28.) As the dew and the rain are given first to cause the seed to germinate, and then to ripen the harvest, so the Holy Spirit is given to carry forward, from one stage to another, the process of spiritual growth. The ripening of the grain represents the completion of the work of God's grace in the soul. By the power of the Holy Spirit the moral image of God is to be perfected in the character. We are to be wholly transformed into the likeness of Christ. The latter rain, ripening earth's harvest, represents the spiritual grace that prepares the church for the coming of the Son of man. But unless the former rain has fallen, there will be no life; the green blade will not spring up. Unless the early showers have done their work, the latter rain can bring no seed to perfection."[7]

The earth before it was transformed, was without form, void, and darkness was upon the face of the deep. Then, the Spirit of God moved upon the face of the waters. The "Word" then spoke light into this darkness. A fertilized egg lies in the womb of darkness; new life also starts in

6. White, *Last Day Events*, 187.
7. White, *Last Day Events*, 183–84.

darkness. Similarly, a seed has to be buried in the darkness of the earth to take root and germinate. From the bowels of the deep, the bowels of the womb, and the bowels of the soil, God masterfully brings life and light from darkness.

Christians are at first seeds; dying to self by recognizing the darkness of sin and surrendering their will to the light of God's words and commandments. As maturing, germinating Christians, we cannot remain as new babes in Christ. We must grow by drawing sap from the vine of Jesus Christ, via the conduit of the abiding Holy Spirit. Neither can we remain as a tree with only rustling leaves; having a form of godliness and being tossed around by every wind of doctrine. All members of the Godhead are active participants in the transformation of the character of sinful man, imbuing them with power to bear spiritual fruits and reflect the image of Christ. The fruit of our character is to be ripe for the harvest for the soon return of Christ the Savior!

— 14 —

3 Wrappings, 1 Gift

Righteousness

(Imputed. Imparted. Imprinted)

Righteousness is the moral equity of Christ's nature given freely to man. Character is the only asset that will be taken to heaven. Christian character must embody and reflect the righteousness of Christ. The three acts or stages of righteousness are imputed, imparted, and imprinted. One gift with three wrappings.

Imputed righteousness is the sinner being justified and placed in "right standing" with God through the merits of the righteousness of Jesus Christ. Imparted righteousness is the on-going daily bestowing of Christ's nature and righteousness through the conduit of the Holy Spirit, enabling the Christian to grow. Imprinted righteousness is the ultimate outcome of a Christian; immovable, unshakeable in their faith in Christ and one who reflects in totality the character of Christ—the sealing of faith.

"The righteousness by which we are justified is imputed. The righteousness by which we are sanctified is imparted. The first is our title to heaven; the second is our fitness for heaven."[1]

---

1. White, *Qualifications for the Worker*, para. 7.

Impute

> Jas 2:23—"And the scripture was fulfilled which saith, Abraham believed God, and it was imputed unto him for righteousness, and he was called the friend of God."

> Gal 3:6—"Even as Abraham believed God, and it was accounted to him for righteousness."

Impute means to credit something to a person or a cause. The word impute has its Latin origin from the word *imputare* which means to attribute or ascribe. The greatest transaction the world has ever been given was the deposit of Christ's righteousness into the morally bankrupt souls of mankind. The deficit account of this fallen race was allocated and credited with the righteousness of Christ. This "bank account" of righteousness brims over with love. It was opened by God the Father and registered into the name of the son Jesus Christ. It is a bank account that is open for all to withdraw from. It is a free gift for the taking. Only those who obediently accept and draw from this account will receive this precious imputed righteousness. There is no secret pin code or number, the access is by believing; you only need to believe and accept the offer by calling on the name of Jesus. Come and withdraw is Christ's beckoning. When a sinner accepts this offer the sinner is justified and righteousness is imputed; the sinner receives the title to heaven. This is the first step.

Impart

The word impart in Latin is *nutriunt*. Clearly this brings to mind the word nutrient. It is fitting that imparted righteousness is the process of sanctification. Sanctification is a lifetime process and not an instantaneous transformation. It is the daily on-going nourishment imparted to the Christian by the abiding Holy Spirit. This sustaining nourishment, i.e., the drawing in of Christ's righteousness, can only be achieved by abiding in Christ and in the Word of God (Scripture.)

> John 15:4–8—"Abide in me, and I in you. As the branch cannot bear fruit of itself, except it abide in the vine; no more can ye, except ye abide in me. I am the vine, ye are the branches, he that abideth in me, and I in him, the same bringeth forth much fruit, for without me ye can do nothing. If a man abides not in me, he is cast forth as a branch, and is withered, and men gather them,

and cast them into the fire, and they are burned. If ye abide in me, and my words abide in you, ye shall ask what ye will, and it shall be done unto you. Herein is my Father glorified, that ye bear much fruit, so shall ye be my disciples."

Christians must be grafted into this righteous tree. The grafting is imputed righteousness and the daily drawing of sap to sustain spiritual life is imparted righteousness. Over time this grafted branch will become a part of the tree or vine and will mirror the likeness of the vine so much so that it will become inseparable and indistinguishable. Without daily sustenance, the grafted branch will wither and die and be cast from the vine and is ultimately burned which represents eternal damnation and eternal separation from God. Without daily sustenance the Christian becomes spiritually malnourished. Daily at our disposal we are being offered a part of Christ's righteousness if we make a conscious and conscientious effort to abide in Christ. We will not be passively fed this nourishment, we must draw into the spiritual sap of this imparted righteousness. We abide in Christ when we keep his word; obey God's commandments, love God, and love others. Abiding in Christ also encompasses the infilling and leading of the Holy Spirit, daily reading of the Scripture and prayer. These are all emblems we saw in the chapter on the Sanctuary, which is the process of sanctification.

Abiding in Christ also means bearing fruit and exhibiting the fruit of the Spirit; love, joy, peace, longsuffering, gentleness, goodness, faith, meekness, and temperance (Gal 5:22-23.) What would be the point of being an apple tree without bearing apples?

Imprinted

Rev 22:11—"He that is unjust, let him be unjust still and he which is filthy, let him be filthy still, and he that is righteous, let him be righteous still, and he that is holy, let him be holy still."

Mark 4:29—"But when the fruit is brought forth, immediately he putteth in the sickle, because the harvest is come."

Imprinted means unable to be changed; to be fixed. When a branch bears fruit it is impossible for the fruit to revert into the process of being a seed or to change into another fruit. When a Christian receives imprinted righteousness, they will reflect the true character of Christ and they will have no desire to return to the old life of sin or alter their beliefs founded upon the word of God. They are fixed, sealed, immovable, and immutable, and will remain "righteous still." This imprinted righteousness is the glorification stage of salvation. Christ is coming back for a church and Christians that reflect his character. As we near the soon return of Christ, God will dispatch the sealing angel who will be sent forth to seal or imprint the righteous in their foreheads (Rev 7:3—9:4.)

> "Seal is a settling into truth—just as soon as the people of God are sealed in their foreheads—it is not any seal or mark that can be seen, but a settling into the truth, both intellectually and spiritually, so they cannot be moved—just as soon as God's people are sealed and prepared for the shaking, it will come. Indeed, it has begun already; the judgments of God are now upon the land, to give us warning, that we may know what is coming."[2]

The word imprint in Latin is *vestigium* which means footstep, footprint, track and trace. Before the final judgment is unleashed upon earth, the servants of God will be sealed. This supernatural seal will protect the righteous from the wrath of God that will be poured out upon the earth and upon those who accept the mark of the beast.

> Rev 7:2-3—"And I saw another angel ascending from the east, having the seal of the living God and he cried with a loud voice to the four angels, to whom it was given to hurt the earth and the sea 'saying, hurt not the earth, neither the sea, nor the trees, till we have sealed the servants of our God in their foreheads.'"

Nearing the imminent second coming of Jesus, God will dispatch angels to imprint or seal the righteousness of Christ in their foreheads. This is not a visible marking like what we see in various religions that mark the forehead to signify a deity. Although this will not be a physical seal there are spiritual parallels. God is described as the potter and Christians are the clay. God will imprint the righteous character of Christ upon the saints, the spiritual clay. This imprint will also assure and ensure their security during the outpouring of God's final judgment upon the unrighteous. The imprinted internal righteousness is the seal, showing who belongs to God and has obeyed him and has the character Christ.

> Rev 9:3-4—"And there came out of the smoke locusts upon the earth and unto them was given power, as the scorpions of

---

2. White, SDA Bible Commentary, 1161.

the earth have power. And it was commanded them that they should not hurt the grass of the earth, neither any green thing, neither any tree, but only those men which have not the seal of God in their foreheads."

The imprinted internal seal of God will be somehow externally distinguishable to the angels and even to the locusts; the saints of God will not be harmed during the outpouring of final judgment upon the earth. The saints of God have made up their minds to obey God's commands, follow in the footsteps of Christ, and accept the free gift of righteousness. This heavenly track and trace system will be their seal, shield, and protection. This one beautiful free gift of righteousness with three wrappings is available to all. The Bible symbolically describes these wrappings as fine, clean, white linen (Rev 19:8), a robe (Isa 61:10), as clothing (Job 29:14), a breastplate (Isa 59:17), and a crown (2 Tim 4:8.)

> Fun Fact: In ancient times documents would be tied up with string and a blob of clay placed over the string; a seal would then be impressed into the clay to identify the sender and assure the security of the document. Seals were often set in signet rings and were inscribed with the owner's name. Seals were used to authenticate and protect documents and vessels.[3]

Righteousness and Salvation

Isa 61:10-11—"I will greatly rejoice in the Lord, my soul shall be joyful in my God, for he hath clothed me with the garments of salvation, he hath covered me with the robe of righteousness, as a bridegroom decketh himself with ornaments, and as a bride adorneth herself with her jewels. For as the earth bringeth forth her bud, and as the garden causeth the things that are sown in it to spring forth, so the Lord God will cause righteousness and praise to spring forth before all the nations."

Matt 5:20—"For I say unto you, that except your righteousness shall exceed the righteousness of the scribes and Pharisees, ye shall in no case enter into the kingdom of heaven."

2 Pet 3:13—"Nevertheless we, according to his promise, look for new heavens and a new earth, wherein dwelleth righteousness."

---

3. Korpel, Jezebel's Seal, para. 1.

The kingdom of God is a kingdom where righteousness dwells. Only those who have accepted this free gift will be saved.

> Questions to ponder: What role does faith, works, grace, and the law play in the plan of salvation and into achieving righteousness in Christ? How can these be harmonized?

Faith, Works, Grace, and Law

The raging debate amongst vast religions for centuries has been the question of salvation and righteousness. Are we saved and made righteous by faith, by grace, by works, by the law or a combination of some or all of these principles? How can they all be harmonized in the plan of salvation and righteousness?

The Godhead knew that a time would come when varying religious interpretations would seek to elevate one of these principles to a higher echelon over another. However, they all play a vital role in the plan of salvation and in the righteousness of saints. We will look at various Bible verses in the quest to harmonize and arrive at a coherent synthesis.

Grace

> Acts 15:11—"But we believe that through the grace of the Lord Jesus Christ we shall be saved, even as they."

> Rom 3:24—"Being justified freely by his grace through the redemption that is in Christ Jesus."

> Rom 5:14-17—"Nevertheless death reigned from Adam to Moses, even over them that had not sinned after the similitude of Adam's transgression, who is the figure of him that was to come. But not as the offense, so also is the free gift. For if through the offense of one many be dead, much more the grace of God, and the gift by grace, which is by one man, Jesus Christ, hath abounded unto many. And not as it was by one that sinned, so is the gift; for the judgment was by one to condemnation, but the free gift is of many offenses unto justification. For if by one man's offense death reigned by one, much more they which receive abundance of grace and of the gift of righteousness shall reign in life by one, Jesus Christ."

Grace and Faith

Eph 2:8—"For by grace are ye saved through faith, and that not of yourselves, it is the gift of God."

Grace, Faith, Law, and Works

Rom 4:1-6, 11-16, 24-25—"What shall we say then that Abraham our father, as pertaining to the flesh, hath found? For if Abraham were justified by works, he hath whereof to glory, but not before God. For what saith the scripture? Abraham believed God, and it was counted unto him for righteousness. Now to him that worketh is the reward not reckoned of grace, but of debt. But to him that worketh not, but believeth on him that justifieth the ungodly, his faith is counted for righteousness. Even as David also describeth the blessedness of the man, unto whom God imputeth righteousness without works, and he received the sign of circumcision, a seal of the righteousness of the faith which he had yet being uncircumcised, that he might be the father of all them that believe, though they be not circumcised, that righteousness might be imputed unto them also. And the father of circumcision to them who are not of the circumcision only, but who also walk in the steps of that faith of our father Abraham, which he had being yet uncircumcised. For the promise, that he should be the heir of the world, was not to Abraham, or to his seed, through the law, but through the righteousness of faith. For if they which are of the law be heirs, faith is made void, and the promise made of none effect, because the law worketh wrath; for where no law is, there is no transgression. Therefore, it is of faith, that it might be by grace, to the end the promise might be sure to all the seed, not to that only which is of the law, but to that also which is of the faith of Abraham, who is the father of us all. But for us also, to whom it shall be imputed, if we believe on him that raised up Jesus our Lord from the dead, who was delivered for our offenses, and was raised again for our justification."

Grace and Law

Rom 6:13-15—"Neither yield ye your members as instruments of unrighteousness unto sin, but yield yourselves unto God, as those that are alive from the dead, and your members as instruments of righteousness unto God. For sin shall not have dominion over you, for ye are not under the law, but under grace. What then, shall we sin because we are not under the law, but under grace? God forbid." (*Note: Paul was referring to the works of circumcision.*)

Faith

Rom 5:1-2—"Therefore being justified by faith, we have peace with God through our Lord Jesus Christ. By whom also we have access by faith into this grace wherein we stand and rejoice in hope of the glory of God."

Faith and Law

Gal 3:23-26—"But before faith came, we were kept under the law, shut up unto the faith which should afterwards be revealed. Wherefore the law was our schoolmaster to bring us unto Christ, that we might be justified by faith. But after that faith is come, we are no longer under a schoolmaster. For ye are all the children of God by faith in Christ Jesus."

Rom 10:3-10—"For they being ignorant of God's righteousness, and going about to establish their own righteousness, have not submitted themselves unto the righteousness of God. For Christ is the end of the law for righteousness to everyone that believeth. For Moses describeth the righteousness which is of the law, that the man which doeth those things shall live by them. But the righteousness which is of faith speaketh on this wise, say not in thine heart, who shall ascend into heaven, that is, to bring Christ down from above? Or who shall descend into the deep, that is, to bring up Christ again from the dead? But what saith it? The word is nigh thee, even in thy mouth, and in thy heart, that is, the word of faith, which we preach. That if thou shalt confess with thy mouth the Lord Jesus, and shalt believe in thine heart that God hath raised him from the dead, thou shalt be saved. For with the heart man believeth unto righteousness, and with the mouth confession is made unto salvation."

Law

> Matt 5:17—"Think not that I am come to destroy the law, or the prophets, I am not come to destroy, but to fulfill."

Works, Law, and Faith

> Gal 2:16—"Knowing that a man is not justified by the works of the law, but by the faith of Jesus Christ, even we have believed in Jesus Christ, that we might be justified by the faith of Christ, and not by the works of the law; for by the works of the law shall no flesh be justified."

How can we harmonize faith, works, law, and grace without contradictions? By using the analogy of seed, fruit, and tree.

- Faith is like the seed. Planting the seed is exhibiting faith.
- Works is the act of watering, fertilizing the seed and the soil. Faith led you to works. Without works, i.e., watering and fertilizing, the seed would die. Faith without works is dead. If someone has works without faith this is likened to watering and fertilizing the soil where no seed is planted. They are laboring in vain. One cannot be saved by works alone. It is by and with faith. When the seed is planted in the hidden earth, you believe that it will grow; this is faith. You do not see what is taking place in the unseen earth and how the seed is being transformed but you believe by faith. So it is with Christians; we accept Jesus by faith, and we are transformed by the unseen workings of the Holy Spirit and by God's words and obedience to his will. A life of faith leads to good works.
- Law is like the structure of the tree and branches. The Latin word for branch is virga which means rod. The tree is like the law, the rod of correction and commands. The tree is firm and solid. It does not change its structure. Likewise, the law and commandments of God are firm, solid, and unchanging. It is the moral structure upon which mankind is governed. Paul describes it as a schoolmaster. The branches bring out the buds and eventually the fruit. The branch (law) allows the fruit to grip and cling and be nourished and live.

- Grace is like the fruit. The fruit is the end result of the watered and fertilized seed and the end result of the tree. Likewise, Christ is the end result of the law as Paul described. Christ himself also declared that he came to fulfill the law. It is the planted seed (faith) that was watered and fertilized (works) that unveiled the tree and branches (law) that led to the fruit (grace.) It is by the grace of Christ we are saved through faith. It is the fruit that is eaten to sustain life. The fruit also has within itself new seeds. Hence, grace cannot be separated from faith. Neither can faith be separated from works nor from law. Neither can law be separated from grace. We are saved by grace through faith. The seed, the tree, and the fruit along with the watering and fertilizing, all cohesively bring about the symbiotic whole. All are needed and required. They cannot be separated or elevated above the other. The same is true for faith, works, law, and grace. All are required to bring about a cohesive whole. Faith, works, law, and grace all harmonize in perfect synthesis through Jesus Christ. Christ is the fulfillment of faith. The love for Christ and others propels us to do good works. Christ is the fulfillment of the law. Christ is the fulfillment of grace. Christ is the only hope for eternal life.

Key Summary Points From Verses:

- righteousness is a gift of grace through Christ—(Jesus placed grace inside the gift box of righteousness)
- righteousness comes by believing—(it requires faith in the gift-giver (Jesus) to accept the gift of righteousness)
- salvation is by the grace of Christ—(Jesus' grace accredits salvation)
- salvation is by grace through faith—(it requires faith to accept grace which leads to salvation)
- salvation begins with confession—(repentance is a first step towards salvation)
- justification by grace through Jesus—(Jesus' grace leads to justification; first stage of salvation)
- justification is by faith—(it requires faith to be justified)

- justification is not works of the law but faith of Christ—(Jesus' faith justifies; not by works)
- faith leads to works—(faith germinates and activates good works)
- faith without works is dead—(faith without the evidence of good works is dead faith)
- we are not under the law but under grace—(we are no longer under the ceremonial mosaic laws, e.g., circumcision of flesh but under grace, the circumcision of the heart)
- Jesus Christ is the end of the law—(the fulfillment of all the laws is through Jesus)

How can salvation, justification, and righteousness harmonize with faith, works, law, and grace?

The common thread that is woven into all these salvific requirements is Jesus Christ. Christ is the embodiment of them all. Christ is the embodiment of salvation, justification, and righteousness. Christ is also the embodiment of faith, works, law, and grace.

Dead Faith, Dead Works, Dead Law Keeping

Jas 2:26—"For as the body without the spirit is dead, so faith without works is dead also."

Heb 6:1—"Therefore leaving the principles of the doctrine of Christ, let us go on unto perfection, not laying again the foundation of repentance from dead works, and of faith toward God."

Gal 2:16—"Knowing that a man is not justified by the works of the law, but by the faith of Jesus Christ, even we have believed in Jesus Christ, that we might be justified by the faith of Christ, and not by the works of the law, for by the works of the law shall no flesh be justified."

Dead faith is faith without works. Faith requires the manifestation of good works. A barren tree that does not bear fruit is akin to a Christian with dead faith. Faith unveils works and works reveal your faith. Faith drives a Christian to do good works, however for many, works drive their faith. They perform good deeds, rituals, pieties, spiritual exercises, and traditions to earn salvation. This is false religion. This is dead works. Likewise, keeping the law without having a relationship with the lawgiver will not lead to salvation. Salvation is the free gift of grace through faith in Christ—the gift-giver. The motivation for doing good works, having faith, obeying the law should be our love for God, the son, Jesus Christ, and the abiding Holy Spirit. The motivation is not for a reward but for a relationship. Righteousness and salvation cannot be attained without abiding in Christ. The seed, tree, and fruit grows in stages, likewise Christian character evolves in stages of nurtured growth and maturity.

Summary—Seed Stage

The birth of new life is like a seed. It is planted and watered in order to release its potential and grow. Jesus likens faith to a mustard seed. (Matt 17:20) By faith, we come to Christ to receive the free gift of grace in order to receive his righteousness and be justified. Receiving this justification is to be endowed with imputed righteousness—Jesus accrediting the sinner his righteousness. This is the first stage of salvation.

Summary—Tree/Vine/Branch Stage

Christ is the vine and Christians are the branches. The branches must daily draw nutrients from the vine in order to survive. At this stage, faith, grace, works, and law are all activated and the Christian begins to sprout spiritual antennas. They are fueled by the guidance of the Holy Spirit, daily worshipping of God, prayer, reading the Word (Bible), obedience to God's laws, performing good works, and actively witnessing. This daily growth is imparted righteousness which is sanctification, the second stage of salvation.

Summary—Fruit Stage

This is the evidentiary stage of Christian maturity; developing buds of the fruits of the Spirit. Faith, grace, works, and law continue to be a daily part of the character and is more externally visible in their lifestyle and their interactions with others. Receiving the final "seal of approval" from God is imprinted righteousness. God will dispatch his angles to seal the servants of God as we near the second coming of Christ. This will be the crowning act given to a Christian who fully reflects the character of Christ. This is glorification and the final stage of salvation. Achieving this stage, is a life-long process and this is only achieved through Christ, who told the disciples that he is the vine and that they are the branches and unless they abide in him they cannot bear fruit.

— 15 —

3 Final Breaking News, 1 Channel

Three Angels' Messages

(True Worship. False Worship. Judgment)

Earth's final three breaking headline news are heralded by the three angels' messages found in Revelation chapter 14. The Latin for angel is *angelus*, the Greek is *angelos,* and Hebrew is *malach* which means messenger. The three angels' messages are end-time prophetic and apocalyptic messages.

First Angel's Message—True Worship

> Rev 14:6–7—"And I saw another angel fly in the midst of heaven, having the everlasting gospel to preach unto them that dwell on the earth, and to every nation, and kindred, and tongue, and people, saying with a loud voice, 'fear God, and give glory to him, for the hour of his judgment is come, and worship him that made heaven, and earth, and the sea, and the fountains of waters.'"

The headliner of the first angel's message broadcasts a call to true worship of the true God. It is interesting to note that there are three references to the true God—"glory to him," "his judgment," and "worship him."

The first angel's message answers the questions—Who is the true God? Why do we need to worship the true God? How do we worship the true God?

True worship of the true God has three components; fear of God, giving glory, and judgment.

To fear God means to give reverence or awe. To give glory means to praise, exalt, or honor. Judgment means the act of investigating, coming to a divine decision and carrying out (executing) that decision.

Before we can examine these three components of true worship, we must answer the three key questions. Who is the true God? Why do we need to worship the true God? How do we worship the true God?

Who is the True God?

> Rev 14:7—"... *and worship him that made heaven, and earth, and the sea, and the fountains of water.*"
>
> Isa 45:12,18—"I have made the earth, and created man upon it, I, even my hands, have stretched out the heavens, and all their host have I commanded. For thus saith the Lord that created the heavens; God himself that formed the earth and made it; he hath established it, he created it not in vain, he formed it to be inhabited. I am the Lord, and there is none else."
>
> Acts 14:15—"And saying, sirs, why do ye these things? We also are men of like passions with you and preach unto you that ye should turn from these vanities unto the living God, which made heaven, and earth, and the sea, and all things that are therein."
>
> Eph 3:9—"And to make all men see what is the fellowship of the mystery, which from the beginning of the world hath been hid in God, who created all things by Jesus Christ."

(Additional verses: Ps 96:5; Gen 2:4; Jer 10:10–16; Col 1:16; Job chapter 38.)

The true God is the one true living Godhead who made heaven, the earth, the sea, and the fountains of water. If there were polytheistic gods, then there would be multiple heavens, earths, seas, and waters. The different gods would have created their own distinct, unique impression of their own interpretation of creation. Additionally, all these different gods would have had to exist at the same time to collaborate on this vast unique cohesive creative project. The heavens, earth, sea, and fountain of waters could not have been created over vast epochs of time by different gods.

Why did God speak the world into existence? Perhaps in divine wisdom, the Godhead knew that if they made it with hands, the archenemy might attempt to copy or manipulate the creative process. Man has also tried to re-create life in laboratories but can never masterfully replicate the creative wisdom of the Godhead. Why is there only one heaven, one earth, one collective body of seas? That is because there is only one creative force who could have done this. There is only one Creator.

> Questions to ponder: Do the other gods of the vast religions profess to the creation of the heavens, earth, and sea? If not, why not? Wouldn't a tremendous feat like creating the heavens, sea, the earth, and fountains of water be something to proudly proclaim as a tenet of who they are?

The inhabitants of earth in these last days will be confronted with this profound question and will have to make a paramount decision as to who to worship. There are thousands of religions and theocratic beliefs that have permeated the psyche of human consciousness since the beginning of time. However, end-time, final climactic events will catapult these questions to the forefront. Who is the true God that should be worshipped? The real Armageddon will be a battle of mindset. Who will you choose? The true God or the false god (antichrist)? The battle of Armageddon will be fought out upon the plains of the human psyche.

The first angel's message is calling everyone to return to the true God; the one and only true and living God who made the heavens, the earth, the seas, and the fountains of water. There is no denying that we can see the heavens, we see the earth because we live in it; we see the seas and the fountains of water because we are surrounded by it. Seeing is believing. Even if you do not know the Creator's name you can begin by calling on the name of the one true God, "him who made the heavens, the earth, the sea, and fountains of water." Worship the Creator!

Why Do We Need to Worship the True God?

> Rev 4:11—"Thou art worthy, O Lord, to receive glory and honor and power, for thou hast created all things, and for thy pleasure they are and were created."

Ps 148:5—"Let them praise the name of the Lord, for he commanded, and they were created."

Neh 9:6—"Thou, even thou, art Lord alone, thou hast made heaven, the heaven of heavens, with all their host, the earth, and all things that are therein, the seas, and all that is therein, and thou preservest them all, and the host of heaven worshippeth thee."

Ps 104:24-25,30-34—"O Lord, how manifold are thy works, in wisdom hast thou made them all, the earth is full of thy riches. So is this great and wide sea, wherein are things creeping innumerable, both small and great beasts. Thou sendest forth thy spirit, they are created and thou renewest the face of the earth. The glory of the Lord shall endure forever, the Lord shall rejoice in his works. He looketh on the earth, and it trembleth, he toucheth the hills, and they smoke. I will sing unto the Lord as long as I live, I will sing praise to my God while I have my being. My meditation of him shall be sweet, I will be glad in the Lord."

The true God is to be worshipped because of the worthiness of who he is; the all-wise, powerful, supreme Creator who made the vastness of the heavens, the expanse of earth, the sea and its lifeforms, and the fountains of water to sustain and preserve all life.

How Do We Worship the True God?

Ps 95:6—"O come, let us worship and bow down, let us kneel before the Lord our maker."

2 Chr 29:30-31—"Moreover Hezekiah the king and the princes commanded the Levites to sing praise unto the Lord with the words of David, and of Asaph the seer. And they sang praises with gladness, and they bowed their heads and worshipped. Then Hezekiah answered and said, 'now ye have consecrated yourselves unto the Lord, come near and bring sacrifices and thank offerings into the house of the Lord.' And the congregation brought in sacrifices and thank offerings, and as many as were of a free heart burnt offerings."

God is worshipped as the Creator when we acknowledge him in prayer, songs, offerings, and in general daily praise, whether physically kneeling or bowing our hearts in contrite reverence. When we pray, we should offer thanksgiving, and praise him as the Creator of heaven, the earth, seas, and fountains of water. Strategically embedded into the Ten Commandments is the fourth commandment that details God's requirement for worship.

> Exod 20:8–11—"Remember the sabbath day, to keep it holy. Six days shalt thou labor and do all thy work. But the seventh day is the sabbath of the Lord thy God; in it thou shalt not do any work, thou, nor thy son, nor thy daughter, thy manservant, nor thy maidservant, nor thy cattle, nor thy stranger that is within thy gates. For in six days the Lord made heaven and earth, the sea, and all that in them is, and rested the seventh day, wherefore the Lord blessed the sabbath day, and hallowed it."

Grafted into the fourth commandment is the same wording of the first angel's message; the call to worship the true God, *who is the Creator of heavens, the earth, and sea.* True worship therefore requires the seventh-day Sabbath be kept holy.

> Question to ponder: Why would God tie true worship to creation and to worshipping on the seventh-day Sabbath?

Sabbath

> Exod 31:13—"Speak thou also unto the children of Israel, saying, verily my sabbaths ye shall keep, for it is a sign between me and you throughout your generations; that ye may know that I am the Lord that doth sanctify you."

> Isa 66:23—"And it shall come to pass, that from one new moon to another, and from one sabbath to another, shall all flesh come to worship before me, saith the Lord."

> Matt 12:8—"For the Son of man is Lord even of the sabbath day."

God in divine wisdom knew that mankind would be drawn away by false worship, i.e., to a man-made day of worship. Who changed God's day of worship from Sabbath to Sunday? God knew that mankind would forget the holy Sabbath day, so he engraved the word "remember" to draw attention back to the true Sabbath (day of rest.) God's fourth commandment draws us back to the seventh-day Sabbath which God sanctified and made holy as a commemoration of the six days of creation; a memorial of his creative power.

The Sabbath is also a time to commune with God. From the foundations of the earth, our foreparents Adam and Eve enjoyed the first Sabbath as they communed with the Creator in Eden. Spending time in nature is an act of honoring God's creative power. Adam's job was to tend and keep the garden, not to worship nature. The true day of worship, Sabbath, and worship of the Creator, versus the spurious man-made day of worship, Sunday, and worship of creation (pantheism), will become the divisive Armageddon moment. There are millions of sincere Christians who are not yet aware—for many it will be breaking news. It is not just about a day, but it is about being obedient to God's commandments.

This first angel's message is a call for God's people to return to the ordained true worship. Worship of the one true living God who created the heavens, the earth, the sea, and the fountains of water.

Let's now examine the three core components of true worship; fear God, give glory, and judgment.

Fear God

Fear God means reverential awe for God. It is worshipful respect for who God is—the supreme, holy, Creator, who is God over all creation and mankind. To fear God also means, living a life that brings honor to him.

> Eccl 12:13—"Let us hear the conclusion of the whole matter; fear God and keep his commandments for this is the whole duty of man."

> Job 1:1—"There was a man in the land of Uz, whose name was Job, and that man was perfect and upright, and one that feared God, and eschewed evil."

> Acts 10:2—"A devout man, and one that feared God with all his house, which gave much alms to the people and prayed to God always."

Give Glory

To give glory means to give God praise, exaltation, thanks, offerings, acknowledgments, and respect by our verbal or non-verbal declarations and living a life that pleases and honors him.

Isa 42:12—"Let them give glory unto the Lord and declare his praise in the islands."

Ps 50:23—"Whoso offereth praise glorifieth me, and to him that ordereth his conversation aright will I shew the salvation of God."

1 Cor 10:31—"Whether therefore ye eat, or drink, or whatsoever ye do, do all to the glory of God."

1 Chr 16:28-29—"Give unto the Lord, ye kindreds of the people, give unto the Lord glory and strength. Give unto the Lord the glory due unto his name, bring an offering, and come before him, worship the Lord in the beauty of holiness."

Judgment

The Greek root word for judgment is *krinos* which means to separate, to make distinction between, to bring to trial. God is merciful but is also a just God who must bring all things into judgment. True worship in the context of judgment means that true worshippers will be a distinct group, separated from worldliness, and who will be called to give account to a just God. True worshippers accept that God's judgment is fair and just and live their lives in accordance to his will.

1 Pet 4:17—"For the time is come that judgment must begin at the house of God, and if it first begin at us, what shall the end be of them that obey not the gospel of God?"

Eccl 3:17—"I said in mine heart, God shall judge the righteous and the wicked, for there is a time there for every purpose and for every work."

Matt 12:36—"But I say unto you, that every idle word that men shall speak, they shall give account thereof in the day of judgment."

2 Cor 5:10—"For we must all appear before the judgment seat of Christ, that everyone may receive the things done in his body, according to that he hath done, whether it be good or bad."

There are three phases of judgment; investigative, sentencing, and executive. The first angel's message heralds the beginning of the investigative phase of judgment. The investigative judgment began in 1844 in heaven when Christ moved from the Holy Place into the Most Holy Place to begin judgment of the dead. The investigative judgment against the living will take place in heaven after the investigative judgment of the dead is completed. However, no one knows when this will begin, nor how long it will last. Upon its completion, probation will end, and God will dispatch angels with the seven last plagues to execute judgment upon the earth. Earth and all mankind are currently under this solemn time of probation. It is a time to yield to the solemn message of the first angel while precious time avails. God is calling forth true worshippers who will worship him in spirit and in truth. (See Appendix: The Investigative Judgment.)

Summary of the First Angel's Message

- True worship of the true God has three components; fear of God, giving glory, and judgment.
- The true God is the Creator; the only living God who made the heavens, the earth, and the sea.
- The Godhead (Father, Jesus, and Holy Spirit) created all things and thus should be feared, reverenced, and worshipped.
- The true God is to be worshipped because of the worthiness of who he is—the Supreme Creator.
- True worshippers fear God and give him glory, i.e., praise, adoration, exaltation, and live a life pleasing to him.
- True worship requires keeping the seventh-day Sabbath which is the sign acknowledging God as the Creator.
- Judgment began in heaven in 1844 with the investigative phase—the judgment of the dead. Judgment of the living will follow. Before Jesus returns to earth, the Godhead will complete the judgment of the living.

Second Angel's Message—False Worship

Rev 14:8—"And there followed another angel, saying, 'Babylon is fallen, is fallen, that great city, because she made all nations drink of the wine of the wrath of her fornication.'"

The headliner of the second angel's message broadcasts the collapse of the false system of worship. Babylon is referred to as "she," which implies a church or religious system as opposed to a financial or corporate entity. This religious system, however, has infiltrated and negatively influenced all nations. The second angel's message answers the questions—Who is the false god (trinity)? Why are people worshipping the false god? How will people worship the false god? Before we can answer these questions, we must first unveil the components of false worship. False worship has three components; false religion, false church, and false doctrine. The clues are in the caption of this breaking news. "Babylon" is a pen name or pseudonym denoting false religion; "she" implies a church (the Bible symbolically identifies a woman as a church) and "wine" symbolically means doctrine.

False Religious System

The false religious system is described as Babylon, which means confusion. It is derived from the word Babel. After the flood, the post-diluvian world decided to build a tower that would reach towards the heavens in defiance of God's punishment by flood. They wanted to seek their own way of safety and salvation should God bring another punishment via a flood. The book of Genesis 11 verses 1–9 records that when God saw what they were doing, he came down and confused the language and they began speaking different languages (tongues), not being able to understand or communicate with each other. Thus, halting the building of the tower of Babel and they were scattered to different parts of the earth.

"*Bab*" is an Arabic word meaning gateway. Babel was man's way of building their own gateway to salvation, in defiance of God's edict. It is from this story of the tower of Babel that the word *babble* is derived. To babble means to utter sounds or words imperfectly, indistinctly, or without meaning. To utter in an incoherent, or meaningless fashion. It is from this concept that the word "baby" originated. The tower of Babel was built in the ancient land of Shinar (Babylonia.) Babylon was the capital city of Babylonia, a kingdom in ancient Mesopotamia, dating between the eighteenth century BC and sixth century BC. It was built along the left and right banks of the Euphrates and was deemed to be the largest city at that time. Today, the uninhabitable remnants of Babylon lie as mud brick buildings in Iraq, fifty miles south of Baghdad. Ancient

Babylon no longer exists as a thriving city so why is the second angel's message proclaiming its coming destruction? It is not literal Babylon but now spiritual Babylon that will collapse. It is a false religious system that is seeking a false way to salvation. There are eleven references to "Babylon" in the New Testament (KJV.) This within itself is quite interesting. Twelve is symbolic of Jesus' complete church, therefore, eleven implies a religious system not fully reflective of God's ideal. Eleven also signifies twelve disciples minus one; Judas who betrayed Jesus. This false religion is a betrayer of Christ and the commandments.

> Rev 17:5—"And upon her forehead was a name written, Mystery, Babylon The Great, The Mother Of Harlots And Abominations Of The Earth."

> Isa 21:9—"And, behold, here cometh a chariot of men, with a couple of horsemen. And he answered and said, 'Babylon is fallen, is fallen, and all the graven images of her gods he hath broken unto the ground.'"

> Jer 50:2,29—"Declare ye among the nations, and publish, and set up a standard; publish, and conceal not, say, Babylon is taken, Bel is confounded, Merodach is broken in pieces, her idols are confounded, her images are broken in pieces. Call together the archers against Babylon, all ye that bend the bow, camp against it roundabout, let none thereof escape, recompense her according to her work, according to all that she hath done, do unto her, for she hath been proud against the Lord, against the Holy One of Israel."

> Rev 18 :1–7—"And after these things I saw another angel come down from heaven, having great power, and the earth was lightened with his glory. And he cried mightily with a strong voice, saying, 'Babylon the great is fallen, is fallen, and is become the habitation of devils, and the hold of every foul spirit, and a cage of every unclean and hateful bird. For all nations have drunk of the wine of the wrath of her fornication, and the kings of the earth have committed fornication with her, and the merchants of the earth are waxed rich through the abundance of her delicacies.' And I heard another voice from heaven, saying, 'come out of her, my people, that ye be not partakers of her sins, and that ye receive not of her plagues. For her sins have reached unto heaven, and God hath remembered her iniquities. Reward her even as she rewarded you, and double unto her double according to her works, in the cup which she hath filled fill to her double.

How much she hath glorified herself, and lived deliciously, so much torment and sorrow give her, for she saith in her heart, I sit a queen, and am no widow, and shall see no sorrow.'"

Although literal ancient Babylon no longer exists, the ancient religious beliefs and practices have woven their way into the fabric of a vast number of modern-day religions.

Ba.by.lon—What's in a Name?

Ba—The mystery religion called "Ba" was an ancient Egyptian religion with the ka and the akh, a principle aspect of the soul; the "ba" appears in bird form, thus expressing the mobility of the soul after death. Originally written with the sign of the jabiru bird and thought to be an attribute of only the god-king, the "*ba*" was later represented by a man-headed hawk often depicted hovering over mummies of kings and commoners alike."[1] The jabiru bird is a black necked stork found mostly near marshes. "The *ba* (often translated as "the soul") conveyed notions of "the noble" and "the sublime." It could enter the body or become incorporeal at will. It was represented as a human-headed falcon, presumably to emphasize its mobility. The *ba* remained sentimentally attached to the dead body, for whose well-being it was somehow responsible. It is often depicted flying about the portal of the tomb or perched on a nearby tree. Although its anatomical substratum was ill-defined, it could not survive without the preserved body."[2]

Bab—Arabic origins meaning gate, gateway, "gate of God"

Baba—Persian origins meaning father, grandfather, wise man

By—near, in, about

Lon—has its origin from the Welsh word *llyn* meaning groves. Also, Welsh origin from *llon* and Irish and Gaelic roots *lon dubh* meaning blackbird. Also means fierce, strong, ready for battle, noble

The root of Babylonian religion and this false religious system is Egyptian. These false religious "beasts" were given their power and authority by the Dragon or Satan (Rev 13:2.)

---

1. Britannica.com, s.v., "Ba."
2. Britannica.com, s.v., "Ba."

> Rev 18:2—"And he cried mightily with a strong voice, saying, 'Babylon the great is fallen, is fallen, and is become the habitation of devils, and the hold of every foul spirit, and a cage of every unclean and hateful bird.'"
>
> Jer 5:26-27—"For among my people are found wicked men, they lay wait, as he that setteth snares, they set a trap, they catch men. As a cage is full of birds, so are their houses full of deceit, therefore they are become great, and waxen rich."
>
> Deut 7:5—"But thus shall ye deal with them, ye shall destroy their altars, and break down their images, and cut down their groves, and burn their graven images with fire."

Both the old and new Testament, through the inspiration of the Holy Spirit, points to Babylon as a cage of hateful birds and a hold of every foul spirit. Every foul demonic spirit exists in Babylon. It is a habitation of devils and full of deceits and deceptions. God's profound love to save humanity and urgency to call his people out of Babylon is proclaimed loudly in the second angels' message. Modern-day Babylon continues to espouse false doctrines such as immortality of the soul, which stems from this ancient pagan Egyptian religion of "Ba." Many are unaware of the dark and demonic spiritual origins of these false religious beliefs.

> Question to ponder: Today we have religions such as kabbalah (kab.ba.lah.) There are also worship rituals performed in groves to worship birds such as owls in Bohemian groves. Are there connections to ancient Egyptian and Babylonian worship?

Modern-Day False Religions

Many have often asked, why are there so many religions if there is only one true God and one true religion? The answer is simple—Babylon. Ancient beliefs and practices have seeped and woven their way into the religious tapestry of today's religious landscape. In many instances shamelessly and unapologetically mowing down the commandments of God; planting tares amongst the wheat and seeding false religious rituals and traditions. God's only way to call his people out of such tangled webs of religious falsehood is to hold the bullhorn of the three angels and proclaim loudly that the only way out is to seek the true God, who created the heavens, the earth, the sea, and the fountains of water. It is a simple, pure, truthful, and salvific broadcast. The shining light out of the darkness of religious tares.

Let's examine the historical origins of this tangled web of inherited religious beliefs, practices, and rituals.

Mesopotamian Religion (4000 BC–3000 BC)

Sumeria, the southern city of ancient Mesopotamia was the cradle of religious birth. It was a polytheistic civilization—the worship of thousands of gods that were deemed to be human, yet immortal. "Ea" was the god of creation and the priests were the rulers who were mediators and represented the gods. "Ea" also ruled over the practices of sorcery, witchcraft, magic spells, and chants. Gods were believed to inhabit and reside in temples. Most temples were built with three rooms and the farthest room housed the "god-statue." Some of the main gods were Nergal and Ereshkigal who ruled the underworld where the soul went after death. Utu judged the soul and was also god of the sun. The spirit of the dead was paid homage with daily offerings of food and drinks. Nanna was the full moon god, and Su-en (Sin) was the crescent moon god, and the crescent was often represented by horns of a bull. Nanna blessed cowherds and each year worshippers enacted worship rituals by bringing their first dairy produce of the year. "Su-en" or "Sin" god was depicted as an old man with a flowing beard wearing a headdress of four horns surmounted by a crescent moon.

Mesopotamian Religion—What It Passed On

Some of the pagan beliefs and practices that has assimilated into modern religions and cultures include; religious diversities, polytheism, idolatry, immortality of the soul, purgatory, the afterlife, priests acting as spiritual mediators, temples and shrines housing statues and relics, religions with symbols of moon or horn emblems, religions that worship sacred animals, religions that offer food and drinks to statues, religious chants, witchcraft, Santa Claus (old man with flowing beard.)

Egyptian Religion (3100 BC)—What They Believed

Ancient Egyptian civilization believed that creation was birthed from chaos. Nun (Nu) was the oldest known god and represented the turbulent waters that created the universe. His son, "Re" was the sun god. "Re" is also identified as "Atum" and was known to have an evil "all-seeing eye" that could destroy those that opposed him. The eye of "Re" was associated with the disk of the sun. "Re-Atum" assimilated into the god Horus, who along with Osiris, Isis, Set, and Nephtys became the five most prominent gods. These pagan gods along with many others were deified and worshipped. Egyptians believed that gods lived in trees and associated plants and flowers with gods. The afterlife was the belief that the soul lived on after death if that soul lived a good life, and pyramids were used as vessels to transport the soul to the afterlife. The "A'Aru" was the paradise of the afterlife, which interpreted to mean, "field of reeds." Osiris lived and ruled in this afterlife paradise. The theology of "negative confession after death" involved the confession of sins to Osiris where sins were weighted. Other beliefs and practices were religious festivals to honor gods, music and dancing to communicate with gods, stars influenced personality, spiritualism, magic, and herbology.

Egyptian Religion—What It Passed On

Some of the pagan beliefs and practices that has assimilated into modern religions and cultures include; polytheism, idolatry, pantheism (nature worship), immortality of the soul, salvation by works, confession of sins to a priest, spiritualism, Hegelian dialect (order out of chaos), religious leaders using initials of Egyptian gods on their garbs (pope wearing IHS symbol), festivals for gods, loud music, dancing with timbrels in worship, magic, sorcery (pharmacology), astrology, all-seeing eye symbols placed on images and accessories or as hand placed over eye to signal allegiance to paganism and occult beliefs.

Babylonian Religion (606 BC–536 BC)

Babylon was the recipient of various inherited religious myths of Mesopotamia and Egypt. Pagan gods were rebranded and given Babylonian names. The chief or patron god was Marduk, also known as Bel or Lord.

He was thought to be the son of the Mesopotamian god "Ea." Marduk means "calf of the sun," or "solar calf." He was also the deity of agriculture and was worshipped and immortalized in statues. Gods were believed to live inside of statues and concurrently in the spirit realm of what they represented, e.g. the sky, water, trees, sun etc. A dragon with a forked tongue was his symbolic animal who he conquered. His symbol was a triangular spade. His name was derived from *amarutu*, which means the "immortal son of Utu," or "bull calf of the sun god." Utu as was noted earlier was the Mesopotamian god who judged souls in the afterlife and was also the sun god. His temple was the model and blueprint for the tower of Babel. The rebranding of Marduk extended to the Greek and Roman religious cultures where he was known as Zeus and Jupiter respectively. The act of divination, the pagan practice of trying to foresee the future was prevalent in Babylon. It is recorded in Ezek 21:21 that the king of Babylon practiced divination by studying the entrails of the liver of a sacrifice, seeking to determine the future.

Babylon Religion—What They Passed On

Some of the pagan beliefs and practices that has assimilated into modern religions and cultures include; idolatry, worship of deities and statues, temples of worship where patrons bow before statues or bring offerings to gods, serpents and snake handling in religious services, dragons symbolically used as emblems of worship or as icons, "bull" is part of religious edict (papal bull), pantheism, nature worship, care for the planet movements, Gaia worship, sun worship and sunrise services.

Roman Religion (27 BC–AD 476)

Roman civilization was the melting pot of polytheism. There was a convergence of Egyptian, Babylonian, Persian, and Greek gods, that fused with Roman paganism. Animism, the belief that everything has a spirit, including lifeless objects was inherited from Egypt. These animistic credence gave birth to the belief that spirits possessed souls and dead ancestors watched over loved ones. Among the vast array of gods, were three that were worshipped on Capitoline hill (temple.) Temples were always built on the highest hills. Mars, Romulus, and Jupiter were known as the Capitoline Triad. This trio was later rebranded as Jupiter,

Juno, and Minerva. Rebranding and the storytelling of the roles of gods, was anchored in mythology. Chief priests were the pontifex maximus ("greatest bridge-builder") and were the mediator between God and man. Individualism was disregarded and adherence to strict rituals was enforced. Augury was the practice wherein priests studied flights of birds or animal entrails to interpret omens, or the will of the gods. This practice was inherited from Babylon and was also termed divination. Diviners or haruspices were always consulted and it was considered dangerous to ignore the omens. Emperors were deified. It was during the Roman era that millions of Christians were persecuted and killed because they defied and refused to worship Roman gods. One of the most significant markers in the history and timeline of the Roman religion occurred in AD 321 when Emperor Constantine changed the day of worship from Sabbath (Saturday) to Sunday in the Council of Laodicea.

Roman Religion—What They Passed On

The impact of Roman theology has potently influenced various religions. Some of the pagan beliefs and practices that have assimilated into modern religions and cultures include; Sunday worship, immortality of the soul, worship of statues and idols in ornate temples, priests as mediators to God, believers not encouraged to develop personal contact with God, church dogmas supersede God's commandments, false trinity, spiritism, mythology, witchcraft using animals and birds to cast omens or predict the future, palm reading, fortune telling, and séance.

> Question to ponder: What are some specific inherited rituals, traditions, and beliefs that modern-day religions have adopted from these false ancient religions?

Rebranding of Paganism

Ancient idolatrous paganistic beliefs and practices have been repackaged and rebranded, giving birth to false religions. This spiritually intoxicating wine of Babylon has inebriated the senses and caused many to unknowingly participate or become cynics of religions. This is not what the true Creator God intended. The three angels messages are the final urgent calls for mankind to flee all false religions and return to the one true and living God. One of the most displeasing pagan practices which God deems abominable is sun worship. How has this been repackaged and rebranded throughout civilizations?

"Ea" (Mesopotamian god of creation) was rebranded as Gaia or Gaea (ancient Greek which means "the earth is a goddess.") "Ea" is incorporated in the word Gaea and in contemporary rebranding, to Gaia. Phonetically, "ea" and Gaia have the same sound. Gaia is now rebranded as Earth Day or Creation Day. "Ea" is also the first two letters of the word earth. Gaia's husband and son was Uranus according to Greek mythology and was god of the sky. Uranus spelt backwards is *"sun-aru."* Ancient religions were steeped in sun worship, pantheism (nature worship) and immortality of the soul. "Aru" was the Egyptian afterlife and translated to mean "field of reeds." It was the heavenly paradise where Osiris lived and ruled. Uranus' son was Cronus, who was rebranded as Saturn to Greek civilization. His name spelt backwards is *"sun-orc."* "Orc" was a mythical horrible sea beast monster and also alluded to a demon. Orcus is the Latin derived version and was the god of the underworld. It is interesting to note that Rev 13:1 describes the beast that rises from under the sea and whose power is derived from the dragon or Satan. It is this terrible non-descript beast that Daniel saw in vision. This first beast will form an alliance with the second beast and deceive and persecute the world in these last days. Those who do not accept the mark of the beast will be threatened with death. As will be discussed in the third angel's message, sun-worship has been rebranded as Sunday worship.

God has declared through the second angel's message, that all these false religious beliefs, practices, rituals, and traditions are Babylonian (confusion)—spiritually intoxicating "wine." Many religions have inherited man-made spiritual exercises, incognizant of their origins. God lovingly wants all to come out of Babylon before it is too late.

> Rev 18:4–5—"And I heard another voice from heaven, saying, come out of her, my people, that ye be not partakers of her sins, and that ye receive not of her plagues. For her sins have reached unto heaven, and God hath remembered her iniquities."

Now that we have identified the origins of the false religious systems, we will explore the topic of false gods and venture to answer three key questions that we posed at the beginning of the chapter. Who is the false god (false trinity)? Why are people worshipping the false god? How will people worship the false god?

Who is This False God?

The false god is the absolute opposite of the true God. It is an unholy alliance; a false trinity consisting of three serpentine origins, identified as spirits of devils.

> Rev 16:13-14—"And I saw three unclean spirits like frogs come out of the mouth of the dragon, and out of the mouth of the beast, and out of the mouth of the false prophet. For they are the spirits of devils, working miracles, which go forth unto the kings of the earth and of the whole world, to gather them to the battle of that great day of God Almighty."

The false god (false trinity) consists of the dragon, the beast, and the false prophets.

The Dragon

> Rev 12:9—20:2—"And the great dragon was cast out, that old serpent, called the Devil, and Satan, which deceiveth the whole world, he was cast out into the earth, and his angels were cast out with him. And he laid hold on the dragon, that old serpent, which is the Devil, and Satan, and bound him a thousand years."

> Isa 27:1—"In that day the Lord with his sore and great and strong sword shall punish leviathan the piercing serpent, even leviathan that crooked serpent, and he shall slay the dragon that is in the sea."

The prophet Isaiah points out that the dragon is in the sea. The sea or waters refers to being amongst the people (Ps 68:22; Rev 17:15.) The dragon is clearly identified as the devil or Satan. The dragon is also the devil that disguised himself as a serpent in the garden of Eden deceiving Eve into eating of the forbidden fruit with cunning lies. He is the architect, originator, and source of sin and the deceptive force behind miracles working through the false religious systems of modern-day Babylon. He is the architect of the Babylonian system.

The Beast

We will now look at two prophecies given to Daniel and John, that will reveal the beast.

> Dan 7:2-8,17,23-24—"Daniel spake and said, 'I saw in my vision by night, and behold, the four winds of the heaven strove upon the great sea. And four great beasts came up from the sea, diverse one from another. The first was like a lion and had eagle's wings; I beheld till the wings thereof were plucked, and it was lifted up from the earth and made stand upon the feet as a man, and a man's heart was given to it. And behold another beast, a second, like to a bear, and it raised up itself on one side, and it had three ribs in the mouth of it between the teeth of it, and they said thus unto it, arise, devour much flesh. After this I beheld, and lo another, like a leopard, which had upon the back of it four wings of a fowl; the beast had also four heads, and dominion was given to it. After this I saw in the night visions, and behold a fourth beast, dreadful and terrible, and strong exceedingly, and it had great iron teeth, it devoured and brake in pieces, and stamped the residue with the feet of it, and it was diverse from all the beasts that were before it, and it had ten horns.
>
> I considered the horns, and behold, there came up among them another little horn, before whom there were three of the first horns plucked up by the roots, and behold, in this horn were eyes like the eyes of man, and a mouth speaking great things. These great beasts, which are four, are four kings, which shall arise out of the earth. Thus, he said, the fourth beast shall be the fourth kingdom upon earth, which shall be diverse from all kingdoms, and shall devour the whole earth, and shall tread it down, and break it in pieces. And the ten horns out of this kingdom are ten kings that shall arise, and another shall rise after them, and he shall be diverse from the first, and he shall subdue three kings.'"

> Rev 13:2,18—"And the beast which I saw was like unto a leopard, and his feet were as the feet of a bear, and his mouth as the mouth of a lion, and the dragon gave him his power, and his seat, and great authority. Here is wisdom; let him that hath understanding count the number of the beast, for it is the number of a man, and his number is six hundred threescore and six."

> Rev 15:2—"And I saw as it were a sea of glass mingled with fire, and them that had gotten the victory over the beast, and over

his image, and over his mark, and over the number of his name, stand on the sea of glass, having the harps of God."

The Beast—Background on Daniel and John's Visions

Daniel and Revelation are two profound prophetic books with detailed visions given by God of end-time events. Daniel was a Jewish captive taken from Jerusalem to Babylon in 605 BC during the siege by King Nebuchadnezzar. Daniel's vision in chapter 7 must be studied in conjunction with Daniel chapter 2. In chapter 2, a dream was given to King Nebuchadnezzar which showed an image of a statue.

> Dan 2:32–34—"This image's head was of fine gold, his breast and his arms of silver, his belly and his thighs of brass, his legs of iron, his feet part of iron and part of clay. Thou sawest till that a stone was cut out without hands, which smote the image upon his feet that were of iron and clay, and brake them to pieces."

The King did not remember his dream and it was Daniel who interpreted the dream after God revealed it to Daniel. The interpretation revealed the order of the succession of earthly kingdoms from Babylon to the second coming of Christ. The prophet John wrote the book of Revelation in the first century, around AD 95 or AD 96, while exiled on the deserted Grecian island of Patmos for his Christian beliefs. Both visions of John and Daniel, though given centuries apart, are in perfect harmony as they were given by the one true God. Daniel was shown the panoramic history of earthly kingdoms that would dominate from Babylon to Medo-Persia, to Greece and finally to pagan Rome. The lion represented Babylon, the bear was Medo-Persia, the leopard was Greece, and the "dreadful and terrible" beast was pagan Rome. It was not just political dominance but also religio-political undercurrents that shaped the beliefs of earth's populace over these centuries. It was this fourth beast and specifically the "little horn" that emerged out of it that would have world dominance, and stealthily work behind the scenes. However, this fourth kingdom with its little horn power will not reign forever. The final kingdom after the fourth earthly beast kingdom will be the kingdom of God, i.e., the stone cut out without hands that will smite the image and demolish all false religions and all earthly kingdoms.

This fourth beast kingdom is a complex mélange of centuries of religious metamorphosis cloaked in the garb of false religio-political traditions and doctrines. Daniel and John saw in vision this nondescript beast. The little horn power that Daniel saw paralleled the beast in Revelation that John saw. Three animals were used to describe this beast. Feet like a bear, mouth like a lion, and a leopard body. The leopard body is fitting as a leopard never changes its spot. Infused in its religious traditions and beliefs are the handed-down practices of ancient Babylon, Medio-Persia, Greece, and pagan Rome. However, the dominant religious beliefs are from Greece. It is the same antichrist power, but now garbed in the disguise of true religion.

Identifying This Fourth Beast with a Little Horn

✓ it came after the third beast, i.e., after leopard (ancient Greece)

✓ in three words: dreadful, terrible, strong

✓ it was dominant; it devoured, stamped on, and broke up others

✓ had ten horns (ten kingdoms)

✓ was known as the iron kingdom ("iron teeth")

✓ was diverse from the other beasts

✓ had an image, a mark, and a number representing his name

✓ had a little horn kingdom emerging from within

✓ had a diverse little horn that plucked up three other horns; this little horn had eyes like the eyes of man, and a mouth speaking great things

History confirms Daniel's God-inspired vision. After Babylon, the kingdom of Medio-Persia emerged, then Greece, then pagan Rome and finally papal Rome (little horn.)

In October 539 BC, Persian king Cyrus the Great invaded and conquered Babylon. History records that Cyrus had already conquered the Medes and other surrounding regions and then set his sights on Babylon. Babylon was considered impregnable as it was surrounded by the river that flowed from the Euphrates. Cyrus cleverly diverted the water upstream allowing the water level to drop, thus allowing his army to wade into the canals under the walls. The gates were opened to him without resistance. October 29 has been named, Cyrus The Great Day, and is still recognized in Iran, however, as an unofficial holiday. In God's encyclopedia, the Bible, God had long foretold Isaiah the prophet, that Cyrus would have many conquests, including Babylon, and specifically how it would be conquered. Isaiah had visions during periods of 740 BC to 646 BC, before Cyrus was born. Cyrus was born between 590 BC and 580 BC.

> Isa 45:1-3—"Thus saith the Lord to his anointed, to Cyrus, whose right hand I have holden to subdue nations before him, and I will loose the loins of kings, to open before him the two leaved gates, and the gates shall not be shut. I will go before thee and make the crooked places straight; I will break in pieces the gates of brass and cut in sunder the bars of iron. And I will give thee the treasures of darkness, and hidden riches of secret places, that thou mayest know that I, the Lord, which call thee by thy name, am the God of Israel."

The kingdom of Medo-Persia was later conquered by Greece under Alexander the Great. Alexander, an avid admirer of Cyrus, conquered most of the empire by 330 BC. In 323 BC Alexander died and his vast empire was divided between four of his generals. God had revealed to Daniel in vision that the third kingdom depicted as the leopard (Greece), would have four wings on its back and four heads (Dan 7:6.) The four heads and wings represented the four generals amongst whom Alexander's empire was divided. History records that these four generals were Cassander, Ptolemy, Antigonus, and Seleucus (known as the Diadochi or successors.) In 168 BC, in the battle at Pydna (a town in Greece), the Romans defeated the Macedonian army. Greece fell to Rome. The pagan Roman Empire was this fourth kingdom of Daniel's vision. This empire, in vision, was the dreadful, terrible, and strong beast. Rome adopted many of the Greek gods, myths, and traditions, and infused them into their own culture. The leopard body of the beast, implied that the religious beliefs of Greece played a great role in shaping the religious beliefs of Rome. The Book of Revelation is very detailed and covers several verses on this beast. There is no doubt that this beast has an important role to play in these last days of earth's history. God wants everyone to be aware of who the beast is and to come out of her false religious institutions.

The Roman Empire was home to many cultures and as a result it allowed the worship of vast numbers of deities. However, when Catholic Christianity became the state religion, anyone who did not conform to its teachings was persecuted. Church and state clasped hands to enforce persecution against those who chose to worship according to the dictates of God's true commandments and to the dictates of their conscience. In the third century, Cassius Dio, a Roman and Greek historian outlined the Roman imperial policy towards religious tolerance by stating that, "you should not only worship the divine everywhere and in every way in accordance with our ancestral traditions, but also force all others to honor it. Those who attempt to distort our religion with strange rites you should hate and punish, not only for the sake of the gods but also because such people, by bringing in new divinities, persuade many folks to adopt foreign practices, which lead to conspiracies, revolts, and factions, which are entirely unsuitable for monarch."[3]

> Titus Livius (Livy), noted to be one of the great Roman historians, identifies who was the "divine," to whom Rome worshipped. "Now, if any nation ought to be allowed to claim a sacred origin and point back to a divine paternity, that nation is Rome. For such is her renown in war that when she chooses to represent Mars as her own and her founder's father, the nations of the world accept the statement with the same equanimity with which they accept her dominion."[4]

The divine god, the foundation of pagan and papal Rome was Mars. Prophecy foretells that Rome will again speak, enforcing worship by joining hands with churches and states. Those who will choose to follow the true God and the dictates of their conscience will again be labeled as inciting conspiracies. By AD 325 approximately two million Christians were killed. They were primarily persecuted and martyred because they refused to offer sacrifice to the Roman gods. Those who did not worship these false gods were blamed for calamities that befell the Roman Empire. Emperor Nero blamed them for starting the fire that burned Rome, dubbed "The Great Fire of Rome." It was Nero who started the fires using this as a gateway to fan flames of persecution and slaughter of Christians. The Inquisition during the twelfth century saw the brutal slaughter of millions more Christians, Jews, and Muslims.

> Rev 17:3,6—"So he carried me away in the spirit into the wilderness and I saw a woman sit upon a scarlet-colored beast, full of names of blasphemy, having seven heads and ten horns. And I saw the woman drunken with the blood of the saints, and with

---

3. Wikipedia.org, s.v., "Roman Empire."
4. Livy, *History of Rome,* preface.

the blood of the martyrs of Jesus, and when I saw her, I wondered with great admiration."

The Roman Empire was as prophecy described—dreadful, terrible, and strong. History frames prophecy. Biblical prophetic truth is framed by historical facts thus leaving no room for doubt, as to the validity of God's words. Will history repeat itself in these end-times? Jesus warned the disciples that one of the signs of the end-times will be persecution. Christians will be delivered up to be afflicted and some will be killed (Matt 24:9.) There will be a time of trouble unwitnessed by any other previous generation (Dan 12:1.) In the 1800s, early Adventist church pioneers were given prophetic visions and revelations of end-time persecutions. Christians will again be blamed for calamities.

> "As men depart further and further from God, Satan is permitted to have power over the children of disobedience. He hurls destruction among men. There is calamity by land and sea. Property and life are destroyed by fire and flood. Satan resolves to charge this upon those who refuse to bow to the idol which he has set up. His agents point to Seventh-day Adventists as the cause of the trouble. These people stand out in defiance of law, they say. They desecrate Sunday. Were they compelled to obey the law for Sunday observance, there would be a cessation of these terrible judgments. Calamities will come—calamities most awful, most unexpected, and these destructions will follow one after another. If there will be a heeding of the warnings that God has given, and if churches will repent, returning to their allegiance, then other cities may be spared for a time. But if men who have been deceived continue in the same way in which they have been walking, disregarding the law of God and presenting falsehoods before the people. God allows them to suffer calamity, that their senses may be awakened"[5]

God's remnant commandment keeping church who observe Sabbath (Saturday) as God's holy day will be primarily blamed for the calamities because they refuse to bow to enforced dictates to observe Sunday. This will usher in a repeat of persecution and a time of trouble and tribulation (Rev 12:17.)

The Roman Empire was eventually broken up into ten barbaric kingdoms, represented by the ten horns of the beast. The kingdoms were: Alemanni (Germany), Suevi (Portugal), Visigoths (Spain), Franks (France),

---

5. White, *Maranatha*, 176.

Burgundians (Switzerland), Anglo-Saxons (England), Lombards (Italy), Heruli (rooted up by the little horn), Ostrogoths (rooted up by the little horn), and Vandals (rooted up by the little horn.)

It is clear that the fourth kingdom, the terrible beast of Daniel's vision, was pagan Rome. Therefore, the little horn that comes out of pagan Rome is papal Rome. The only remaining unfulfilled portion of the vision is the stone cut out without hands that will smite this image. This of course is the second coming of Christ and the kingdom of God.

False Prophets

By way of recapping—there are three components of the false god; the dragon, the beast, and the false prophets. The dragon is Satan, and the beast is pagan Rome which became papal Roman Empire. Now we will look at the false prophets.

> Jer 14:14—"Then the Lord said unto me, the prophets prophesy lies in my name. I sent them not, neither have I commanded them, neither spake unto them; they prophesy unto you a false vision and divination, and a thing of nought, and the deceit of their heart."

> Matt 7:15—24:11,24—"Beware of false prophets, which come to you in sheep's clothing, but inwardly they are ravening wolves. Ye shall know them by their fruits. Do men gather grapes of thorns, or figs of thistles? And many false prophets shall rise and shall deceive many. For there shall arise false Christs, and false prophets, and shall shew great signs and wonders, insomuch that, if it were possible, they shall deceive the very elect."

> 1 John 4:1—"Beloved, believe not every spirit, but try the spirits whether they are of God, because many false prophets are gone out into the world."

CHARACTERISTICS OF FALSE PROPHETS

- they prophesy lies in the name of Christ
- they teach and practice false doctrines or man-made traditions
- they are not in harmony with the Word of God (Bible)

- they are deceitful
- they claim to have visions from God, but those visions do not come true
- they perform false signs, wonders, miracles, and healings
- They solicit for profit (sell merchandise, exploit for money)

Jesus reminds us to test every spirit to see if they are from God. Test the spirits by confirming in Scripture. If it is not in harmony with the Bible, then it is a false prophet. False prophets are described as wolves dressed in a religious garb of sheep clothing. They deceive by "pulling the wool over the eyes" of the masses using false doctrines and traditions. They hide the truth by mixing truth with error and outwardly profess Christ but inwardly and secretly practice doctrines of the dragon. False prophets are not only individuals, churches, religious institutions, teachers, pastors but is described in Revelation 13 as a country or kingdom.

> Rev 13:11-14—"And I beheld another beast coming up out of the earth, and he had two horns like a lamb, and he spake as a dragon. And he exerciseth all the power of the first beast before him, and causeth the earth and them which dwell therein to worship the first beast, whose deadly wound was healed. And he doeth great wonders, so that he maketh fire come down from heaven on the earth in the sight of men, and deceiveth them that dwell on the earth by the means of those miracles which he had power to do in the sight of the beast, saying to them that dwell on the earth, that they should make an image to the beast, which had the wound by a sword, and did live."

This second beast is not only a kingdom (country), but is also a false prophet, who will deceive the masses using false miracles and force worship of the first beast. Outwardly appearing as a docile lamb but inwardly a ravenous dragon.

The False Lamblike Horned Prophet?

> Rev 13:15-17—"And he had power to give life unto the image of the beast, that the image of the beast should both speak, and cause that as many as would not worship the image of the beast should be killed. And he causeth all, both small and great, rich and poor, free and bond, to receive a mark in their right hand,

or in their foreheads. And that no man might buy or sell, save he that had the mark, or the name of the beast, or the number of his name."

This lamblike country appears externally to be Christian, as lamb symbolically represents Christ. However, internally, it speaks on behalf of the dragon (Satan) and is the ambassador of sorts for the first beast. A country "speaks" through legislation or laws. Therefore, laws will be mandated which will be in direct opposition to God's commandments. Which country matches these qualifiers:

- enforces the false doctrines of the first beast (papacy)
- forces the earth to worship the first beast and its image (teachings/doctrines)
- makes fire come down from heaven to deceive (spectacular light shows/wonders)
- deceives with false miracles
- restricts buying and selling to those who refuse to accept the mark of the beast

This false lamblike beast/prophet is the United States of America, as was shown in prophecy.

> "At this point another symbol is introduced. Says the prophet, 'I saw another beast coming up out of the earth, and he had two horns like a lamb' (Rev 13:11.) Both the appearance of this beast and the manner of its rise indicate that the nation which it represents is unlike those presented under the preceding symbols. The great kingdoms that have ruled the world were presented to the prophet Daniel as beasts of prey, rising when the four winds of heaven were stirring up the great sea (Dan 7:2.) In Revelation 17 an angel explained that waters represent peoples, multitudes, nations, and tongues (Rev 17:15.) Winds are a symbol of strife. The four winds of heaven striving upon the great sea represent the terrible scenes of conquest and revolution by which kingdoms have attained to power. But the beast with lamblike horns was seen 'coming up out of the earth.' Instead of overthrowing other powers to establish itself, the nation thus represented must arise in territory previously unoccupied and grow up gradually and peacefully. It could not, then, arise among the crowded and struggling nationalities of the Old World—that turbulent sea of 'peoples, multitudes, nations, and tongues.' It must be sought in

the Western Continent. What nation of the New World was in 1798 rising into power, giving promise of strength and greatness, and attracting the attention of the world? The application of the symbol admits of no question. One nation, and only one, meets the specifications of this prophecy; it points unmistakably to the United States of America."[6]

America, the world's superpower, will play a pivotal role in enforcing false worship and will enforce laws mandating worship to the beast (papacy.)

False Church

There are three components to false worship—false religion, false church, and false doctrine. Scripture and prophecy define false religion as spiritual Babylon. Babylon is headed by a false trinity, composed of the dragon (Satan), the beast (pagan and papal Roman Empire), and false prophets. Scripture and prophecy define the false church as the little horn that arose out of the fourth beast. It is the woman who sits atop the beast, the pagan Roman Empire (Dan 7:8.) The little horn is the papal Roman Empire. Therefore, the false church is also the Roman papal system. God has given the second angel an urgent message to his people to flee false worship before executive judgment is unleashed upon the earth.

> Rev 18:2–5—"And he cried mightily with a strong voice, saying, 'Babylon the great is fallen, is fallen, and is become the habitation of devils, and the hold of every foul spirit, and a cage of every unclean and hateful bird. For all nations have drunk of the wine of the wrath of her fornication, and the kings of the earth have committed fornication with her, and the merchants of the earth are waxed rich through the abundance of her delicacies.' And I heard another voice from heaven, saying, 'come out of her, my people, that ye be not partakers of her sins, and that ye receive not of her plagues. For her sins have reached unto heaven, and God hath remembered her iniquities.'"

The Little Horn

The prophetic book of Revelation revealed some important pointers that unmasked this little horn. The little horn is papal Rome. Papal Rome is

---

6. White, *The Great Controversy*, 439–40.

the image of the empirical pagan Rome Empire. Papal Rome came out of the heart of the pagan Roman Empire with a mindset pulsating with the tyrannical dogmas of this ancient persecuting power.

> Rev 17:1–5,9—"And there came one of the seven angels which had the seven vials, and talked with me, saying unto me, 'come hither, I will shew unto thee the judgment of the *great whore that sitteth upon many waters,* with whom the kings of the earth have committed fornication, and the inhabitants of the earth have been made drunk with the wine of her fornication.' So, he carried me away in the spirit into the wilderness and I saw *a woman sit upon a scarlet-colored beast, full of names of blasphemy,* having seven heads and ten horns. And the woman was *arrayed in purple and scarlet color, and decked with gold and precious stones and pearls,* having a *golden cup in her hand* full of abominations and filthiness of her fornication. And *upon her forehead was a name written, Mystery, Babylon The Great, The Mother Of Harlots And Abominations Of The Earth.* And here is the mind which hath wisdom. *The seven heads are seven mountains, on which the woman sitteth.*"

(Note: woman is a symbol of church—Jer 6:2)

Papal Rome, also called The Holy See, is headquartered in the independent Vatican City. It was established by the Lateran Treaty in 1929 between Italy and The Holy See to ensure its temporal, diplomatic, and spiritual independence. Vatican City is the smallest country in the world at 0.2 square miles. Vatican Hill is located across the Tiber river from the traditional seven hills of Rome.

Va.ti.can—Vati.can: What's in a Name?

- The word vatican literally means "divining serpent"—vatis means diviner and "can" means serpent
- Va in old Norse means woe, calamity, danger
- Vati in German is papa
- Vati in English is bard which means one skilled in reciting verses
- Vati (vates) has the Latin meaning of soothsayer, poet, prophet or seer, mouthpiece of deity

- Vati in Sanskrit is a kind of aquatic bird, or animal which moves on water. Vati in Hindu and Gujarati means nature
- Vati is a city in Rhodes, Greece dating back to the Mycenaean civilization (1700 BC to 1100 BC.) The city is surrounded by forest and olive groves. The name Vati means crossing point or path. There is also the belief that the name originated because it was surrounded by swamps. The festival of the virgin Mary is celebrated every September.

The word pope in Latin is *papam* and in Greek it is *papas*. This translates to papa in English. This means Father. Perhaps this is where "papal" originated from. Jesus admonished that no earthly religious figure should be called father. The only father is the heavenly Father in heaven.

> Matt 23:9—"And call no man your father upon the earth; for one is your Father, which is in heaven."

Attributes of the False Church (Little Horn/Papal Rome)

> Rev 13:2-8—"And the beast which I saw was like unto a leopard, and his feet were as the feet of a bear, and his mouth as the mouth of a lion, and the dragon gave him his power, and his seat, and great authority. And I saw one of his heads as it were wounded to death, and his deadly wound was healed, and all the world wondered after the beast. And they worshipped the dragon which gave power unto the beast, and they worshipped the beast, saying, 'who is like unto the beast, who is able to make war with him?' And there was given unto him a mouth speaking great things and blasphemies, and power was given unto him to continue forty and two months. And he opened his mouth in blasphemy against God, to blaspheme his name, and his tabernacle, and them that dwell in heaven. And it was given unto him to make war with the saints, and to overcome them and power was given him over all kindreds, and tongues, and nations. And all that dwell upon the earth shall worship him, whose names are not written in the book of life of the Lamb slain from the foundation of the world."

> Dan 7:21,23,25—"I beheld, and the same horn made war with the saints, and prevailed against them. Thus, he said, 'the fourth beast shall be the fourth kingdom upon earth, which shall be

diverse from all kingdoms, and shall devour the whole earth, and shall tread it down, and break it in pieces. And he shall speak great words against the most High and shall wear out the saints of the most High, and think to change times and laws, and they shall be given into his hand until a time and times and the dividing of time.'"

Dan 8:9–11—"And out of one of them came forth a little horn, which waxed exceeding great, toward the south, and toward the east, and toward the pleasant land. And it waxed great, even to the host of heaven, and it cast down some of the host and of the stars to the ground and stamped upon them. Yea, he magnified himself even to the prince of the host, and by him the daily sacrifice was taken away, and the place of the sanctuary was cast down."

Rev 13:18—"Here is wisdom. Let him that hath understanding count the number of the beast, for it is the number of a man, and his number is six hundred threescore and six."

Summary of Attributes:

- persecuted and warred against the saints for forty-two months
- received a deadly wound that was healed
- speaks blasphemies against God
- think to change times and laws
- world will worship him whose names are not in book of life
- arrayed in purple and scarlet, decked in gold with golden cup in hand
- has many blasphemous names (titles)
- has seven heads, i.e., a church sitting on seven mountains
- has a number of six hundred threescore and six (666)

Let's decipher these identifying markers of the little horn power and historical qualifiers.
Rome is a city of seven hills—(Palatine, Capitoline, Quirinal, Viminal, Esquiline, Caelian, and Aventine.)

Papal regalia—consist of a tiara, purple and scarlet robes with the pope holding a golden cup. These colors were worn by the High Priest of Israel in the sanctuary services in the wilderness. However, there were three colors worn by the High Priest; blue, purple, and scarlet. Blue to symbolize divinity. The papal tiara is a triple crown, which the Vatican states is the triple power of the pope, father of kings, governor of the world, and Vicar of Christ. Vicar of Christ means to stand in place of Christ. Another meaning of the triple crown is sovereignty over heaven, earth, and purgatory. The Bible calls these titles blasphemous.

Persecuting power—forty-two months is equivalent to one thousand two hundred and sixty days. In biblical prophetic time, there is a day-for-a-year principle (Ezek 4:6; Num 14:34.) One prophetic day equals one literal year. The papal Roman Empire initially reigned for forty-two prophetic months (1260 prophetic days, which equals 1,260 literal years)—from AD 538 to AD 1798. During this period the Roman Empire persecuted and killed millions of Christians and those they deemed to be heretics. God's church as described in Revelation 12:6, had to flee persecution for "one thousand two hundred and threescore days" or 1260 literal years. The Bible was taken away and there was a period of spiritual darkness, known as the Dark Ages. However, God still had witnesses (the word), professing the truth for "one thousand and threescore days, clothed in sackcloth" (Rev 11:3.) History records that in 1798 French General Berthier invaded the Vatican and took Pope Pius VI prisoner. This was the "deadly wound" given to the beast (Rev 13:3.) The Lateran Treaty signed on February 11, 1929, between the Vatican and Italian prime minister Benito Mussolini restored power to the Vatican and the wound began to heal.

The number 666—number of the beast (six hundred, threescore and six) is derived by adding up the numerical values of the papal title, "*Vicarius Filii Dei.*"

V = 5	F = 0	D = 500
I = 1	I = 1	E = 0
C = 100	L = 50	I = 1
A = 0	I = 1	
R = 0	I = 1	
I = 1		
U = 5		
S = 0		
Sum = 112	Sum = 53	Sum = 501

Total 112+53+501 = 666. The number matches the title. There is only one religious entity that perfectly meets all the prophetic Biblical markers and qualifiers, and that is the papal Roman Empire.

The birth of the Protestant Movement in the sixteenth century, led by Augustinian monk Martin Luther brought Romanism to the forefront when he challenged the unscriptural dogmas and traditions of the church. Many Protestants fled from Europe to America seeking refuge from religious persecutions.

"The Protestant reformers, including Martin Luther, John Calvin, Thomas Cranmer, John Thomas, John Knox, and Cotton Mather, felt the early church had been led into apostasy by the Papacy and identified it as the antichrist. Many broke away from the Catholic church. The Centuriators of Magdeburg, a group of Lutheran scholars in Magdeburg headed by Matthias Flacius, wrote the 12–volume Magdeburg Centuries to discredit the papacy and identify the pope as the antichrist."[7]

> "Romanism is now regarded by Protestants with far greater favor than in former years. In those countries where Catholicism is not in the ascendancy, and the papists are taking a conciliatory course in order to gain influence, there is an increasing indifference concerning the doctrines that separate the reformed churches from the papal hierarchy; the opinion is gaining ground that, after all, we do not differ so widely upon vital points as has been supposed, and that a little concession on our part will bring us into a better understanding with Rome. The time was when Protestants placed a high value upon the liberty of conscience which had been so dearly purchased. They taught their children to abhor popery and held that to seek harmony with Rome would be disloyalty to God. But how widely different are the sentiments now expressed! The papal church will never relinquish her claim to infallibility. All that she has done in her persecution of those who reject her dogmas she holds to be right, and would she not repeat the same acts, should the opportunity be presented? Let the restraints now imposed by secular governments be removed and Rome be reinstated in her former power, and there would speedily be a revival of her tyranny and persecution. It is true that there are real Christians in the Roman Catholic communion. Thousands in that church are serving God according to the best light they have. They are not allowed access to his word, and therefore they do not discern the truth. They have never seen the contrast between a living heart

---

7. Wikipedia.org, s.v., "Apostasy."

service and a round of mere forms and ceremonies. God looks with pitying tenderness upon these souls, educated as they are in a faith that is delusive and unsatisfying. He will cause rays of light to penetrate the dense darkness that surrounds them. He will reveal to them the truth as it is in Jesus, and many will yet take their position with his people."[8]

Over the centuries since the Protestant Reformation, this great theological divide appears to have narrowed. The gaps have become indistinguishable, as modern-day Protestants embrace the doctrines and worship styles of Romanism. What is the attraction back to Romanism? Studies and articles highlight reasons such as, the search for ancient wisdom and traditions, repeating beautiful liturgy, a more subdued style of worship, and the rebranded image of popery. By adopting and modeling Catholic papal practices, Protestant churches are unknowingly but slowly forming an image of the beast. According to Scripture and prophecy, the persecuting mindset of the beast and the little horn (pagan and papal Rome), will again arise once the restraints of governments are relaxed. Church and state will soon reunite. The second angel's message of Revelation 14 is an urgent call by God to flee Babylon. Scripture warns that the lamblike beast (America) will align with the first beast whose deadly wound was healed (papacy.) By default, both having allegiance to the dragon (Satan.) This alliance will be the union of church and state that will enforce terrible persecutions upon planet earth (Rev 13:11–15.)

Blasphemy

There are two biblical definitions for blasphemy; claiming or taking on the prerogatives of God and claiming to forgive sins (John 10:33; Luke 5:20–21.) The papal title of "Vicar of Christ," means to act for and in the place of Christ. The Council of Florence also describes the office of the Pope as the master of all Christians. The papacy also deems that the power to forgive sins was conferred to the apostles hence the pope has power to forgive sins. The basis for this dogma (Sacrament of Penance) is drawn from John 20:23 when Jesus imparted the Holy Spirit upon the disciples. *"Receive the Holy Spirit. Whose sins you shall forgive, they are forgiven; whose sins you shall retain, they are retained."* The verse quoted was made by Jesus shortly after the resurrection.

---

8. White, *The Great Controversy*, 564.

> John 20:17-24—"Jesus saith unto her, 'touch me not, for I am not yet ascended to my Father, but go to my brethren, and say unto them, I ascend unto my Father, and your Father, and to my God, and your God.' Mary Magdalene came and told the disciples that she had seen the Lord, and that he had spoken these things unto her. Then the same day at evening, being the first day of the week, when the doors were shut where the disciples were assembled for fear of the Jews, came Jesus and stood in the midst, and saith unto them, 'peace be unto you.' And when he had so said, he shewed unto them his hands and his side. Then were the disciples glad when they saw the Lord. Then said Jesus to them again, 'peace be unto you, as my Father hath sent me, even so send I you.' And when he had said this, he breathed on them, and saith unto them, *'receive ye the Holy Ghost; whose soever sins ye remit, they are remitted unto them, and whose soever sins ye retain, they are retained.'* But Thomas, one of the twelve, called Didymus, was not with them when Jesus came."

Jesus used several pronouns in his discourse; "me," "my," "your," "you," and "ye." Jesus used *"you"* when he referred to the disciples, e.g., "peace be to *you*" or "so send I *you.*" Jesus breathed on them and said, "receive *ye* the Holy Ghost." However, *"ye"* referred to the Holy Ghost. "Whosoever sins *ye* remit, they are remitted unto them, and whose soever sins *ye* retain, they are retained." Again, *"ye"* referred to the power of the Holy Spirit to remit or retain sins. In this context "ye" was not referring to "you," i.e., the disciples. It was a reference to the Holy Spirit. Alternative terms for "ye" are yeah, yes, aye, or ay. Ye is also an old way of writing "the." When we say "praise *ye* the Lord," we are referring *ye* towards the Lord. It does not mean you, the individual or towards us—it refers to the Lord. The serpent in the garden also twisted the word "ye" to tempt Eve into eating the forbidden fruit. The word "ye" has been misconstrued and misinterpreted to substantiate the doctrine of the forgiveness of sins. The power to forgive sins lies solely with the Godhead and not with mortal sinful man.

> Questions to ponder: Thomas was not present when Jesus imparted the Holy Spirit upon disciples. Does this mean Thomas never received the Holy Spirit and hence could not forgive sins? Wouldn't Jesus have waited until all the disciples were present? Are there any examples in the Bible of disciples forgiving sins?

It is clear that Jesus did not give the disciples power to forgive sins. There is no scriptural evidence of this. Religious theology on the forgiveness of sins cannot be based on one scripture that was misinterpreted. The book of Acts chapter 7 records that Stephen, being full of the Holy Spirit while being stoned, looked up to heaven and saw the glory of God and Jesus at the right hand. Stephen asked the Lord to forgive those stoning him. If Stephen had the power to forgive sins, why did he not forgive the stoners himself? Christ, on the cross, prayed to the Father to forgive those who crucified him. When the disciples asked Jesus to teach them to pray, Jesus was clear that sins are forgiven by the Father in heaven (Luke 11:2–4.)

> 1 Tim 2:5—"For there is one God, and one mediator between God and men, the man Christ Jesus."

> Eph 1:7—"In whom we have redemption through his blood, the forgiveness of sins, according to the riches of his grace."

Jesus forgave sins because he was earth's representative for the Godhead and was sent by the Father to atone for sins. The Godhead did not designate any earthly man or church as the mediator for sins. There is access for the sinner to receive pardon and forgiveness by seeking God directly in prayer and supplication.

Think to Change Time and Laws

One of the most profound changes made by the Roman Empire to God's commandment was the change of the day of worship from the seventh day, Saturday (Sabbath) to the first day, Sunday. History records that on March 7, AD 321, Roman Emperor Constantine I issued a civil decree. "On the venerable day of the sun let the magistrate and people residing in cities rest, and let all workshops be closed. In the country however, persons engaged in agricultural work may freely and lawfully continue their pursuits; because it often happens that another day is not so suitable for grain growing or for vine planting; lest by neglecting the proper moment for such operations the bounty of heaven should be lost."[9]

Constantine used this civil decree as a bridge to connect paganism to Christianity. The pagan worship of the sun known as Mithraism was the primary religion of the Roman Empire. This decree now officialized pagan worship and assigned a specific day for worship which was dubbed "the venerable day of the sun." This day was the first day of the week, Sunday. Modern-day Romanism, within its ranks, has conceded that nowhere in the Bible does it advocate worship on the first day of the week, Sunday.

---

9. Wikipedia.org, s.v., "Sunday."

> "A rule of faith, or a competent guide to heaven, must be able to instruct in all the truths necessary for salvation. Now the Scriptures alone do not contain all the truths which a Christian is bound to believe, nor do they explicitly enjoin all the duties which he is obliged to practice. Not to mention other examples, is not every Christian obliged to sanctify Sunday and to abstain on that day from unnecessary servile work? Is not the observance of this law among the most prominent of our sacred duties? But you may read the Bible from Genesis to Revelation, and you will not find a single line authorizing the sanctification of Sunday. The Scriptures enforce the religious observance of Saturday, a day which we never sanctify. The Catholic Church correctly teaches that our Lord and His Apostles inculcated certain important duties of religion which are not recorded by the inspired writers. For instance, most Christians pray to the Holy Ghost, a practice which is nowhere found in the Bible."[10]

This admission is astute, as nowhere in Scripture was Sunday, the first day of week sanctified by God. It was the seventh-day Sabbath that God sanctified and made holy (sunset Friday to sunset Saturday.) Cardinal Gibbons also noted that Christians should not pray to the Holy Spirit as it is not biblical. However, the Bible states that Christians should pray in the Holy Spirit and that the Holy Spirit intercedes for and with us in prayer (Jude 18:20; Rom 8:26–27.)

God's desire is that all come to an understanding of these solemn yet salvific prophetic books of Revelation and Daniel. The sum of these two books crescendos into the loud cries of the three angels' messages. It is fitting that the triune Godhead has chosen to use three angels to give the loud cry. Scripture has unmasked the beast to be the pagan Roman Empire. History confirms that the little horn that rose up from among the horns of the beast, is the papal Roman religio-political system. History validates this and the Protestant reformers witnessed and confirmed it. Other early church pioneers from various denominations came to the same conclusion; they pointed to Romanism as the "man of sin" and perdition, i.e., antichrist.

> 2 Thess 2:2–4—"That ye be not soon shaken in mind, or be troubled, neither by spirit, nor by word, nor by letter as from us, as that the day of Christ is at hand. Let no man deceive you by any means for that day shall not come, except there come a falling away first, and that man of sin be revealed, the son of

---

10. Gibbons, *Faith of Our Fathers*, 89.

perdition, who opposeth and exalteth himself above all that is called God, or that is worshipped; so that he as God sitteth in the temple of God, shewing himself that he is God."

Two quotes raised earlier bear repeating, Cassius Dio, a Roman and Greek historian noted that the "*divine*" was to be worshipped everywhere and in every way and all should be forced to conform to this worship. Titus Livius (Livy), the Roman historian, identified the divine source to whom Rome worshipped as Mars and that the nations of earth should likewise submit. "Divine" originated from the Latin word *divinus*, which means pertaining to a god, eternal, holy, or godlike.

On October 11, 1962, Pope John XXIII led an ecumenical convocation dubbed Vatican II. This was in essence the rebranding of the church, its practices, and doctrines. Vatican II was the bridge and the springboard to connect the church in a modernized way to the rest of the other religions and denominations. The thesis of the initiative as outlined in the manifest was to bring all of mankind back to the church. It was both an outreach and an in-reach. Romanism, however, has always claimed infallibility and immutability of her dogmas. If Rome never changes, how would it now incorporate all the various religions and religious beliefs? Are there two doctrines, one for the masses, i.e., general congregation and the other for the secret inner circles? The second angel's message of Revelation 14 and 18, prophetically defined this event as spiritual wine being drunk by the world. History frames prophecy. History confirms what Biblical prophecy foretold.

False Doctrine

The third component of false worship is false doctrine. False doctrines have seeped into a vast number of religions creating a myriad of false theologies and many are unaware of their origins. The Bible likens false doctrine to intoxicating wine. This doctrinal wine is theological dogmas that have been supped by many through inherited traditions. The word dogma is from sixteenth-century Latin which means philosophical tenet. It originated from the Greek word *dokein* and translates to mean "to seem good," "to accept," or "opinion." It is interesting to note that the word dogma, if spelt backwards, reveals the words "am god." Is this an inference to false man-made doctrines usurping the true God and the true commandments of God? Let's examine some of these false doctrines and see how they differ from the truth found in the Word of God.

Divine revelation includes tradition—the belief that divine revelation and the rule of faith is drawn from Scripture and tradition, e.g., liturgy, sacraments, and mass. However, the Word of God describes man-made traditions and theologies as unavailing worship.

> Mark 7:9,13—"And he said unto them, 'full well ye reject the commandment of God, that ye may keep your own. Making the Word of God of none effect through your tradition, which ye have delivered and many such like things do ye.'"
>
> Col 2:8—"Beware lest any man spoil you through philosophy and vain deceit, after the tradition of men, after the rudiments of the world, and not after Christ."
>
> Matt 15:9—"But in vain they do worship me, teaching for doctrines the commandments of men."

Chantings—the use of melodic repetitions to reach altered state of consciousness or to repeat names of deities to harness their spiritual powers. The history of chanting began with shamans who used to communicate with the spirit world. In ancient Greece chanting was a means to reach a mystical state and harness magical powers. In contemporary terms, repetitive worship songs are used to create a hypnotic state. However, the Word of God describes this as heathenism.

> Matt 6:7—"But when ye pray, use not vain repetitions, as the heathen do, for they think that they shall be heard for their much speaking."

Praying or talking to statues—the belief that statues or images have spiritual powers. However, the Word of God calls this idolatry. Idolatry is the veneration of an idol or making an image of a deity for the purpose of worship. "*Idolum*" is Latin for image. Idols can be physical or mental. Anything that replaces the true God is an idol. Perhaps there might be a connection to the word doll. The first and second commandment forbids idolatry and explicitly admonishes against idol worship.

> Exod 20:3–5—"Thou shalt have no other gods before me. Thou shalt not make unto thee any graven image, or any likeness of anything that is in heaven above, or that is in the earth beneath, or that is in the water under the earth. Thou shalt not bow down thyself to them, nor serve them, for I the Lord thy God am a

> jealous God, visiting the iniquity of the fathers upon the children unto the third and fourth generation of them that hate me."
>
> Rev 9:20—"And the rest of the men which were not killed by these plagues yet repented not of the works of their hands, that they should not worship devils, and idols of gold, and silver, and brass, and stone, and of wood, which neither can see, nor hear, nor walk."
>
> Judg 3:7—"And the children of Israel did evil in the sight of the Lord, and forgat the Lord their God, and served Baalim and the groves."

Worship of idols which can be physical, e.g., images, statues, worship of people, temples etc. It can also be mental, e.g., self-worship and self-exaltation. Worship should be given only to the one true God who made heaven, earth, and sea.

Worship of nature or heavenly bodies—Worship of nature or creation is known as pantheism. Gaia worship is the modernized version of pantheism. This is another form of idolatry. Nature worship in ancient times took the form of worship of celestial bodies; sun, moon, stars, and sacred groves, woods, and trees. There is a resurgence of pantheism and nature worship and climate awareness disguised under different banners and names. God reminds us that we ought to worship the Creator not creation.

> 2 Kgs 23:5—"And he put down the idolatrous priests, whom the kings of Judah had ordained to burn incense in the high places in the cities of Judah, and in the places roundabout Jerusalem, them also that burned incense unto Baal, to the sun, and to the moon, and to the planets, and to all the host of heaven."
>
> Deut 17:3—"And hath gone and served other gods, and worshipped them, either the sun, or moon, or any of the host of heaven, which I have not commanded."
>
> Col 2:18—"Let no man beguile you of your reward in a voluntary humility and worshipping of angels, intruding into those things which he hath not seen, vainly puffed up by his fleshly mind."

Monetary sacrifices—this false doctrine includes the belief that money should be given to receive or purchase blessings or to receive spiritual endowments. However, God's Word calls this wickedness.

> Acts 8:18-22—"And when Simon saw that through laying on of the apostles' hands the Holy Ghost was given, he offered them

money, saying, 'give me also this power, that on whomsoever I lay hands, he may receive the Holy Ghost.' But Peter said unto him, 'thy money perish with thee, because thou hast thought that the gift of God may be purchased with money. Thou hast neither part nor lot in this matter, for thy heart is not right in the sight of God. Repent therefore of this thy wickedness, and pray God, if perhaps the thought of thine heart may be forgiven thee.'"

God's salvation, blessings, and healings cannot be purchased. They are free gifts from God. He only requires that we offer ourselves as living sacrifices, holy and acceptable which is our reasonable service (Rom 12:1)

Scripture is produced by the church—the church espouses that the Bible is her book, her production and that she is the only one with the authority to decipher its meanings. However, the Word of God attributes the Bible and Scripture to be the inspiration of the Godhead, given to all for personal study and edification.

> 2 Tim 3:16—"All scripture is given by inspiration of God, and is profitable for doctrine, for reproof, for correction, for instruction in righteousness."
>
> Rom 16:26—"But now is made manifest, and by the scriptures of the prophets, according to the commandment of the everlasting God, made known to all nations for the obedience of faith."
>
> 2 Pet 1:20-21—"Knowing this first, that no prophecy of the scripture is of any private interpretation. For the prophecy came not in old time by the will of man but holy men of God spake as they were moved by the Holy Ghost."
>
> 2 Tim 2:15-16—"Study to shew thyself approved unto God, a workman that needeth not to be ashamed, rightly dividing the word of truth. But shun profane and vain babblings, for they will increase unto more ungodliness."

The Godhead not of same origin—the belief that each member of the Godhead has a distinct origin. However, Jesus while on earth declared that he was one with the Father and that he came from the Father.

> John 10:30—"I and my Father are one."
>
> John 16:27—"For the Father himself loveth you, because ye have loved me, and have believed that I came out from God."
>
> 1 John 5:7—"For there are three that bear record in heaven, the Father, the Word, and the Holy Ghost and these three are one."

> John 1:12—"In the beginning was the Word, and the Word was with God, and the Word was God. The same was in the beginning with God."

The triune Godhead is one from the beginning, all three have the same origin. Jesus did not originate in isolation. He was sent to earth by the Father and was manifested via the conduit of a virgin birth. He was one with the Father from the beginning; the Word at creation who became flesh.

Sins can be forgiven by a religious leader—the belief that an earthly intercessor is needed for the confession and forgiveness of sins and for the reconciliation of the sinner. However, the Word of God says, "there is one God, and one mediator between God and men, the man Christ Jesus" (1 Tim 2:5.)

> Matt 6:1,6,9—"Take heed that ye do not your alms before men, to be seen of them, otherwise ye have no reward of your Father which is in heaven. But thou, when thou prayest, enter into thy closet, and when thou hast shut thy door, pray to thy Father which is in secret, and thy Father which seeth in secret shall reward thee openly. After this manner therefore pray ye, our Father which art in heaven, hallowed be thy name."

> Acts 5:31—"Him hath God exalted with his right hand to be a prince and a Savior, for to give repentance to Israel, and forgiveness of sins."

God is the only one who can forgive sins because it is against his commandments that we have transgressed. Jesus while on earth also forgave sins as he was the fulfillment of God in bodily form; he was the divine God in human form. Jesus commissioned us to go privately to God in prayer and confess our sins and not through earthly mediators.

Day of worship (Sunday)—The day of worship was changed from Sabbath (sunset Friday to sunset Saturday) to Sunday by Roman Empire Constantine on March 7, AD 321. However, the Word of God validates that the seventh-day Sabbath is to be kept perpetually until eternity.

> Isa 66:23—"And it shall come to pass, that from one new moon to another, and from one sabbath to another, shall all flesh come to worship before me, saith the Lord."

> Ezek 20:12—"Moreover also I gave them my sabbaths, to be a sign between me and them, that they might know that I am the Lord that sanctify them."

> Exod 20:8–11—"Remember the sabbath day, to keep it holy. Six days shalt thou labor, and do all thy work, but the seventh day is the sabbath of the Lord thy God; in it thou shalt not do any work, thou, nor thy son, nor thy daughter, thy manservant, nor thy maidservant, nor thy cattle, nor thy stranger that is within thy gates. For in six days the Lord made heaven and earth, the sea, and all that in them is, and rested the seventh day, wherefore the Lord blessed the sabbath day, and hallowed it."
>
> Matt 12:8—"For the Son of man is Lord even of the sabbath day."

The Sabbath was never changed by God. Jesus kept the Sabbath as validation that it was never intended to be changed and declared that he did not come to destroy the law but to fulfill it (Matt 5:17.) Both Jews and Gentiles and the disciples kept the Sabbath, even after Jesus' resurrection. The Sabbath was not only for the Jews but is for all mankind (Mark 2:27.) John 20 verse 19 is often used to justify that, because the disciples gathered together the first day of the week, that meant the Sabbath was changed to the first day, Sunday. On the contrary, after the crucifixion, the disciples had assembled together because they were hiding from the Jews. Jesus appeared to them, however, there is no record of Jesus validating that the Sabbath had changed. John 20 versus 24 points out that Thomas was absent. If the Sabbath was changed to Sunday would Thomas not also be worshipping with the disciples? It was not a worship session as there was no change to God's Sabbath. Many philosophize that any day can be the Sabbath because Sabbath generically means "rest." However, the Sabbath was instituted from creation as the seventh day of the week.

Immortality of the soul—the belief that there is life after death and when one dies, they either go to purgatory or go directly to heaven or hell. However, the Word of God is in direct opposition to this belief.

> Eccl 9:5—For the living know that they shall die, but the dead know not anything, neither have they anymore a reward, for the memory of them is forgotten."
>
> Job 7:7–10—"O remember that my life is wind, mine eye shall no more see good. The eye of him that hath seen me shall see me no more, thine eyes are upon me, and I am not. As the cloud is consumed and vanisheth away, so he that goeth down to the grave shall come up no more. He shall return no more to his house, neither shall his place know him anymore."

> 1 Thess 4:16—"For the Lord himself shall descend from heaven with a shout, with the voice of the archangel, and with the trump of God, and the dead in Christ shall rise first."

The dead will only live again at the second coming of Christ, i.e., the righteous who died in Christ. Jesus is the resurrection and the life (John 11:25.)

Secret rapture or pre-tribulation—this is the belief that the second coming of Christ will be a secret and the church is raptured before the tribulation. However, the Word of God confirms that the tribulation will precede the second coming, which will be a spectacular event with lightning, powers of heaven shaken, dead being raised etc. Every eye will see him, even those who pierced him (Rev 1:7.)

> Matt 24:21-27—"For then shall be great tribulation, such as was not since the beginning of the world to this time, no, nor ever shall be. And except those days should be shortened, there should no flesh be saved, but for the elect's sake those days shall be shortened. Then if any man shall say unto you, lo, here is Christ, or there, believe it not. For there shall arise false Christs, and false prophets, and shall shew great signs and wonders, insomuch that, if it were possible, they shall deceive the very elect. Behold, I have told you before. Wherefore if they shall say unto you, behold, he is in the desert, go not forth, behold, he is in the secret chambers, believe it not. For as the lightning cometh out of the east, and shineth even unto the west, so shall also the coming of the Son of man be."

> Mark 13:24-27—"But in those days, after that tribulation, the sun shall be darkened, and the moon shall not give her light, and the stars of heaven shall fall, and the powers that are in heaven shall be shaken. And then shall they see the Son of man coming in the clouds with great power and glory. And then shall he send his angels and shall gather together his elect from the four winds, from the uttermost part of the earth to the uttermost part of heaven."

> Rev 7:14—"And I said unto him, sir, thou knowest. And he said to me, 'these are they which came out of great tribulation, and have washed their robes, and made them white in the blood of the Lamb.'"

God wants all to be alert, watchful, and ready for the tribulation and not to be alarmed or fearful. Jesus comforts the disciples and by extension everyone, with these words "these things I have spoken unto you, that in me ye might have peace. In the world ye shall have tribulation, but be of good cheer, I have overcome the world" (John 16:33.)

Miracles, signs, and wonders—this is the belief that miracles, signs, and wonders are indicators of a true prophet. The Word of God calls this deception. Satan will deceive many with false miracles, signs, and wonders. The word miracle means a supernatural act of God for the glory of God (John 2:11; Num 14:22.) The Latin is *miraculum* which means "object of wonder," and the Greek is *semeion* which means sign.

> Rev 13:13-14—"And he doeth great wonders, so that he maketh fire come down from heaven on the earth in the sight of men. And deceiveth them that dwell on the earth by the means of those miracles which he had power to do in the sight of the beast, saying to them that dwell on the earth, that they should make an image to the beast, which had the wound by a sword, and did live."

> Rev 16:13-14—"And I saw three unclean spirits like frogs come out of the mouth of the dragon, and out of the mouth of the beast, and out of the mouth of the false prophet. For they are the spirits of devils, working miracles, which go forth unto the kings of the earth and of the whole world, to gather them to the battle of that great day of God Almighty."

> Matt 16:4—"A wicked and adulterous generation seeketh after a sign, and there shall no sign be given unto it, but the sign of the prophet Jonas. And he left them and departed."

Deceptive miracles, signs and wonders are tools of the devil and will proliferate even more so in these last days. In Matthew 16, the Pharisees sought to tempt Jesus by asking for a sign from heaven. Why did Jesus refer to the sign of Jonas (Jonah)?

Story of Jonah and End-Time Deception of Signs, Wonders, Miracles

Miracles, signs, and wonders are oftentimes promoted as a means to garner church growth and profit. Jesus warned against these false lures and deemed them as wickedness and spiritual adultery that draws the masses into its underbelly; likened to the ship that carried the prophet Jonah. Jonah was sent by God to warn and "cry against" the evil city of Nineveh where idolatry and the worship of false gods were prevalent. Jonah defied

God and boarded a ship going in the opposite direction and hid in the belly of the ship from the crew, but he could not hide from the eyes of God. God sent a mighty wind that stirred the seas, and the ship began to break apart. The crew were frightened and cried out to their own gods. They began unloading their cargo in a vain effort to save themselves. Realizing the futility of their efforts they approached Jonah who was asleep in the belly of the ship. They beckoned for him to arise and call upon his God. They cast lots to see who had brought this evil upon them as they deemed it. The lot fell upon Jonah. He was thrown overboard and was swallowed up by a whale that God had prepared. Jonah's prayer was heard by God while still in the whale's belly. He was eventually spat out from this putrid womb after three days and three nights with weeds wrapped around his head.

> Jonah 2:7-10—"When my soul fainted within me, I remembered the Lord, and my prayer came in unto thee, into thine holy temple. They that observe lying vanities forsake their own mercy. But I will sacrifice unto thee with the voice of thanksgiving, I will pay *that* that I have vowed. Salvation is of the Lord. And the Lord spake unto the fish, and it vomited out Jonah upon the dry land."

Jonah's prayer was one of self-confession and renouncement of vanity or pride. It was also a rebuke against those that practiced lying vanities, i.e., false doctrines and theologies. He acknowledged that the only means of salvation was from the Lord God. There are many analogies and parallels to draw from the story of Jonah. The weeds wrapped around his head can be likened to the false doctrines and beliefs that he was exposed to. It was also the idolatrous practices he observed in those around him. Weeds are also the tares—false Christians planted amongst the wheat, real Christians.

Some false religions and churches solicit payment to perform miracles, blessings, prayers, removal of sins, prayers for deceased loved ones etc. Jesus likens this to spiritual adultery. Jonah realized that salvation was free, and he only had to offer himself; a living sacrifice of thanksgiving to the Lord God (Rom 12:1).

Before Jonah was thrown overboard where his tribulation was to begin, he witnessed and gave his testimony that he was a believer in the true God, the one who made heaven, earth, and sea.

> Jonah 1:9—"And he said unto them, I am a Hebrew and I fear the Lord, the God of heaven, which hath made the sea and the dry land."

Jonah's public confession that he feared God and that he was a follower of the true God who created heaven, earth, and sea, mirrors the loud cry of the first angel's message. Another parallel that Jesus wanted to highlight and especially to us living in these end-times, is that those who profess to be followers of Christ will be thrown into tribulation. There will be personal tribulation, e.g., those who refuse to accept the mark of the beast will not be able to buy or sell (Rev 13:17.) There will be global tribulation, wars, natural disasters, earthquakes, floods, fires, hurricanes, famine, and economic hardships (Matt 24:7; Mark 13:8.) The crew parallels those who are worshippers of false gods (Jonah 1:5.) They began praying and unloading their cargo into the sea. In their own efforts they tried to save themselves by praying to false gods, by absorbing and practicing false doctrines, and false religious beliefs—seeking a false way to salvation. However, spiritually they had unloaded themselves of truth and of the true God and sought-after false gods and false traditions of man. The only enduring truth is found in the true God who created the heavens, the earth, and the sea. God unleashed a mighty wind upon their ship, and it began to break. Instead of humbling themselves before God they turned their attention to Jonah. In these end-times, there will be many natural disasters, many of which will be caused by satanic forces. Those who are the true worshippers will be blamed as the cause for these disasters. After throwing Jonah overboard, the raging sea came to a quiet calm. The crew repented and worshiped the true God by offering sacrifices and making vows (Jonah 1:16.) This parallels the first angel's message; a call for worship of the true God.

After the whale spat Jonah on dry land, the Lord reminded him of the mission to declare the loud cry against Nineveh, the "great city." Although Nineveh was a three day's journey, Jonah went swiftly and arrived in a day heralding the loud cry that in forty days Nineveh would be overthrown (Jonah 3:1–4.) This parallels the swiftness of the second angel's message that the "great city" of Babylon is fallen. Nineveh was rife with idolatry. Babylon likewise represents false worship. After hearing Jonah's prophetic warning message, the Ninevites repented. God relented from punitive executive judgment. The third angel's message is a warning of punitive executive judgment in these last days. Only those who heed and forsake false worship will escape the wrath of God. The three angels' messages will be proclaimed more loudly throughout the world as a witness, then the end will come. This will be God's mighty wind; the end-time prophetic word that will blow "upon the seas." Seas represent people. God's true church and Christians will proclaim these messages as we near the second coming of Christ. Jonah was in the darkness of the whale's belly for three days and three nights, and it was not until he confessed and forsook his sins that God answered and spewed him out. Jesus drew another analogy to this significant number three.

> Matt 12:40—"For as Jonas was three days and three nights in the whale's belly, so shall the Son of man be three days and three nights in the heart of the earth."

Beginning from Thursday night, in the dark and perhaps cool garden of Gethsemane, before he was to be crucified, Jesus agonized with God. Jesus took three disciples; Peter, John, and James. Jesus prayed three times. The Bible does not specify how long he prayed but perhaps one could deduce it might have been three hours as he admonished the disciples that they could not stay awake for an hour, and he returned three times and found them sleeping at each of these three intervals.

> Matt 26:39—"And he went a little farther, and fell on his face, and prayed, saying, 'O my Father, if it be possible, let this cup pass from me, nevertheless not as I will, but as thou wilt.'"

> Luke 22:44—24:46—"And being in an agony he prayed more earnestly, and his sweat was as it were great drops of blood falling down to the ground. And said unto them, 'thus it is written, and thus it behooved Christ to suffer, and to rise from the dead the third day.'"

> Jonah 1:17—"Now the Lord had prepared a great fish to swallow up Jonah. And Jonah was in the belly of the fish three days and three nights."

> Jonah 2:3-6—"For thou hadst cast me into the deep, in the midst of the seas, and the floods compassed me about, all thy billows and thy waves passed over me. Then I said, I am cast out of thy sight, yet I will look again toward thy holy temple. The waters compassed me about, even to the soul, the depth closed me roundabout, the weeds were wrapped about my head. I went down to the bottoms of the mountains, the earth with her bars

was about me forever, yet hast thou brought up my life from corruption, O Lord my God."

- Jonah was sent by God to a sinful city to cry against their wickedness. Jesus was sent by God to a sinful world to pay the penalty for sin and to reconcile the sinner back to God.
- Both Jesus and Jonah surrendered their will for God's perfect will.
- Jonah had a crown of weeds; Jesus had a crown of thorns.
- Jonah was awash with water, waves, and weeds. Jesus was awash with sweat, blood, and the incredible weight of the world's sin; both agonized with God.
- Lots were cast against them (Jonah 1:7; Matt 27:35.)
- Jonah was in the whale's belly three days and three nights. Jesus was in the heart of earth three days and three nights (from Gethsemane Thursday night to his crucifixion Friday morning, to a cold tomb, and then resurrection Sunday morning.)
- Jonah died spiritually to his sins. Jesus died physically for our sins; yet he was sinless.

Christians must agonize with God and seek him with their whole heart. Jonah was releasing his sins to God and Jesus was taking on the sins of the world. Salvation is not through a religion or church or a priest or pastor nor seeking after miracles, signs, or wonders. Salvation is through Jesus Christ alone.

Summary of Second Angel's Message

The second angel's message is a cry to all to come out of false worship (Babylon.) True worship has a true God, likewise, false worship has a false god. We started off by asking three key questions; who is the false god? why do people worship the false god? how will they worship the false or counterfeit god?

- Who—the false god is a false trinity; the dragon (Satan), the beast (pagan Rome and papal system), and the false prophets (religions and churches who adapt the false doctrine of Babylon's wine)

- Why—people worship the false god because they have unknowingly "drank of the wine" (doctrine) of the false god
- How—by adopting and practicing false doctrines and theologies
- False worship has three components—false religion, false church, and false doctrine
- False religion is Babylon; a melange of various ancient pagan beliefs and practices that have been handed down to many of today's religions
- False church is the little horn or the woman sitting upon the beast; the Roman papal system that sprung from the pagan Roman Empire
- False doctrine is the "wine" of false theology, teachings, traditions, practices, and observances. These doctrines have given birth to various other religions, churches, and factions that inherited these paganistic dogmas

Third Angel's Message—Judgment

The final angel's message is the third angel's message.

> Rev 14:9-11—"And the third angel followed them, saying with a loud voice, 'if any man worship the beast and his image, and receive his mark in his forehead, or in his hand. The same shall drink of the wine of the wrath of God, which is poured out without mixture into the cup of his indignation, and he shall be tormented with fire and brimstone in the presence of the holy angels, and in the presence of the Lamb.' And the smoke of their torment ascendeth up forever and ever, and they have no rest day nor night, who worship the beast and his image, and whosoever receiveth the mark of his name."

Judgment has three phases; investigative, sentencing, and executive. The first, second, and third angels' messages all have aspects of these three phases of judgment. The first angel's message was the proclamation that the investigative judgment had begun. This investigative judgment began in 1844 in heaven when Jesus moved from the Holy Place to the Most Holy Place to begin the judgment of the dead. After the judgment of the dead, Jesus will begin the judgment of the living, but we do not know when this will begin. (Refer to the Appendix for more details on the Investigative Judgment.) After the first angel gives warning of the start of judgment, the second angel announces judgment against Babylon (false worship.)

> Rev 14:8—"And there followed another angel, saying, 'Babylon is fallen, is fallen, that great city, because she made all nations drink of the wine of the wrath of her fornication.'"

> Rev 18:1-8,16,23-24—"And after these things I saw another angel come down from heaven, having great power, and the earth was lightened with his glory. And he cried mightily with a strong voice, saying, 'Babylon the great is fallen, is fallen, and is become the habitation of devils, and the hold of every foul spirit, and a cage of every unclean and hateful bird. For all nations have drunk of the wine of the wrath of her fornication, and the kings of the earth have committed fornication with her, and the merchants of the earth are waxed rich through the abundance of her delicacies.' And I heard another voice from heaven, saying, 'come out of her, my people, that ye be not partakers of her sins, and that ye receive not of her plagues. For her sins have reached unto heaven, and God hath remembered her iniquities. Reward her even as she rewarded you, and double unto her double according to her works, in the cup which she hath filled fill to her double. How much she hath glorified herself, and lived deliciously, so much torment and sorrow give her, for she saith in her heart, I sit a queen, and am no widow, and shall see no sorrow. Therefore, shall her plagues come in one day, death, and mourning, and famine, and she shall be utterly burned with fire, for strong is the Lord God who judgeth her.' And saying, 'alas, alas that great city, that was clothed in fine linen, and purple, and scarlet, and decked with gold, and precious stones, and pearls' And the light of a candle shall shine no more at all in thee and the voice of the bridegroom and of the bride shall be heard no more at all in thee, for thy merchants were the great men of the earth, for by thy sorceries were all nations deceived. And in her was found the blood of prophets, and of saints, and of all that were slain upon the earth.'"

The second angel's message is twofold. It is an investigative phase because God outlines why there will be judgment against Babylon. The charges and evidence are brought against Babylon. The evidence and charges include, intoxicating many with false religious doctrines (wine), causing the death of saints and prophets, performing sorcery, deceiving the nations, and pride. The charges also include having unholy and unethical relations with the kings and merchants of the world. In today's narrative this means partnering and deceiving world political leaders, presidents, prime ministers, business leaders, CEOs, financiers, bankers etc. A pre-sentencing warning is given to everyone to come out of Babylon because God has investigated her and found her guilty of intoxicating the world with false doctrines and deceptions.

The second phase is the pronouncement of punishment, which is the sentencing phase of judgment. Babylon will be punished with plagues, famine, torment, sorrow, fire, and ultimately death.

The third angel's message is the sentencing phase and also a preview of the executive phase of judgment. The sentencing phase highlights the punishment upon those who worship the beast, his image, or receive his mark in their forehead or hand. To receive the mark of the beast in the forehead is to philosophically agree with the tenets of the beast system. To receive the mark in the hand is to accept the tents of the beast system for the convenience of retaining employment, material possessions, access to buying and selling, and other cherished freedoms. It is these two groups that will receive the wrath of God, which will be poured out without mercy. They will also be tormented with fire and brimstone. The executive phase which is the final phase of judgment is the actual pouring out of the plagues upon the beast, the false prophets, and anyone who has not heeded the call to come out of these false religious systems and has accepted the mark of the beast. The pouring out of these plagues will precede the second coming of Christ.

The apostle John was shown in vision, the dreadful scenes of the executive judgment; the pouring out of the seven last plagues.

> Rev 16:1–4,8–12,17–21—"And I heard a great voice out of the temple saying to the seven angels, 'go your ways, and pour out the vials of the wrath of God upon the earth.' And the first went, and poured out his vial upon the earth, and there fell a noisome and grievous sore upon the men which had the mark of the beast, and upon them which worshipped his image. And the second angel poured out his vial upon the sea, and it became as the blood of a dead man, and every living soul died in the sea. And the third angel poured out his vial upon the rivers and fountains of waters, and they became blood. And the fourth angel poured out his vial upon the sun, and power was given unto him to scorch men with fire. And men were scorched with great heat, and blasphemed the name of God, which hath power over these plagues, and they repented not to give him glory. And the

fifth angel poured out his vial upon the seat of the beast, and his kingdom was full of darkness, and they gnawed their tongues for pain. And blasphemed the God of heaven because of their pains and their sores and repented not of their deeds. And the sixth angel poured out his vial upon the great river Euphrates, and the water thereof was dried up, that the way of the kings of the east might be prepared. And the seventh angel poured out his vial into the air and there came a great voice out of the temple of heaven, from the throne, saying, 'It is done.' And there were voices, and thunders, and lightnings, and there was a great earthquake, such as was not since men were upon the earth, so mighty an earthquake, and so great. And the great city was divided into three parts, and the cities of the nations fell, and great Babylon came in remembrance before God, to give unto her the cup of the wine of the fierceness of his wrath.

And every island fled away, and the mountains were not found. And there fell upon men a great hail out of heaven, every stone about the weight of a talent, and men blasphemed God because of the plague of the hail, for the plague thereof was exceeding great."

It is interesting to note that the Babylonian city will be divided into three parts. The Godhead is making a clear point that the false trinity will be destroyed in totality (Rev 17:1—18:21—19:20.) Three phases of judgment reflect a just and righteous God who is patient and merciful and has given humanity time to repent and forsake the false religious systems. God never executes judgment without first investigating and sending clear warnings of imminent danger—not to worship the beast, or its image, or receive its mark.

Mark of the Beast

Rev 13:15-17—"And he had power to give life unto the image of the beast, that the image of the beast should both speak, and cause that as many as would not worship the image of the beast should be killed. And he causeth all, both small and great, rich and poor, free and bond, to receive a mark in their right hand, or in their foreheads. And that no man might buy or sell, save he that had the mark, or the name of the beast, or the number of his name."

Severe persecution described as a time of trouble or tribulation is prophesied, when no one will be able to buy or sell except they accept the mark of the beast. The beast and its image are the conglomerate of the Roman Empire and the papal system. The old pagan Roman Empire no longer exists in theory, but it has merged the theologies, dogmas, and mindset into the papal Roman system. The word "mark" has its origin from Latin, *mart-kos*, which means consecrated to Mars—god of war or warlike. The Latin root origin of the word "image" is *imitor* which means to imitate. The image of the beast means the imitator of the beast. The beast and his imitator have the same likeness and mindset. The inherited tendencies of the pagan Roman Empire were transferred over into the papal Roman system. In order to determine what the mark of the beast is we must first understand the beast in modern-day end-time application.

> Dan 7:7-8—"After this I saw in the night visions, and behold a fourth beast, dreadful and terrible, and strong exceedingly, and it had great iron teeth, it devoured and brake in pieces, and stamped the residue with the feet of it, and it was diverse from all the beasts that were before it, and it had ten horns. I considered the horns, and behold, there came up among them another little horn, before whom there were three of the first horns plucked up by the roots, and behold, in this horn were eyes like the eyes of man, and a mouth speaking great things."
>
> Rev 17:3-6,18—"So he carried me away in the spirit into the wilderness and I saw a woman sit upon a scarlet-colored beast, full of names of blasphemy, having seven heads and ten horns. And the woman was arrayed in purple and scarlet color, and decked with gold and precious stones and pearls, having a golden cup in her hand full of abominations and filthiness of her fornication. And upon her forehead was a name written, Mystery, Babylon The Great, The Mother Of Harlots And Abominations Of The Earth. And I saw the woman drunken with the blood of the saints, and with the blood of the martyrs of Jesus, and when I saw her, I wondered with great admiration. And the woman which thou sawest is that great city, which reigneth over the kings of the earth."

We have already identified the beast as the pagan Roman Empire. The little horn that sprang up on its head (mindset), was the papal Roman system. The papal Roman Empire is also the "image of the beast." Who is this woman (church) riding the beast and sits as a fixture upon the beast? The woman (church) is also the papal Roman church; she has her seat upon the beast, which signifies her authority over the beast. Who gave her this seat and authority?

> Rev 13:2—"And the beast which I saw was like unto a leopard, and his feet were as the feet of a bear, and his mouth as the mouth of a lion, and the dragon gave him his power, and his seat, and great authority."

The dragon (Satan) gave the beast its power, seat, and authority, and now the woman (papal Roman church) sits in authority on this seat.

Seat

The prophet Ezekiel who lived during the sixth century received a profound vision from God. It is imperative to analyze this vision in order to unmask the seat, the woman, the beast, and the mark.

> Ezek 8:1–18—"And it came to pass in the sixth year, in the sixth month, in the fifth day of the month, as I sat in mine house, and the elders of Judah sat before me, that the hand of the Lord God fell there upon me. Then I beheld, and lo a likeness as the appearance of fire, from the appearance of his loins even downward, fire, and from his loins even upward, as the appearance of brightness, as the color of amber. And he put forth the form of a hand, and took me by a lock of mine head, and the spirit lifted me up between the earth and the heaven and brought me in the visions of God to Jerusalem, to the door of the inner gate that looketh *toward the north, where was the seat of the image of jealousy*, which provoketh to jealousy. And behold, the glory of the God of Israel was there, according to the vision that I saw in the plain. Then said he unto me, 'son of man, lift up thine eyes now the way toward the north.' So, I lifted up mine eyes the way toward the north and behold *northward at the gate of the altar this image of jealousy in the entry*. He said furthermore unto me, '*son of man, seest thou what they do, even the great abominations* that the house of Israel committeth here, that I should go far off from my sanctuary, *but turn thee yet again, and thou shalt see greater abominations*.' And he brought me to the door of the court, and when I looked, behold a hole in the wall. Then said he unto me, 'son of man, dig now in the wall,' and when I had digged in the wall, behold a door. And he said unto me, 'go in, and behold the *wicked abominations that they do here*.' So, I went in and saw, and behold *every form of creeping things, and abominable beasts,*

and all the idols of the house of Israel, portrayed upon the wall roundabout. And there stood before them seventy men of the ancients of the house of Israel, and in the midst of them stood Jaazaniah the son of Shaphan, with every man his censer in his hand, and a thick cloud of incense went up. Then said he unto me, 'son of man, hast thou seen what the *ancients of the house of Israel do in the dark, every man in the chambers of his imagery,* for they say, the Lord seeth us not, the Lord hath forsaken the earth.' He said also unto me, 'turn thee yet again, and thou shalt see *greater abominations that they do.*' Then he brought me to the door of the gate of the Lord's house which was *toward the north, and behold, there sat women weeping for Tammuz.* Then said he unto me, 'hast thou seen this, O son of man, turn thee yet again, and thou shalt *see greater abominations than these.*' And he brought me into the inner court of the Lord's house, and behold, at the door of the temple of the Lord, between the porch and the altar, were about five and twenty men, *with their backs toward the temple of the Lord, and their faces toward the east, and they worshipped the sun toward the east.* Then he said unto me, 'hast thou seen this, O son of man? Is it a light thing to the house of Judah that they *commit the abominations* which they commit here, for they have filled the land with violence, and have returned to provoke me to anger, and, lo, they put the branch to their nose. Therefore, will I also deal in fury, mine eye shall not spare, neither will I have pity, and though they cry in mine ears with a loud voice, yet will I not hear them.'"

Who Was Tammuz?

Tammuz was an ancient Mesopotamian god associated with shepherds, springtime, and fertility. He was also worshipped as a sun god called Dumuzu to the Babylonians, as Osiris to the Egyptians, as Adonis to the Greeks. He was the husband of Ishtar. She too was a deity who was worshipped in various cultures, as Isis to the Egyptians, as Aphrodite to the Greeks, and as Venus to the Romans. According to the myth, Tammuz was killed annually by a wild boar. Ishtar went into mourning and descended into the underworld to rescue him from death and brought him back to life and became the god of springtime. Ishtar in her own right was a powerful and famous goddess in the ancient Near East (area in Mesopotamia near Tigris and Euphrates.) It is believed that Easter derived its name from Ishtar. It is interesting to note that she was the goddess of the East, so perhaps Easter was also given its name to reflect her influence. Regardless of the name origin of Easter, we see yet again, how paganism seeped its way into modern-day religious observances. God was displeased with the worshippers who were crying for Tammuz.

Ezekiel was shown the spiritual downward deterioration, attributable to the various pagan practices. Gradually and progressively, God's people debased themselves in idolatry, drinking the abominable wine of Babylon. "And upon her forehead was a name written, Mystery, Babylon The Great, The Mother Of Harlots And Abominations Of The Earth" (Rev 17:5.)

Progression of Abominations

A. "Great abominations"—door of inner gate toward the north; at gate of altar ⇒ seat of jealousy

B. Greater than "great abominations" (wicked abominations)—door of the court ⇒ creeping things, abominable beasts, idols, priests with censers doing rituals in the cloak of darkness ⇒ leading to modern-day spiritualism, idol worship, animal sacrifices

C. Greater than greater than "great abominations" (wicked abominations) than "great abominations"—door of gate of the Lord's house towards the north ⇒ women sat (seated) weeping for Tammuz ⇒ modern-day "women" are churches (congregations) worshipping false gods, idols, performing pagan rituals, and services

D. Greater than greater than greater than "great abominations" (wicked abominations) than "great abominations" than greater than "great abominations" (wicked abominations) than "great abominations"—inner court of the Lord's house at the door of temple between the porch (temple) and the altar ⇒ twenty-five high priests with their backs to the temple of the Lord and faces towards the east worshipping the sun ⇒ modern-day church leaders, religious heads worshipping on the day of the sun (Sunday.) Religions that require bowing to the direction of the sun when they pray; praying towards the east; use of sundials.

Every rung of the ladder of abomination was aggregately greater and worse than the one before. Of all the abominations, God described the greatest of all abominations to be the worshipping of the sun. This pagan worship of the sun was not just in the ancient time of Ezekiel but also in the Roman Empire. The Roman sun god was called sol. The Roman Emperor Elagabalus built a temple called Sol Invictus, "the invincible sun," in honor of the sun god. Empire Constantine on March 7 AD 321 modernized this into Sunday worship. Jesus highlighted the significant end-time relevance of this abominable act when he spoke to the disciples and referenced the prophet Daniel. This will be the proverbial last straw. The resurgence of this abomination will climax into the great tribulation and then the second coming of Christ.

> Dan 11:31—"And arms shall stand on his part, and they shall pollute the sanctuary of strength, and shall take away the daily sacrifice, and they shall place the *abomination that maketh desolate.*"

> Matt 24:14-22,29-33—"And this gospel of the kingdom shall be preached in all the world for a witness unto all nations, and then shall the end come. When ye therefore shall see the *abomination of desolation, spoken of by Daniel the prophet, stand in the holy place*, whoso readeth, let him understand. Then let them which be in Judaea flee into the mountains. Let him which is on the housetop not come down to take anything out of his house. Neither let him which is in the field return back to take his clothes. And woe unto them that are with child, and to them that give suck in those days! But pray ye that your flight be not in the winter, neither on the sabbath day. For then shall be great tribulation, such as was not since the beginning of the world to this time, no, nor ever shall be. And except those days should be shortened, there should no flesh be saved, but for the elect's sake those days shall be shortened. Immediately after the tribulation of those days shall the sun be darkened, and the moon shall not give her light, and the stars shall fall from heaven, and the powers of the heavens shall be shaken. And then shall appear the sign of the Son of man in heaven, and then shall all the tribes of the earth mourn, and they shall see the Son of man coming in the clouds of heaven with power and great glory. And he shall send his angels with a great sound of a trumpet, and they shall gather together his elect from the four winds, from one end of heaven to the other. Now learn a parable of the fig tree, when his branch is yet tender, and putteth forth leaves, ye know that summer is nigh. So likewise, ye, when ye shall see all these things, know that it is near, even at the doors."

Jesus emphasized that end-time signs will be indicators of the nearness of his coming—"even at the door." It is interesting to note that in Ezekiel's vision, God brought him to four doors; the door of the inner gate, the door of the court, the door of the gate of the Lord's house, and the door of the temple. The greatest abomination was at the door of the temple where sun worship was being practiced. The second coming of Christ will be "at the door" when this same abomination that causes desolation resurges and unfolds in these end-times, but this time as a mandated and forced day of worship. God never changes, nor does his commandments change. He is the same God that gave Daniel, Ezekiel, and John these visions. He still abhors the ancient pagan practices of worshipping the sun. Many religions worship on Sunday, not aware of the pagan origins carried over by Roman influences. Congregations and church leaders have unknowingly been seated (placed) into these false doctrinal practices and traditions of man. Jesus calls this abomination—the abomination of idolatry; the abomination of blasphemy, i.e., a priest making himself like God and claiming to forgive sins and act as God; the abomination of sun worship. The abomination that maketh desolate—*de.sol.late* (sol/sun worship), will be restored by the papal Roman system. There will be mandated laws forcing the world to worship on Sunday—also known as The Sunday Law (Blue Laws.) The three angels' messages are urgent cries to God's people to come out of false worship before it is too late. In both the Old and New Testaments, the cry of a loving God in a voice of warning and rebuke is consistent against those who refuse to abandon false idolatrous worship.

> Ezek 8:18—"Therefore will I also deal in fury, mine eye shall not spare, neither will I have pity, and though they cry in mine ears with a loud voice, yet will I not hear them."

> Rev 16:10—"And the fifth angel poured out his vial upon the *seat of the beast*, and his kingdom was full of darkness, and they gnawed their tongues for pain."

God's executive judgment will see wrath poured out upon the seat of the beast and upon the woman (church) who sits upon the beast.

Mark (Seal) of God Versus Mark of the Beast

Ezekiel was shown the slaughter of those who did not have the mark (seal) of God on their foreheads.

> Ezek 9:3–7—"And the glory of the God of Israel was gone up from the cherub whereupon he was, to the threshold of the house. And he called to the man clothed with linen, which had the writer's inkhorn by his side. And the Lord said unto him, 'go through the midst of the city, through the midst of Jerusalem, and *set a mark upon the foreheads of the men that sigh and that cry for all the abominations that be done in the midst thereof.*' And to the others he said in mine hearing, 'go ye after him through the city, and smite, let not your eye spare, neither have ye pity. Slay utterly old and young, both maids, and little children, and women, *but come not near any man upon whom is the mark* and begin at my sanctuary.' Then they began at the ancient men which were before the house. And he said unto them, 'defile the house, and fill the courts with the slain, go ye forth.' And they went forth and slew in the city."

There was a faithful remnant who did not cry or weep for the sun god Tammuz, but instead was crying against all the abominations of idolatry and against sun worship. God instructed an angel dressed in white linen to place a mark upon their forehead so that they would be spared from the slaughter. Anyone without this special mark of God was to be slain, beginning in the sanctuary. Judgment must begin at the house of God (1 Pet 4:17.)

What Was This Mark or Seal of God?

The mark of God is obviously not a microchip as microchips were not invented in the time of Ezekiel. Nor was it a stamp or physical inscription. It is the same mark of God in Ezekiel's time as will be in these end-times. Therefore, it is imperative to understand what this mark or seal is.

> Rev 7:2–3—"And I saw another angel ascending from the east, having the seal of the living God and he cried with a loud voice to the four angels, to whom it was given to hurt the earth and the sea, saying, 'hurt not the earth, neither the sea, nor the trees, till we have sealed the servants of our God in their foreheads.'"

> Rev 9:3-4—"And there came out of the smoke locusts upon the earth, and unto them was given power, as the scorpions of the earth have power. And it was commanded them that they should not hurt the grass of the earth, neither any green thing, neither any tree, but only those men which have not the seal of God in their foreheads."
>
> 2 Tim 2:19—"Nevertheless the foundation of God standeth sure, having this seal, the Lord knoweth them that are his. And, let everyone that nameth the name of Christ depart from iniquity."
>
> Isa 8:16—"Bind up the testimony, seal the law among my disciples."
>
> John 3:33—"He that hath received his testimony hath set to his seal that God is true."

In Ezekiel's vision the faithful remnants were marked in their foreheads to shield them from the punishment upon idolatrous Jerusalem. Like Ezekiel, the apostle John in the book of Revelation was shown in vision, an angel commissioned to place the seal of the living God upon the foreheads of the faithful. Before the final judgment begins, the servants of God will be sealed in their foreheads to protect and preserve them from the onslaught of punishment upon the earth. This can be seen as type and antitype—both events parallel each other. The mark of God in Ezekiel's vision is the same as the seal of God in John's vision. Both are placed in the forehead. The mark or seal of God are the laws, commandments, and testimonies that will be mentally sealed into the mindset of the obedient servants of God.

Why the Forehead?

> Ezek 3:4,7-9—"And he said unto me, 'son of man, go, get thee unto the house of Israel, and speak with my words unto them. But the house of Israel will not hearken unto thee, for they will not hearken unto me, for all the house of Israel are impudent and hardhearted. Behold, I have made thy face strong against their faces, and *thy forehead strong against their foreheads. As an adamant harder than flint have I made thy forehead;* fear them not, neither be dismayed at their looks, though they be a rebellious house.'"

Adamant means refusing to be persuaded or to change one's mind—unshakeable, unmoving, unwavering, uncompromising, or firm in your decision. Adamant is from the Latin and Greek *adamas* which means "hard as steel" or a hard stone—invincible. The word diamond originated from adamant. Flint is a hard gray rock. Therefore, God fortified Ezekiel's mindset to be unpersuaded and unshakeable, to empower him to boldly confront the idolaters with God's prophetic warnings. There were two opposing ideologies. The forehead is the *seat* of the mind. It is the *seat* of all decision making. It is the place where we "make up our minds." There is an idiom, "to seal the deal" which means to make an agreement official, to solidify, or finalize. The faithful remnant of God will solidify their decision to accept the true and living God and obey all the commandments thereby receiving the "seal of approval" and thereby "seal their fate" in God.

> "A mark which angels read—(Eph 1:13 quoted.) What is the seal of the living God, which is placed in the foreheads of His people? It is a mark which angels, but not human eyes, can read; for the destroying angel must see this mark of redemption. The angel with the writer's ink horn is to place a mark upon the foreheads of all who are separated from sin and sinners, and the destroying angel follows this angel (Rev 7:2.) Seal is a settling into truth—just as soon as the people of God are sealed in their foreheads—it is not any seal or mark that can be seen, *but a settling into the truth, both intellectually and spiritually, so they cannot be moved*—just as soon as God's people are sealed and prepared for the shaking, it will come. Indeed, it has begun already, the judgments of God are now upon the land, to give us warning, that we may know what is coming."[11]

Eph 1:13—"In whom ye also trusted, after that ye heard the word of truth, the gospel of your salvation, in whom also after that ye believed, ye were sealed with that holy Spirit of promise."

Rev 14:1—"And I looked, and, lo, a Lamb stood on the mount Sion, and with him a hundred forty and four thousand, having his Father's name written in their foreheads."

Rev 22:3-4—"And there shall be no more curse, but the throne of God and of the Lamb shall be in it, and his servants shall serve him. And they shall see his face, and his name shall be in their foreheads."

---

11. White, *Manuscript*, 173.

The mark of God sealed into the forehead is the "settling into the truth" of God's word, commandments, laws, and testimonies—in faithful obedience to the living God. The seal of God also encompasses the acceptance and obedience to the Sabbath truth (the fourth commandment.) The name of God is also in their foreheads because they reflect the character of God.

> Fun Fact: The forehead is an area of the head bounded by three features; two of the skull and one of the scalp.

Mark of the Beast

In a futile effort to usurp God and control humanity, Satan will attempt to copy the seal of God by enforcing the mark of the beast. Anyone who rejects God's words or commandments will be adapting the mindset and ideology of the dragon (Satan) and the beast. God's final three angels' messages are warnings to the earth not to accept false worship, false doctrines nor its idolatrous practices. Those who accept the mark of the beast will be anyone who accepts or takes part in false religions, the false sabbath, or adheres to false doctrines. This group will also include those who take a neutral stance and by default will not be sealed by God. The mark (seal) of God versus the mark of the beast is played out in the battlefield of the mind. The war is over worship and allegiance. There is a war to capture the minds of mankind; this is the real Armageddon. Receiving the seal of God versus the mark of the beast is the climax of the ages, upon which the souls of all humanity hinges. We will now reexamine some key verses that will unmask key characteristics of the beast and its mark.

> Rev 13:11-18—"And I beheld another beast coming up out of the earth and he had two horns like a lamb, and he spake as a dragon. And he exerciseth all the power of the first beast before him, and causeth the earth and them which dwell therein to worship the first beast, whose deadly wound was healed. And he doeth great wonders, so that he maketh fire come down from heaven on the earth in the sight of men, and deceiveth them that dwell on the earth by the means of those miracles which he had power to do in the sight of the beast, saying to them that dwell on the earth, that they should make an image to the beast, which had the wound by a sword, and did live. And he had power to give life unto the image of the beast, that the image of the beast

should both speak, and cause that as many as would not worship the image of the beast should be killed. And he causeth all, both small and great, rich and poor, free and bond, to receive a mark in their right hand, or in their foreheads, and that no man might buy or sell, save he that had the mark, or the name of the beast, or the number of his name. Here is wisdom, let him that hath understanding count the number of the beast, for it is the number of a man, and his number is six hundred threescore and six."

Rev 14:9–12—"And the third angel followed them, saying with a loud voice, 'if any man worship the beast and his image, and receive his mark in his forehead, or in his hand, the same shall drink of the wine of the wrath of God, which is poured out without mixture into the cup of his indignation, and he shall be tormented with fire and brimstone in the presence of the holy angels, and in the presence of the Lamb.' And the smoke of their torment ascendeth up forever and ever, and they have no rest day nor night, who worship the beast and his image, and whosoever receiveth the mark of his name. Here is the patience of the saints, here are they that keep the commandments of God, and the faith of Jesus."

Rev 16:2—"And the first went and poured out his vial upon the earth and there fell a noisome and grievous sore upon the men which had the mark of the beast, and upon them which worshipped his image."

Rev 19:20—"And the beast was taken, and with him the false prophet that wrought miracles before him, with which he deceived them that had received the mark of the beast, and them that worshipped his image. These both were cast alive into a lake of fire burning with brimstone."

Rev 20:4—"And I saw thrones, and they sat upon them, and judgment was given unto them, and I saw the souls of them that were beheaded for the witness of Jesus, and for the Word of God, and which had not worshipped the beast, neither his image, neither had received his mark upon their foreheads, or in their hands, and they lived and reigned with Christ a thousand years."

The common thread in all these verses is the word *worship*—it will be an end-time spiritual warfare. The word *worship* appears seventy-three times in the New Testament and strikingly, twenty-two of these references are in the end-time prophetic book of Revelation.

CHARACTERISTICS OF THE BEAST AND ITS MARK

- Forces or mandates worship
- Forces all to receive mark in the hand or forehead
- Persecutes and slaughter those who do not worship or receives its mark
- Prohibits buying and selling to those who refuse its mark, name, or number
- Receiving the mark means giving allegiance to the beast
- Having the name of the beast means adapting its character of disobedience to God
- Number of the beast is number of man = 666 (papal "Vicarius Filii Dei"/Vicar of Christ)

How will the mark of the beast unfold in the last days? The trojan horse that will be used as a springboard for the mark of the beast is the mandated or enforcement of Sunday worship, i.e., the Sunday Law. The trojan horse that will be used to springboard the Sunday Law mandate might be pandemics, pestilences, natural disasters, economic financial collapses, civil unrest, political strife etc. Revelation identifies two beasts—the first beast, papal Rome and the second beast, the United States of America. These beasts along with false prophets, false churches, and apostate Protestantism will align, thus giving their allegiance to the mindset of the dragon (Satan.) This unholy alliance between church and state will be the catalyst for the lamblike beast (America) to enact pseudo-religious laws enforcing worship. These laws will be adapted globally. "These have one mind and shall give their power and strength unto the beast" (Rev 17:13.)

MARK OF BEAST—IN THE HAND OR FOREHEAD

Unlike the seal of God, which is only in the forehead, the mark of the beast will be in the hand or forehead. Forehead is the mind and the seat of all decision making. Those who receive the mark of the beast in their forehead will be deceived and will accede to the false religious doctrines and participate in mandated false worship. They will mentally accept and believe the tenets of the beast system. Those who receive the mark in their hands will not necessarily believe the false doctrines but acquiesce for the convenience of being able to buy and sell or to not lose cherished comforts. This lack of faith in God who promises to provide for their needs will be evident once they align with the beast power.

Forehead—What's in a Name?

The Latin word for forehead is *imminens fronti pontificis*. Latin was the mother language of Rome.

> *Imminens* = projecting, threatening, menacing
>
> *Fronti* = on forehead
>
> *pontificis* = Roman supreme college of priests, pope

Therefore, the mark of the beast will be a threatening enforcement of false worship; seeking to indoctrinate and control the mindset of humanity in the form of a mandated Sunday Law worship. This is done in defiance of God's true Sabbath, the seventh day of the week. God's true Sabbath is from sunset Friday to sunset Saturday. True worship is never forced or coerced. The true God never forces worship. Worship should be done out of love for God and the sacrifice of Jesus Christ in the power of the Holy Spirit. The three angels' messages are given from a loving and long-suffering God to warn of the dangers of forming an alliance with the beast and accepting the mark of the beast. The first vial of God's wrath will be upon those who receive the mark of the beast.

> Rev 16:1-2—"And I heard a great voice out of the temple saying to the seven angels, 'go your ways, and pour out the vials of the wrath of God upon the earth.' And the first went, and poured out his vial upon the earth, and there fell a noisome and grievous sore upon the men which had the mark of the beast, and upon them which worshipped his image."
>
> Question to ponder: To whom will you give your allegiance

For many, a mandated Sunday Law might seem far-fetched, however the Bible and prophecy foretells of events soon to take place that will signal its approach. Since the emergence of the covid pandemic the world has plateaued to a new era of globalization and unification of enforced mandates that the planet has never seen before. If mandates are enforced globally for health reasons, could they be enforced for worship?

Will church and state unite and how will this unfold? Which religious institution will be involved?

In an open letter to celebrate the World Day of Prayer for the Care of Creation, dated September 1, 2020, the papacy highlighted the need to develop new ways of living in light of the pandemic. Key points highlighted were restoration and rest for the earth and all creation, a return to a simpler lifestyle, energy usage, consumption, transportation, diet, trade, transport of goods, cancellation of debt to poorer nations, social justice, legislation and investment for the common good, global goals, social goals, and environmental goals, emission reduction, and a call for the U.N. to safeguard thirty percent of earth as protected habitats by 2030. This lengthy list was a religio-political laced message; a directive addressed to the U.N., world leaders, economic leaders, faith communities, and the general populace to come together to perhaps reshape the world into a one world government for the betterment of the "common good." It also emphasized the need for the world and creation to return to the rhythm of Sabbath "rest." It is also interesting to note that posters promoting Earth Day or creation, or the jubilee of the earth featured the sun as a prominent fixture. The cross is placed over the sun, worshippers raise their hands towards the sun, or kneel in front of the sun, or the Vatican logo is placed over the sun. The Earth Day poster of April 2020 also featured a postage stamp with the number thirty. Is this a reference to the year 2030, which is a U.N. led agenda for the transformation of the world towards "sustainable development" as stated openly on their website? Are church and state clasping hands? What was the historical origin of church, state, and sun worship? This dates back to the pagan Roman Empire. Emperor Constantine was a pagan monotheist, and an admirer of the sun god Sol Invictus—the unconquered sun. Before the Milvian Bridge battle (October 28, 312), he and his army saw a cross of light in the sky above the sun with words in Greek that are generally translated into Latin as *in hoc signo vinces* (in this sign conquer.)[12] The sign was composed of two Greek letters, *chi* and *rho*, X and P superimposed over each other. ☧—the Chi Rho symbol is still used in many religions although its origin is pagan. The cross superimposed over the sun is a symbol of sun worship. Constantine became the first emperor to convert to Christianity and is responsible for the change of the Sabbath (seventh day of worship) to Sunday (first day of the week.) Church and state clasped hands

---

12. Wikipedia.org, s.v., "Constantine."

through the legislation of sun worship when Constantine modernized it into Sunday as a worship day (sun's day.) Scripture and prophecy foretell that church and state will again unite to legislate and mandate this false worship—this will be the mark of the beast. There will be a renewed mandated Sunday Law. If God is urgently calling his people out of Babylon's false churches and false worship, where should they go? Who or what is God's remnant church?

True Remnant Church

How does Scripture define the true remnant church and what are the qualifiers and key indicators? A remnant means residual remainder, a small surviving group.

> John 10:16—"And other sheep I have, which are not of this fold, them also I must bring, and they shall hear my voice, and there shall be *one fold, and one shepherd.*"
>
> Jer 23:3—"And I will gather the *remnant of my flock out of all countries* whither I have driven them, and will bring them again to their folds, and they shall be fruitful and increase."
>
> Rom 11:4-5—"But what saith the answer of God unto him? I have reserved to myself seven thousand men, *who have not bowed the knee to the image of Baal.* Even so then at this present time also *there is a remnant according to the election of grace.*"
>
> John 4:23-24—"But the hour cometh, and now is, when the *true worshippers shall worship the Father in spirit and in truth,* for the Father seeketh such to worship him. God is a Spirit and they that worship him *must worship him in spirit and in truth.*"
>
> Rev 12:17—"And the dragon was wroth with the woman and went to make war with the remnant of her seed, which *keep the commandments of God, and have the testimony of Jesus Christ.*"
>
> Rev 19:10—"And I fell at his feet to worship him. And he said unto me, 'see thou do it not, I am thy fellow servant, and of thy brethren that have the testimony of Jesus, worship God; for the *testimony of Jesus is the spirit of prophecy.*'"
>
> Rev 12:4-6—"And his tail drew the third part of the stars of heaven, and did cast them to the earth, and the dragon stood before the woman, which was ready to be delivered, for to devour her child as soon as it was born. And she brought forth a

man child, who was to rule all nations with a rod of iron, and her child was caught up unto God, and to his throne. And *the woman fled into the wilderness,* where she hath a place prepared of God, that they should feed her there *a thousand two hundred and threescore days."*

Rev 14:12—"Here is the patience of the saints, here are they that *keep the commandments of God, and the faith of Jesus."*

Rev 11:13—"And the same hour was there a great earthquake, and the tenth part of the city fell, and in the earthquake were slain of men seven thousand, and the remnant were affrighted, and *gave glory to the God of heaven."*

Characteristics of the Remnant Church

- Believes in the triune Godhead—Father (God), son (Jesus), and the Holy Spirit (Comforter)
- Worships in spirit and truth
- Keeps all the commandments of God
- Has the faith of Jesus
- Has the testimony of Jesus, which is the spirit of prophecy
- Is persecuted by the dragon (Satan) and fled into the wilderness for 1260 prophetic days (1260 years)
- Arises after the 1260 years of being in wilderness; after the Dark Ages, i.e., after 1798
- Has not bowed to Baal, i.e., does not partake in worship of the sun, memorialized as Sunday worship, that was constituted by Roman Empire Constantine in AD 321
- Remnant will be gathered from all countries and all denominations into one core fold

Spirit and Truth—in a conversation with the woman at the well in Samaria, Jesus expounded on what it means to worship God in spirit and in truth. It means that one does not have to go to a physical place, i.e., a religious site, temple, or shrine to worship God. God is an omnipresent Spirit, who can be worshipped anywhere and at any time. The Holy

Spirit is also an omnipresent force of the Godhead that is accessible at any time and at anywhere. God desires a personal intimate relationship with mankind. He desires that we worship with a reverend and contrite heart of faith.

> John 4:21,23-24—"Jesus saith unto her, 'woman, believe me, the hour cometh, when ye shall neither in this mountain, nor yet at Jerusalem, worship the Father. But the hour cometh, and now is, when the true worshippers shall worship the Father in *spirit and in truth*, for the Father seeketh such to worship him. God is a Spirit, *and they that worship him must worship him in spirit and in truth.*'"

> John 15:26—"But when the *Comforter is come*, whom I will send unto you *from the Father, even the Spirit of truth*, which proceedeth from the Father, he shall testify of me."

> 2 Thess 2:13—"But we are bound to give thanks always to God for you, brethren beloved of the Lord, because God hath from the beginning chosen you to salvation through *sanctification of the Spirit and belief of the truth*."

> 1 John 5:5-6—"Who is he that overcometh the world, but he that believeth that Jesus is the Son of God? This is he that came by water and blood, even Jesus Christ not by water only, but by water and blood. And it is the Spirit that beareth witness because the *Spirit is truth*."

What is truth? There are three key definitions of truth in the Bible; Jesus, the word, and the commandments.

> John 14:6—"Jesus saith unto him, I am the way, the truth, and the life, no man cometh unto the Father, but by me."

> John 17:17—"Sanctify them through thy truth; thy word is truth."

> Ps 119:151—" Thou art near, O Lord, and all thy commandments are truth."

God's true remnant church worships the triune Godhead in spirit and truth. The remnant church also keeps all the commandments and has the testimony of Jesus, i.e., the spirit of prophecy. It believes in and teaches prophecy. This church keeps the seventh-day Sabbath holy. This church came into fruition after the wilderness experience when Christians from various denominations fled persecutions during the Dark Ages.

There is a particular church that fits these qualifiers, and this is the Seventh-day Adventist Church, which came into fruition around the 1860s.

> "Before becoming Seventh-day Adventists, the founders of the denomination were sitting in the pews of other protestant churches in the early-to-mid 1800s. They were farmers, lawyers, teachers, and a handful of Adventism's prominent early leaders were already involved in pastoral ministry. The roots of Adventism can be traced back to the Second Great Awakening, which inspired a spirit of revival throughout the United States in the late 1700s and early 1800s. More people had Bibles in their homes and began to study Scripture themselves rather than leaving that to the clergy. Many biblical truths were brought back into light, such as the seventh-day Sabbath and the literal Second Coming of Christ. Tent meetings and Bible studies led people to a deeper understanding of God's love and his plans for humanity. People began to crave a more authentic Christian walk, beyond the traditions and rituals that had been routine for so long. Several separate groups of these devout Christians were dispersed throughout the northeastern United States. But God brought them together, and what began as the "Advent Movement" is now a worldwide Christian protestant denomination with over twenty million members"[13]

The triune Godhead has given three final salvific messages via the three angels. These are the three final breaking news for planet earth. These are and will be the most important and urgent messages that must be preached throughout the ends of the earth as we near the soon return of Christ. The angels flew swiftly and cried with loud voices imparts a sense of urgency to all to return to true worship and to flee false worship before the plagues of punishment fall. A call for the revival of the Advent Movement undergirds these messages. God desires that no one should perish but heed these warning messages. The epic spiritual battle of the ages is about to reach a climactic conclusion—light versus darkness, life versus death, likeness versus diverseness, truth versus lies, and love versus fear.

---

13. www.adventist.org, s.v., "Adventist."

— 16 —

3 Verbs, 1 Action
Love

(Give. Believe. Live)

John 3:16—"For God so loved the world, that he *gave* his only begotten Son, that whosoever *believeth* in him should not perish, but have everlasting *life*."

The Godhead's definition of love encompasses three core attributes; to give, to believe, and to live.

love = giving + believing + living

The suffix "ive" means a tendency, causing, making something happen, inclination, nature of character, or belonging to. These are all action words. The suffix "eve" means living. It is derived from the Hebrew *chawah* or *chayah*, which means to live or to breathe. The first woman was called Eve which means mother of all living (Gen 3:20.) The Hebrew word for love is *ahava*. Ahava also means to give. God is love, that is why he gave. You cannot love without having a natural inclination to give. Love is an action with three verbs. The carnal understanding of love is focused on self-pleasure, emotions, and feelings. However true love is the act of giving, believing, and living. The immeasurable depth of God's love towards humanity is the giving of his son Jesus Christ. The immeasurable depth of Jesus' love for humanity is the giving of his life for us. This was and is the greatest act of love.

Give—Heart

"For God so loved the world that he gave his only begotten son..."
Giving Jesus to us was akin to a heart transplant. God gave us his heart when he gave us Jesus.

> John 1:17-18—"For the law was given by Moses, but grace and truth came by Jesus Christ. No man hath seen God at any time, the only begotten Son, which is in the bosom of the Father, he hath declared him."
>
> Luke 23:34—"Then said Jesus, 'Father, forgive them, for they know not what they do.' And they parted his raiment and cast lots."
>
> Luke 7:47—"Wherefore I say unto thee, her sins, which are many, are forgiven, for she loved much, but to whom little is forgiven, the same loveth little."

Reciprocating God's love is to accept his heart in the form of his son Jesus Christ. The forgiveness of sin through Jesus Christ is God's great demonstration of his love. The word forgive consists of two words—for and give. The word "give" anchors this word. Forgiving someone of a trespass is an act of giving love.

Believe—Mind (Brain)

"... that whosoever believeth in him..."
Giving Jesus was akin to a mind (brain) transplant from God. Believing is central to the mind; it all starts in the mind. It is the medium through which God communicates with mankind.

> John 16:27—"For the Father himself loveth you, because ye have loved me, and have believed that I came out from God."
>
> 1 John 5:7—"Whosoever believeth that Jesus is the Christ is born of God, and everyone that loveth him that begat loveth him also that is begotten of him."

> Phil 2:5-8—"Let this mind be in you, which was also in Christ Jesus. Who, being in the form of God, thought it not robbery to be equal with God. But made himself of no reputation, and took upon him the form of a servant, and was made in the likeness of men. And being found in fashion as a man, he humbled himself, and became obedient unto death, even the death of the cross."

God's desire for us to believe in him was revealed when he gave his son Jesus. Believing requires trusting and this begins with a new mindset. Believing is a requirement of love. Reciprocating that love is to truly believe in the triune Godhead. We also reciprocate that love when we choose to submit our mind and thoughts to God, spiritual thoughts over carnal thoughts.

> Rom 12:2—"And be not conformed to this world but be ye transformed by the renewing of your mind, that ye may prove what is that good, and acceptable, and perfect, will of God."
>
> Rom 8:6—"For to be carnally minded is death, but to be spiritually minded is life and peace."
>
> 2 Tim 1:7—"For God hath not given us the spirit of fear but of power, and of love, and of a sound mind."

Live—Soul (Blood)

". . . should not perish but have everlasting life."
Giving Jesus was analogous to a blood transfusion. Life is in the blood. Jesus shed his precious blood to demonstrate his love. Reciprocating that love is to accept Christ and the sacrifice of his shed blood which afforded everyone eternal life.

> Rev 1:5—"And from Jesus Christ, who is the faithful witness, and the first begotten of the dead, and the prince of the kings of the earth. Unto him that loved us and washed us from our sins in his own blood."
>
> John 15:13—"Greater love hath no man than this, that a man lay down his life for his friends."
>
> John 6:53—"Then Jesus said unto them, 'verily, verily, I say unto you, except ye eat the flesh of the Son of man, and drink his blood, ye have no life in you.'"

God gave his heart, his mind, and his soul through his beloved son Jesus. God poured everything out when he gave Jesus. The human race was dead in sin and on spiritual life support, God intervened and sent his only begotten son to save us. Mankind is the recipient of a heart transplant, a brain (mind) transplant, and blood transfusion (soul.) Reciprocating that love is to love the Godhead with all our heart, mind, and soul. There are three occurrences in Scripture that these three key words are spoken together by Jesus and recorded by three apostles.

> Matt 22:37—"Jesus said unto him, 'thou shalt love the Lord thy God with all thy heart, and with all thy soul, and with all thy mind.'"

> Mark 12:30—"And thou shalt love the Lord thy God with all thy heart, and with all thy soul, and with all thy mind, and with all thy strength, this is the first commandment."

> Luke 10:27—"And he answering said, 'thou shalt love the Lord thy God with all thy heart, and with all thy soul, and with all thy strength, and with all thy mind, and thy neighbor as thyself.'"

Modern-Day Love

A heart is often used as a symbol for love. This is fitting as it is the heart that pumps the life-giving blood throughout the body. There are four categories of love.

- Agape—God's love for mankind and mankind's love for God
- Philia—brotherly love for each other
- Eros—romantic love
- Storage—familial love (family)

Although there are different kinds of love, the core foundation for expressing love should be giving, believing, and living. Ahava means to give, and it also means love. Love begins with giving, not seeking to get or take. Believing means to establish trust and have faith in someone or the principles they represent. Living means nurturing and being nurtured in a loving relationship. It is being alive, happy, joyful, and engaging each other in a lifelong journey with God, or in a marriage with a spouse, or with family, or friends. We live in a world where sin and selfishness has marred the true essence of what God intended love to be. Our world today reflects three types of interpersonal love relationships. Scenarios one and two are toxic love; the third is the ideal.

1. To be in someone's life but not a part of it
2. To be a part of someone's life but not really in it
3. To be in someone's life and be a part of it

"I Am in Your Life but, Not a Part of It"

This scenario describes a couple that are in a relationship but are living separate lives. They do not share mutual experiences, e.g., rarely go out together, rarely share common interests, or hobbies and do not effectively communicate. They are a couple in name only. There are some internal expressions of love but no overt external expressions of love. Oftentimes, Christians have a similar lukewarm relationship with God. God is in their life but is not a daily part of it. They rarely attend church (virtual or otherwise), they rarely spend time in the Scripture or in prayer, yet they profess their belief in God. They have a surface relationship and only seek God in an emergency or in times of need. They have some internal expressions of love or belief towards God but rarely transfer this externally.

> Isa 4:1—"And in that day seven women shall take hold of one man, saying, we will eat our own bread, and wear our own apparel, only let us be called by thy name, to take away our reproach."

They seek God only in name only and do not desire a deep, committed, and spiritually exclusive relationship.

"I Am a Part of Your Life but, I Am Not Really in It"

They are not really in an exclusively committed relationship but are emotionally connected. One person may even feel like an adjunct—marginally, emotionally attached to the other. They may do things together, e.g., go out on dates, but one party cannot or will not give full commitment or access to their heart. There are some external expressions of love but no strong, solid internal love connection. Parallels can be drawn to those who embrace God as being a part of their life, but they do not make him the center of their life. They believe in him but are unwilling to totally surrender to his commands. They have a form of godliness but deny the power thereof (2 Tim 3:5.)

> 1 John 2:15—"Love not the world, neither the things that are in the world. If any man love the world, the love of the Father is not in him."

> Matt 6:24—"No man can serve two masters, for either he will hate the one, and love the other, or else he will hold to the one, and despise the other. Ye cannot serve God and mammon."

"I Am in Your Life, and I Am a Part of It"

Both are in a committed relationship, and both make each other an inclusive and exclusive partner. They spend quality time together and enjoy doing things together. Both still have their own identity but are connected and deeply in love. Their strong internal love for each other is expressed externally. This should also be the ideal in our relationship with God. God must be in our lives internally and also be reflected externally. We must be a part of Christ and also be in Christ. Externally showing that Christ lives internally by the power of the abiding Holy Spirit.

> 2 Cor 5:17—"Therefore if any man be in Christ, he is a new creature, old things are passed away, behold, all things are become new."

> Gal 3:27—"For as many of you as have been baptized into Christ have put on Christ."

> Eph 2:10—"For we are his workmanship, created in Christ Jesus unto good works, which God hath before ordained that we should walk in them."

> 1 Cor 6:19-20—"What, know ye not that your body is the temple of the Holy Ghost which is in you, which ye have of God, and ye are not your own? For ye are bought with a price, therefore glorify God in your body, and in your spirit, which are God's."

The triune Godhead has the perfect ideal love relationship. The Father loved the son and revealed all things unto him and included Jesus in all aspects of the work (John 5:20.) God empowered Jesus with the Holy Spirit to aid and guide him throughout his earthly ministry. The external expression of this anointing was evident in miracles, healings, teaching, casting out of devils etc. True internal love must be expressed externally. The heavenly Father showed his love for us by giving us Jesus that whosoever believes in him will not perish but have everlasting life (John 3:16.) Jesus was this external expression of God's love—the fruit and Word that became flesh. The gift of the Holy Spirit, the Comforter is the active internal love connecting us to Jesus and the Father. Similarly, a Christian that loves Christ must bear internal and external fruits. Parallels can also be drawn to the seed, fruit, and tree. The seed is internal, the fruit is external, and the tree is everlasting. Giving is external, believing is internal and living is everlasting. The ideal love relationship must encompass giving, believing, and living. Both parties give all of themselves to each other. Giving is not restricted to giving gifts or things but giving of your heart, your time, talent, and your support. They believe in each other and trust their hearts with each other. They feel free to express themselves in a safe, happy connection and build that love by effectively communicating and sharing their emotions with each other in a Christ and God centered union.

Love Played as a Game

The wholesome purity of what God intended love to be, has been marred by human selfishness. Broken relationships arise when love is played out as a game. A broken relationship is the absence or deficiency in giving, believing, or living.

"*I am in your life but not a part of it*"—this is like being a guest invited to sit on the bench but not invited on the court to play in the game. This is like a cheerleader on the sideline cheering but not on the court nor in the game. This is like being a coach who is on the court but not really playing the game with you.

"*I am a part of your life but not really in it*"—this is like being a fan who sits in the bleachers cheering but not on the bench nor on the court nor in the game. This is like the water boy or girl bringing water to satisfy a temporary thirst or need but they are not in the game. This is like the mascot who wears a mask and offers jokes to boost you emotionally from the sideline but is not in the game.

What role have you been relegated to play? Are you a cheerleader, a guest, a fan, a coach, a mascot, or a player? Love was not intended to be played as a game. True, pure, wholesome love reflects the Godhead, for God is love. God is the source of true love.

Developing a Love Relationship with the Godhead

Jesus, and the Father want to be special guests who are invited into your life and become a part of your life.

> Luke 19:5—"And when Jesus came to the place, he looked up, and saw him, and said unto him, 'Zacchaeus, make haste, and come down, for today I must abide at thy house.'"

> Exod 25:8—"And let them make me a sanctuary, that I may dwell among them."

Jesus and the Holy Spirit want to be your cheerleader who is invited into your life to root for you and to encourage you.

> John 16:33—"These things I have spoken unto you, that in me ye might have peace. In the world ye shall have tribulation but be of good cheer, I have overcome the world."

> John 14:16-18—"And I will pray the Father, and he shall give you another Comforter, that he may abide with you forever, even the Spirit of truth whom the world cannot receive, because it seeth him not, neither knoweth him, but ye know him, for he dwelleth with you, and shall be in you. I will not leave you comfortless, I will come to you."

Jesus and the Holy Spirit want to be your coaches who are invited into your life to teach and guide you.

> Matt 11:29—"Take my yoke upon you, and learn of me, for I am meek and lowly in heart, and ye shall find rest unto your souls."

> John 14:26—"But the Comforter, which is the Holy Ghost, whom the Father will send in my name, he shall teach you all things, and bring all things to your remembrance, whatsoever I have said unto you."

Jesus and the Father want to satisfy your hunger and thirst and supply all your needs.

> John 6:35—"And Jesus said unto them, 'I am the bread of life, he that cometh to me shall never hunger and he that believeth on me shall never thirst.'"

> John 4:13-14—"Jesus answered and said unto her, 'whosoever drinketh of this water shall thirst again. But whosoever drinketh of the water that I shall give him shall never thirst, but the water

that I shall give him shall be in him a well of water springing up into everlasting life.'"

Phil 4:19—"But my God shall supply all your need according to his riches in glory by Christ Jesus."

There is a hunger in the human heart for love; an unquenchable thirst that only God can satisfy. God is the architect of true love. Sin marred this perfect design and tainted the human heart. Jesus, the perfect son of God, came to repair, restore, and reconnect us to the source of true love.

Rev 7:16–17—"They shall hunger no more, neither thirst anymore, neither shall the sun light on them, nor any heat. For the Lamb which is in the midst of the throne shall feed them and shall lead them unto living fountains of waters and God shall wipe away all tears from their eyes."

— 17 —

3 Thoughts, 1 Emotion

Fear

(Afraid. Naked. Hide)

These were the first three words of fear spoken on earth by Adam in the garden of Eden after he and his wife Eve had partaken of the forbidden fruit. Fear is the absence of love. Fear is the opposing force of love.

> Gen 3:6–10—"And when the woman saw that the tree was good for food, and that it was pleasant to the eyes, and a tree to be desired to make one wise, she took of the fruit thereof, and did eat, and gave also unto her husband with her, and he did eat. And the eyes of them both were opened, and they knew that they were naked, and they sewed fig leaves together, and made themselves aprons. And they heard the voice of the Lord God walking in the garden in the cool of the day and Adam and his wife hid themselves from the presence of the Lord God amongst the trees of the garden. And the Lord God called unto Adam, and said unto him, 'where art thou?' And he said, 'I heard thy voice in the garden, and I was *afraid*, because I was *naked*, and I *hid* myself.'"

The sin of disobedience brought fear into the hearts of our first parents—the emotional and moral DNA of humanity forever alerted. The human psyche now knew what it felt like to be fearful and emotionally separated from the loving heavenly Father. These three thoughts of being afraid, naked, and hiding one's shame, forever encapsulated the human genome giving birth to the emotion of fear. Fear was and still is a spiritual weapon used by the devil to attack the three areas of the human experience—physical (body), emotional (mind), and spiritual (soul.) Fear is spiritual warfare against humanity. It is interesting to note that the word warfare has the word "fare" as its anchor and these four letters spell "fear," and phonetically sound the same. We wrestle not against flesh or blood but against spiritual wickedness in high places (Eph 6:12.)

"I Was Afraid"

Adam felt afraid because he knew he had disobeyed God's command. He thought God would no longer love him because he had disobeyed. This fear came from the devil in the form of the serpent. Adam felt afraid of God and also afraid of the punishment of death. If Adam had remembered that God loved him unconditionally, he would not have said "I am afraid." Fear became a figment of the imagination. God did not abandon Adam and Eve but instead came down searching for them. "Where art thou?" was a rhetorical question. God knew Adam's physical location, but God wanted Adam to do some internal spiritual introspection and take responsibility for his actions. The weapon of fear seeks to separate man from God. God is love and the source of true love, so fear seeks to separate us from the source of love. It sought to separate Adam and Eve physically, emotionally, and spiritually. The voice of fear says, "I am afraid," "God will punish me," "no one will love me." But the voice of a loving God beckons, "come now, and let us reason together, though your sins be as scarlet, they shall be as white as snow, though they be red like crimson, they shall be as wool" (Isa 1:18.)

"I Was Naked"

> Gen 2:25—"And they were both naked, the man and his wife, and were not ashamed."

> Gen 3:7,21—"And the eyes of them both were opened, and they knew that they were naked, and they sewed fig leaves together, and made themselves aprons. Unto Adam also and to his wife did the Lord God make coats of skins and clothed them."

Before sin Adam and Eve were naked but not ashamed. After sin they became ashamed and sought to cover their shame with their own pseudo robes of righteousness (fig leaves.) Sin always seeks to cover up.

> Prov 28:13—"He that covereth his sins shall not prosper, but whoso confesseth and forsaketh them shall have mercy."

Their garments of fig leaves were not enough to cover their sins. This grave sin of disobedience required the shedding of blood. God made coats of skin to cover Adam and Eve, by shedding the blood of an animal (Gen 3:21.) This was the foreshadowing to the ultimate sacrifice of Jesus, who was slain to pay the penalty and redeem the world from sin. Being naked means feeling stripped of power, feeling powerless, loss of control, emotionally vulnerable, or exposed. The voice of fear says, "I have to cover my sins before I approach God," "I have to try to fix myself," "I can find my own salvation." The paradoxical deception in these emotions is the feeling of being exposed and powerless yet believing that you can fix or save yourself on your own. The only coverage for sin is the acceptance of Jesus and the merits of his shed blood. The voice of a loving God still beckons, "come now, and let us reason together, though your sins be as scarlet, they shall be as white as snow; though they be red like crimson, they shall be as wool."

"I Hid"

Adam and Eve hid themselves from the presence of God. They attempted to separate themselves physically from God. Not only were they hiding their shame behind fig leaves but they hid behind the trees. They attempted to put up layers and barriers between themselves and God, but in the presence of God there is no hiding place. Adam's attempt to hide from the all-knowing, all-seeing, all-powerful God was of unsound mind and thinking. The inner voice of fear says, "I must run away and flee from God's presence," "I am going to avoid going to church (virtual or otherwise), reading the Bible, or praying," "I am going to hide behind the busyness of my work or life rather than dedicate time with God." The attempt to avoid God is the attempt not to confront sin. Adam chose to run away from God instead of running away from sin. The voice of a loving God still beckons, "come now, and let us reason together, though your sins be as scarlet, they shall be as white as snow; though they be red like crimson, they shall be as wool."

Overcoming Fear

By biting into the forbidden fruit, the first parents bit off more than they could chew. They bit into the bait, and the world was now exposed to the spirit of fear and many other spiritual ills.

> 2 Tim 1:7—"For God hath not given us the spirit of fear but of power, and of love, and of a sound mind."

God did not give us a "spirit of fear" tells us that this is indeed a spiritual warfare. Fear is the absence of love. Fear is the absence of power. Fear is the absence of a sound mind (thinking.) Feeling fearful is to feel unloved, powerless, or experience irrational thoughts. The root cause of many phobias stem from one, two, or all three of these negative thoughts. Autophobia, the fear of being alone, stems from the fear of feeling unloved or being abandoned by loved ones. Oftentimes this fear is rooted in a childhood hurt of feeling unloved or being emotionally scarred as a child. Acrophobia, fear of height is to feel powerless because we feel vulnerable being at a high elevation. Unsound thinking fuels fear.

The stages of fear parallels Adam's verbal outcries when God confronted him.

- First, he felt afraid—*internal anguish or torment*
- Secondly, he said he was naked—*projecting his internal anguish externally*
- Thirdly, he hid—*flight or avoidance, running away physically or emotionally*

Glossophobia, the fear of public speaking, is to conjure negative internal anxious thoughts of what might happen or of what others might think. This internal anguish is then projected externally—sweaty palms, trembling, panic attack etc. Third phase is flight or to hide—stand behind the podium without moving around, avoid eye contact, or to back out and avoid public speaking altogether.

Adam felt afraid, he thought God would not love him. He felt and saw his nakedness and projected his internal feelings of not being loved to his external circumstance and made external coverings to pacify his inner fear and shame. Feeling powerless, he took flight—ran away and hid behind the trees. This scene has been playing out since the beginning of our first parents. The mirage of fear becomes real when we first allow ourselves to internalize negative self-talk. We might feel that someone doesn't love us, a parent, a child, a spouse, a boss, a friend etc. We then project this negative internal dialogue to our external circumstances, e.g., we try to make ourselves more physically attractive; we buy new clothes to cover up what we deem to be imperfections; we change or suppress our personality to please the other person; we try to please the other person at the expense of our own happiness etc. Feeling powerless we run away physically or emotionally, e.g., a child running away from home; couples running away from each other (divorce); partners avoiding each other though they live in the same house; avoiding conversation etc. How do we overcome fear? We overcome fear with love. Perfect love casts out all fear.

> 1 John 4:18—"There is no fear in love, but perfect love casteth out fear, because fear hath torment. He that feareth is not made perfect in love."

Fear, Disease, and Sin

If fear is a spiritual weapon of the devil to attack the body (physical), the emotions (mind), and soul (spiritual), what role does fear play in terms of disease and sin? What correlations can be made? Jesus encountered and addressed all three. The story is told in Luke 8:43–48 of the woman stricken for twelve years with a sickness, an issue of blood. She had spent all her savings on doctors but only grew worse. She heard about Jesus as he disembarked a ship and was being thronged by a crowd. She made up her mind to reach him, even if that meant limited access. She touched the border (hem) of his garment and was healed completely of her disease. Jesus publicly credited her healing to her faith and declared that virtue had left him. The woman had won this spiritual battle. Though her body was afflicted, her mind and spirit were not dissuaded. Jesus was highlighting perhaps to the others that had thronged him and were not healed, that they lacked faith. Lack of faith is the sin of doubt. The backdrop of this story is that Jesus was on his way to Jairus' house, whose daughter lay dying. While Jesus spoke to the woman, Jairus got word that his daughter had died. Jesus immediately admonished him to "fear not, believe only, and she shall be made whole" (Luke 8:50.) The connection between fear, disease (sickness), and sin is inextricably interwoven in this spiritual warfare. Scripture records many instances wherein Jesus healed and lovingly cautioned to "go and sin no more." Disease is also attributable to disobedience to God's health laws and lifestyle choices. The woman had spent all her living on physicians. If we were to contemporize this story, the woman would probably declare that she "trusted the science." She spent all and got nothing and was even worse; yet it took a little touch on Jesus' garment, and she became whole. Her mustard seed faith was enough.

The COVID-19 pandemic has brought to the forefront an epidemic of fear; an attack upon the human body, an attack upon the mind with fearful dread of what this virus has unleashed, and a spiritual attack as many have become depressed, suicidal, and faithless. Fear, as noted earlier, seeks to separate. During the pandemic families were separated, countries were locked down, isolation, standing six feet apart, no human-to-human hugs were the order of the day. The spiritual context of fear cannot be ignored. Fear causes anxiety, doubt, and feelings of hopelessness. These negative emotions within themselves cause sickness and disease. Throughout Scripture there are numerous declarations by the Godhead to "fear not." Love is the Godhead's weapon to fight fear. Love and faith in the Godhead cures all ills, anxiety, depression, hopelessness, doubt, faithlessness, and fear.

The Triune Godhead—The Source of True Love

The antidote for fear is love, power, and a sound mind. The triune Godhead were all active in the creation of mankind. We were created in the physical and emotional likeness of God. Before the entrance of sin, Adam and Eve had a perfect relationship with God. Sin brought the wedge of fear into the relationship. It was Adam and Eve who sought to run away from God. God's unfailing love for them, brought him down to the garden in pursuit of them, to repair that love relationship. The Godhead wants to repair all broken relationships in our lives. The Father, Son and Holy Spirit are all actively involved in restoring this love relationship.

> 1 John 4:8—"He that loveth not knoweth not God, for God is love."
>
> Phil 2:5—"Let this mind be in you, which was also in Christ Jesus."

Acts 1:8—"But ye shall receive power, after that the Holy Ghost is come upon you, and ye shall be witnesses unto me both in Jerusalem, and in all Judaea, and in Samaria, and unto the uttermost part of the earth."

To completely overcome fear, we must embody and reflect the love of God, have the mindset of Christ, and be filled with the power of the Holy Spirit. Reading God's word and obeying his commands is reflecting this love. In a world crippled by fear, it is only God's perfect love that can permanently cast out the root of all fears.

— 18 —

3 Keys, 1 City
Kingdom of the Godhead

(Book of Life. River of Life. Tree of Life)

"Key to the city" is a term coined that conveys an honor bestowed by a city upon esteemed residents and visitors.[1] It allows the recipient the privilege and honor of entering the city and partaking of what the city has to offer.

> Fun Fact: The term "key to the city" has its origin from medieval times. Ancient cities such as the city of Jericho were protected by defensive walled-in compounds with fortified gates. Cities were built as fortresses to protect the citizens inside from external barbaric invaders. The gates were guarded at day and locked at nights after curfew. Being given the key to the city was a gesture of trust and honor as the key would open the gate allowing access to the city and to enter and leave at free will. This tradition has carried over into contemporary times but is now an ornamental gesture to acknowledge someone's achievement or public status."[2]

What are the keys of access in the kingdom of God? The kingdom of heaven is God's throne (Isa 66:1; Matt 5:34.) This kingdom of the Godhead has a literal city. This walled and gated city is the heavenly New

---

1. Wikipedia.org, s.v., "keys to city."
2. Wikipedia.org, s.v., "keys to city."

Jerusalem (Rev 21:2.) Jerusalem in literal translation means "the city of peace." Jesus described New Jerusalem as the city of God (Rev 3:12.) There are three keys that will be discussed—the book of life which allows access to enter the city, the river of life, and the tree of life which allows access to emblems within the city.

Book of Life

The book of life represents God's judgment. God is a fair and just God. His kingdom is one of obedience, truth, justice, and judgment. There will be clear evidence for all to see in the examination of the books why some are lost whilst others are saved.

> Rev 21:10,27—"And he carried me away in the spirit to a great and high mountain, and shewed me that great city, the holy Jerusalem, descending out of heaven from God. And there shall in no wise enter into it anything that defileth, neither whatsoever worketh abomination, or maketh a lie, but they which are written in the Lamb's book of life."

> Rev 20:12,15—"And I saw the dead, small and great, stand before God, and the books were opened, and another book was opened, which is the book of life, and the dead were judged out of those things which were written in the books, according to their works. And whosoever was not found written in the book of life was cast into the lake of fire."

> Rev 3:5—"He that overcometh, the same shall be clothed in white raiment and I will not blot out his name out of the book of life, but I will confess his name before my Father, and before his angels."

> Rev 13:4,8—"And they worshipped the dragon which gave power unto the beast, and they worshipped the beast, saying, 'who is like unto the beast, who is able to make war with him?' And all that dwell upon the earth shall worship him, whose names are not written in the book of life of the Lamb slain from the foundation of the world."

The book of life is the book from which God will judge mankind. Those who overcome will be given white raiment which represent the righteousness of Christ. They will have their names written in the book of life. However, those that choose to worship the dragon and the beast, the antichrist system which includes false religions, will not have their names written in the book of life and will be cast into the lake of fire. The book of life is a book of names. The Hebrew word for name is *shem*. Shem means character. When Moses encountered God on Mount Sinai, God revealed to Moses his name or his character.

> Exod 34:5–7—"And the Lord descended in the cloud, and stood with him there, and proclaimed the name of the Lord. And the Lord passed by before him, and proclaimed, 'the Lord, the Lord God, merciful and gracious, longsuffering, and abundant in goodness and truth, keeping mercy for thousands, forgiving iniquity and transgression and sin, and that will by no means clear the guilty; visiting the iniquity of the fathers upon the children, and upon the children's children, unto the third and to the fourth generation.'"

Biblical names were given to people or places to reflect their purpose. The purpose then became the character. Jesus was given his name before birth because his purpose was to save mankind from sin (Matt 1:21.) His purpose became his character. He became our Savior because he lived in obedience to the commandments of God and fulfilled the purpose of God; perfectly reflecting the character of God. The prophet Isaiah called him Immanuel, which means "God with us." God was with man in the form of Jesus. Jesus came as our example to restore the character of God in man. Every human being is created with a divine purpose. It is freewill that will guide this purpose in two directions, either to reflect the character of Christ or the character of self, worldliness, and rebellion against God. Those who reflect the character of Christ will have their names written in the book of life also called the Lamb's book of life (Rev 21:27.)

The book of life is not just a one-dimensional list of names. It is multi-dimensional; it details the character of each individual. Jesus will confess our names, i.e., our character to the Father. Our advocate, Christ is now in the heavenly courtroom pleading our names to the Father, and our works before the great judgment seat. The works will be our character; not works of our hands as we are not saved by works but by grace through faith in Christ. We are now living in the anti-typical Day of Atonement; we do not know when our names will come up for review, so it is imperative that everyone accepts the free offer of salvation whilst it avails. This solemn time of probation is soon to close. Christ will take off his priestly robe and leave the Most Holy Place. Shortly thereafter he will return to earth to execute judgment. Before probation ends there will be a great final test upon the earth to determine whose name will remain in the book of life and whose names will be blotted out. Worship of the true God versus worship of the false god will be the ultimate decision. The true God is the Creator of heaven, the earth, and the sea, the Almighty living God. The false god is the dragon (Satan), the beast (false religions), and the false prophets. The true God who created all things also instituted a holy day of worship, i.e., the seventh-day Sabbath. Those who chose to receive the mark of the beast and acquiesce to the mandated worship on Sunday, instituted and enforced by the beast power (Roman Empire and papal system), will have their names blotted out of the book of life. Many are innocently in darkness, not aware of this change in the day of worship, but soon it will become clear that this pivotal axile of obedience hinges on allegiance and worship.

God cannot change his law or his commands because his law reflects his character. That is why God sent his only begotten and beloved son to pay the penalty for our sins and to reconcile mankind. The kingdom of God is a kingdom of love, but it is also a kingdom of obedience, truth, justice, and judgment. Receiving the key to the city and gaining access to the heavenly city means that our name must be written in the Lamb's book of life.

River of Life

The second emblem and key of access is the river of life.

> Rev 22:1—"And he shewed me a pure river of water of life, clear as crystal, proceeding out of the throne of God and of the Lamb."

John the Revelator describes in the prophetic book of Revelation a new heaven and a new earth and a holy city, new Jerusalem descending from heaven to earth. In this new earth is the river of life. The river of life is a literal river, but it also has beautiful spiritual analogies. Another word for river is stream. Spiritual symbolisms include:

- The Holy Spirit or God's breath (Isa 30:28,33)
- Peace (Isa 66:12)
- Judgment and righteousness (Amos 5:24)
- Gladness and happiness (Ps 46:4)

The book of Revelation notes that there will be no more sea (Rev 21:1.) Why is that? A popular and plausible hypothesis is that in the new city there will be no more separation of the nations. Countries today are separated by seas but in the New Jerusalem there will be no seas, all nations will be living together in this new holy city. Another possible explanation is that God wants to remove all reminders of death.

> Rev 21:1—"And I saw a new heaven and a new earth, for the first heaven and the first earth were passed away; and there was no more sea."
>
> Rev 20:12-15—"And I saw the dead, small and great, stand before God and the books were opened, and another book was opened, which is the book of life, and the dead were judged out of those things which were written in the books, according to their works. And the sea gave up the dead which were in it, and death and hell delivered up the dead which were in them, and they were judged every man according to their works. And death and hell were cast into the lake of fire. This is the second death. And whosoever was not found written in the book of life was cast into the lake of fire."

There are three things mentioned that yielded up the dead—the sea, death, and hell. The Hebrew word for hell is *sheol* which means the grave. The Bible refers to the grave as the pit.

> Isa 14:15—"Yet thou shalt be brought down to hell, to the sides of the pit."
>
> Isa 38:18—"For the grave cannot praise thee, death cannot celebrate thee; they that go down into the pit cannot hope for thy truth."
>
> Ezek 32:23—"Whose graves are set in the sides of the pit, and her company is roundabout her grave, all of them slain, fallen by the sword, which caused terror in the land of the living."
>
> Job 26:5-6—"Dead things are formed from under the waters, and the inhabitants thereof. Hell is naked before him, and destruction hath no covering."

The dead that are in the grave, the dead from the sea, and all others who died without being buried, e.g., those who were burned up, cremated, will be brought back to face the judgment of God. Death and hell (graves) will then be cast into the lake of fire, along with all those whose names are not in the book of life. This will be their second death. There will be no more death and no more hell (graves) and no more sea in the new earth. There will be no more reminders of death or anything that held death or represented death. They will be completely destroyed forever. Death will die and all reminders of death will be completely destroyed.

> Rev 21:4-8—"And God shall wipe away all tears from their eyes, and there shall be no more death, neither sorrow, nor crying, neither shall there be any more pain, for the former things are passed away. And he that sat upon the throne said, 'behold, I make all things new.' And he said unto me, 'write, for these words are true and faithful.' And he said unto me, 'It is done. I am Alpha and Omega, the beginning and the end. I will give unto him that is athirst of the fountain of the water of life freely. He that overcometh shall inherit all things, and I will be his God, and he shall be my son. But the fearful, and unbelieving, and the abominable, and murderers, and whoremongers, and sorcerers, and idolaters, and all liars, shall have their part in the lake which burneth with fire and brimstone, which is the second death.'"

God the Father, Jesus, and the abiding Holy Spirit desire that all will choose to partake of the river of life and that none be cast into the lake of fire. The kingdom of the Godhead is a kingdom of life, love, peace, gladness, judgment, and righteousness.

> Rev 7:17—"For the Lamb which is in the midst of the throne shall feed them, and shall lead them unto living fountains of waters, and God shall wipe away all tears from their eyes."

The Lamb (Jesus) will give us the key of access to the River of Life.

Tree of Life

> Gen 2:8-9—"And the Lord God planted a garden eastward in Eden, and there he put the man whom he had formed. And out of the ground made the Lord God to grow every tree that is pleasant to the sight, and good for food; the tree of life also in the midst of the garden, and the tree of knowledge of good and evil."

Trees have played a prominent role in the rise and fall of the human story. It all started with a tree and a fruit. There were three types or categories of trees that were in Eden—trees for food, the tree of the knowledge of good and evil, and the tree of life. The tree of the knowledge of good and evil was intended to be an emblem of obedience and trust between God and Adam. Eve was deceived and beguiled by the subtlety of the serpent who had disguised himself as an attractive creature and perched himself in the tree of the knowledge of good and evil. He engaged Eve in a deadly conversation that made her doubt the words of God and God's admonishment to not eat of that tree lest they would die. After eating the forbidden fruit, they realized that they were naked and made coverings of fig leaves and ran from God and hid behind trees. Leaves became a man-made apron; it was a covering and a cover-up for sin. God found them cowering in fear behind the trees and made them coats of skins. The first sacrifice for sin was in Eden, God had to sacrifice the life of an animal to clothe Adam and Eve. Unbeknownst to the first parents this was pointing to the coming Messiah, Jesus who would one day be the sacrificial Lamb for the whole human race.

The Hebrew word for apron is *chagowr* which means girdle. The first parents believed Satan's lies and in futility girdled themselves with human efforts of righteousness. The pandora's box of spiritual warfare now unleashed upon all mankind required a far greater armor of protection. The plan of redemption and salvation from the foundation of the world was Christ. The human heart must now be girded with the truth of God's word and his commandments and through the sacrificial merits of the righteousness of Christ and in his shed blood.

> Eph 6:12–17—"For we wrestle not against flesh and blood, but against principalities, against powers, against the rulers of the darkness of this world, against spiritual wickedness in high places. Wherefore take unto you the whole armor of God, that ye may be able to withstand in the evil day, and having done all, to stand. Stand therefore, having your loins girt about with truth, and having on the breastplate of righteousness, and your feet shod with the preparation of the gospel of peace. Above all, taking the shield of faith, wherewith ye shall be able to quench all the fiery darts of the wicked. And take the helmet of salvation, and the sword of the Spirit, which is the Word of God."

Paul admonishes in the book of Ephesians, that the first area to protect is the loins which must be girded with truth. The Bible identifies three definitions for truth; Jesus, God's word, and the commandments. These must be the first armor of defense in spiritual warfare. This spiritual warfare will not end until Christ returns to set up his earthly kingdom on earth. In the new holy city Jerusalem, there will be the tree of life.

> Rev 22:1–3,14—"And he shewed me a pure river of water of life, clear as crystal, proceeding out of the throne of God and of the Lamb. In the midst of the street of it, and on either side of the river, was there the tree of life, which bare twelve manner of fruits, and yielded her fruit every month, and the leaves of the tree were for the healing of the nations. And there shall be no more curse, but the throne of God and of the Lamb shall be in it, and his servants shall serve him. Blessed are they that do his commandments, that they may have right to the tree of life and may enter in through the gates into the city."
>
> Rev 2:7—"He that hath an ear, let him hear what the Spirit saith unto the churches, to him that overcometh will I give to eat of the tree of life, which is in the midst of the paradise of God."

This magnificent tree of life will yield twelve manners of fruits every month which the saints will partake of. The leaves will be for healing. There will be no physical sickness in heaven, so what will require healing? Perhaps there is a spiritual explanation for this. The Eden story is one marred by sin—leaves were used to cover-up sin, trees used as a hiding place from God, and the fruit eaten in disobedience. Curse and punishment followed suit. The serpent was cursed, the woman was punished, childbirth cursed, man punished, the ground cursed, and manual labor (work) became punishment. In making all things new again, God will make new experiences that will heal the old connections to past sins. Leaves and the tree will now be an emblem of spiritual restoration and healing for God's people. The key of access, the right to the tree of life is given by Jesus Christ in obedience to the commandments.

> Question to ponder: If Adam and Eve are in the New Jerusalem they will see the tree of life. What will they ask or think? We will not know until we get to heaven.

Emblems and Symbols in the Kingdom

Following the second coming of Christ, the righteous saints will be taken to heaven for one thousand years. After these one thousand years they will return with Christ in the holy city, New Jerusalem (Rev 20:4–6.) John in vision describes the beautiful and glorious new holy city as a bride coming down from heaven adorned for her husband.

> Rev 21:2–3—"And I John saw the holy city, new Jerusalem, coming down from God out of heaven, prepared as a bride adorned for her husband. And I heard a great voice out of heaven saying, 'behold, the tabernacle of God is with men, and he will dwell with them, and they shall be his people, and God himself shall be with them, and be their God.'"

What might some of the emblems and symbols be in New Jerusalem?

National Tree—the tree of life bearing twelve manner of fruits every month.

Currency—love is the currency of the kingdom of the Godhead. For it was God who so loved the world that he sent his beloved son Jesus to purchase mankind back with his own blood. Jesus himself said that there was no greater display of love than for a man to lay down his life for his friends. God's love cannot be bought or sold; it is a free gift. Gone will be the din of the earthly stock exchange trading floors. The value of gold will be relegated to the streets of the holy city, which will be made of pure gold. Precious gemstones will not be mined nor auctioned but will be gates, walls, and foundations.

> Rev 21:10–11,18–21—"And he carried me away in the spirit to a great and high mountain, and shewed me that great city, the holy Jerusalem, descending out of heaven from God, having the glory of God, and her light was like unto a stone most precious, even like a jasper stone, clear as crystal. And the building of the wall of it was of jasper and the city was pure gold, like unto clear glass. And the foundations of the wall of the city were garnished with all manner of precious stones. The first foundation was jasper, the second sapphire, the third a chalcedony, the fourth an emerald, the fifth sardonyx, the sixth sardius, the seventh chrysolyte, the eighth beryl, the ninth a topaz, the tenth a chrysoprasus, the eleventh a jacinth, and the twelfth an amethyst. And the twelve gates were twelve pearls, every several gate was of one pearl, and the street of the city was pure gold, as it were transparent glass."

Motto—perhaps the motto might be, "to love the Lord thy God with all thy heart, and with all thy soul, and with all thy mind, and to love thy neighbor as thyself."

> Matt 22:37–40—"Jesus said unto him, 'thou shalt love the Lord thy God with all thy heart, and with all thy soul, and with all thy mind. This is the first and great commandment. And the second

is like unto it, thou shalt love thy neighbor as thyself. On these two commandments hang all the law and the prophets.'"

Anthem—every nation has a national anthem, perhaps the anthem of New Jerusalem will be, "The Song of Moses and Song of the Lamb."

> Rev 15:2–4—"And I saw as it were a sea of glass mingled with fire and them that had gotten the victory over the beast, and over his image, and over his mark, and over the number of his name, stand on the sea of glass, having the harps of God. And they sing the song of Moses the servant of God, and the song of the Lamb, saying, 'great and marvelous are thy works, Lord God Almighty, just and true are thy ways, thou King of saints. Who shall not fear thee, O Lord, and glorify thy name, for thou only art holy, for all nations shall come and worship before thee, for thy judgments are made manifest.'"

The song of Moses is a song of deliverance that Moses and the children of Israel sang after God delivered them from the hands of Pharaoh and the Egyptian army. In the new Jerusalem, spiritual Israel and those who God will deliver from the antichrist, will join with Moses and the Israelites and sing the song of Moses and the song of the Lamb (Exod 15:1–18.)

Before Jesus departed to heaven, he told the disciples that he was going to prepare a place and return and reunite with them and take them to this heavenly place (John 14:1–4.) Heaven is real and so is the holy city, New Jerusalem. There is much that we do not know but will discover when God reveals it. "Eye hath not seen, nor ear heard, neither have entered into the heart of man, the things which God hath prepared for them that love him" (1 Cor 2:9.)

God's Story for Us

God's love for us is eternal and everlasting as demonstrated by the sacrifice of Jesus. God is a personal God who desires a personal relationship with each and every one of us. He has a specific purpose and plan for each of us. If God was to tell us his story for us it would be woven throughout the rugged terrain of our earthly journey as chronicled in Scripture.

> Jer 1:5—"Before I formed thee in the belly I knew thee, and before thou camest forth out of the womb I sanctified thee, and I ordained thee a prophet unto the nations."

> Gal 1:15-16—"But when it pleased God, who separated me from my mother's womb, and called me by his grace, to reveal his Son in me, that I might preach him among the heathen, immediately I conferred not with flesh and blood."
>
> Jer 29:11—"For I know the thoughts that I think toward you, saith the Lord, thoughts of peace, and not of evil, to give you an expected end."
>
> Luke 12:7—"But even the very hairs of your head are all numbered. Fear not therefore, ye are of more value than many sparrows."
>
> Ps 139:1-2;13-18—"O lord, thou hast searched me, and known me. Thou knowest my downsitting and mine uprising, thou understandest my thought afar off. For thou hast possessed my reins, thou hast covered me in my mother's womb. I will praise thee, for I am fearfully and wonderfully made, marvelous are thy works, and that my soul knoweth right well. My substance was not hid from thee, when I was made in secret, and curiously wrought in the lowest parts of the earth. Thine eyes did see my substance yet being unperfect and in thy book all my members were written, which in continuance were fashioned, when as yet there was none of them. How precious also are thy thoughts unto me, O God! how great is the sum of them! If I should count them, they are more in number than the sand, when I awake, I am still with thee."

Threefold Invitation from the Triune Godhead—"Come"

This beautiful invitation into the Kingdom of heaven is not just for the disciples but for all.

> Rev 22:16-17—"I Jesus have sent mine angel to testify unto you these things in the churches. I am the root and the offspring of David, and the bright and morning star. And the Spirit and the bride say, *'come.'* And let him that heareth say, *'come.'* And let him that is athirst *come*. And whosoever will, let him take the water of life freely."

This threefold appeal to "come" is extended to all from God the Father, Jesus Christ our Savior, and the Comforter the Holy Spirit—the true and faithful triune living Godhead!

— Appendix A —

Events and Occurrences with the Number Three

The theme of threes is profound. The triune Godhead co-exists, speaks, creates, orchestrates, acts, governs, and carries out judgment from a seat of trilateral power. Throughout Scripture we see the Godhead giving instructions to human agents requesting them to carry out tasks in threes, or on the third day or third hour, supernatural events at 3 pm or 3 am, punitive judgment of three curses, three choices, armies of three hundred, three thousand, plagues impacting one-third etc. Warring against the triune Godhead is the archenemy Satan. In a futile attempt to unseat the Godhead's authority, Satan deceived one-third of the angels. Since the expulsion from heaven for this act of rebellion, the spiritual warfare is still being waged on earth from the bowels of the false triunity—the dragon (Satan), beast (pagan and papal Rome), and the false prophets.

Questions to ponder: Why is there a superstitious folklore that death occurs in threes? Why is 3 am considered the witching hour when evil acts disturb the calm of night? Why are there secret societies called thirty-three? Why are news media and news headliners proliferated with the number three, thirteen, thirty-three? We have looked at various themes of three throughout this book, here are some more intriguing occurrences.

Events

- *Feasts*—three major pilgrimage festivals: Passover (feast of unleavened bread or Pesach), Pentecost (feast of harvest or Shavuot), and Tabernacle (feast of booths or Sukkot.)
- *Kingdom of Judah (Ezek 21:27)*—three declarations of "I will overturn, overturn, overturn" made by God for the punishment upon Judah.
- *Last-day events/seven last trumpets (Rev 8:7–13—9:15,18)*—one-third of trees burnt up, one-third of sea becomes blood, one-third of sea creatures die, one-third of ships destroyed, one-third of rivers and waters become bitter, one-third of sun, moon, and stars smitten and become darkened, one-third of day in darkness, thirty minutes (half hour) of silence in heaven, three "woes" uttered by an angel before the final three angels sound their trumpets, three weapons of punishment (hail, fire, and blood), one-third of man slain.
- *Pentecost (Acts 2:15,41)*—three cities mentioned by Jesus to the disciples that they were to begin witnessing to: Jerusalem, Judaea, and Samaria. Third hour of the day, around 9 am, the Holy Spirit fell upon them and they spoke in different tongues (languages.) Three thousand baptized.
- *Plagues in Egypt (Exod 10:22—11:5)*—three days of darkness during the ninth plague. The tenth plague was the death of the firstborn in three groups: firstborn of Pharaoh's household, the maidservant's household, and firstborn of beasts.
- *Spiritual warfare in heaven (Rev 12:4–7)*—one-third of rebellious angels cast out with Satan.

Heaven

- *God's throne/appearance (Rev 4:3)*—three gemstones: jasper, sardine, and emerald.
- *New Jerusalem/holy city (Rev 21:13)*—three sets of gates on each side: three on the east, three on the north, three on the south, and three on the west.

- *Proclamation (Rev 4:8)*—three words repeated of "holy, holy, holy" by four beasts.
- *Throne Room (Rev 4:5)*—three things proceed from the throne: lightning, thunder, and voices.
- *Worshippers (Rev 4:8–11—5:11)*—three categories of worshippers: beasts, elders, and angels.

Creation

- *Colors*—three primary colors: red, blue, and yellow. Three secondary colors: green, orange, and purple.
- *Core foundational elements*—time, space, and matter.
- *Earth*—third planet from the sun.
- *Elohim*—the divine name of God appears thirty-three times in the Genesis story of creation.
- *Galaxies*—three major types: elliptical, spiral, and irregular.
- *Heavens*—three heavens: first heaven (the atmosphere where the birds fly), the second (universe, galaxies, dark space), and third (throne of God/where God dwells.)
- *Light (Gen 1:14–16)*—three sources: sun, moon, and stars. Created for three purposes: signs, seasons, and days/years.
- *Matter*—three forms: solid, liquid, and gas.
- *Metal*—three is the atomic number for lithium and is the lightest of all metals.
- *Organisms*—three types of domains: bacteria, archaea, and eukarya
- *Rainbow*—three requirements of light: reflection, refraction, and dispersion.
- *Realms (Gen 1:6–25)*—heaven, earth, and sea.
- *Space*—three dimensions: length, width, and height.
- *Sun*—divided into three regions: the interior, the solar atmosphere (chromosphere and corona), and the surface (photosphere.) The interior has three main parts: the core, the radiative zone, and the convective zone.

- *Third day of creation (Gen 1:11)*—three things created: grass, herbs, and trees.
- *Time*—three segments: hour, minute, and second.
- *Water*—three forms: solid, liquid, and gas.

Human Anatomy

- *Brain*—three layers of protective coverings (meninges): dura mater (thick outermost layer), arachnoid (thin weblike layer), pia mater (thin membrane.) The brainstem is composed of three parts: midbrain, the pons, and medulla oblongata. The midbrain is divided into three parts: tectum, tegmentum, and ventral tegmental. There are three primary brain vesicles: prosencephalon, mesencephalon, and rhombencephalon.
- *Blood cells*—three types: red, white, and platelets.
- *Ear*—three parts: outer, middle, and inner. Three semicircular canals in the inner ear. Three ossicles (bones) in the middle ear.
- *Eye*—three layers: outer (fibrous tunic), middle (vascular tunic), and inner (retina.) Three types of color receptor cells in the retina; most humans are trichromatic. Most colors that humans can see are made of the three primary colors of red, blue, and yellow.
- *Foot*—three groups of muscles in sole of foot: muscles of big toe, muscles of little toe, and central muscle group.
- *Hair*—three zones of hair shaft: cuticle, cortex, and medulla. Three growth phases: anagen, catagen, and telogen. Three main aspects of hair textures: curl pattern, volume, and consistency. Three consistency of hair: fine, medium, and coarse.
- *Hand*—three phalanx bones in fingers: proximal, middle, and distal.
- *Heart*—three layers of tissue forms the heart wall. It is the first organ to develop and to beat and it begins pumping blood about three weeks into embryogenesis.
- *Intestine*—three regions in small intestine: duodenum, jejunum, and ileum. Three parts of large intestine: ascending, transverse, and descending.

- *Lungs*—three lobes in the right lungs.
- *Mankind*—three dimensions: mental, physical, and spiritual.
- *Muscle*—three main types: skeletal, smooth, and cardiac.
- *Neck*—three pairs of muscle in neck called scalene: anterior, middle, and posterior.
- *Nose*—three shell-like bones on the outer nasal cavity: superior, middle, and inferior conchae.
- *Pharynx*—three sections: nasopharynx, oropharynx, and laryngopharynx.
- *Pregnancy*—three trimesters.
- *Salivary glands*—three major glands: parotid, submandibular, and sublingual.
- *Spinal cord*—three main parts: cervical (neck), thoracic (chest), and lumbar (lower back.) Three functions of nerve messaging: controls body movement and functions, reports senses to the brain, and manages reflexes.
- *Skin*—three layers: epidermis, dermis, and hypodermis. Three main functions: protection, regulation, and sensation.
- *Skull*—three parts: neurocranium, sutures, and facial skeleton.
- *Stomach*—three parts: fundus, body, and pylorus.
- *Teeth*—three layers: enamel, dentin, and pulp. Three primary (deciduous) teeth: incisors, canine, and molars.
- *Vein*—three main layers: outer (connective tissue), middle layer (smooth muscle), inner layer (endothelial cells.)
- *Vertebrae (spine)*—thirty-three bones.

Religious Practices, Tenets, and Covenants

- *Parables (Matt 13:33; Luke 10:36—11:5—13:7—15:1-32—19:12-27)*—stories told by Jesus using simple illustrations to convey a heavenly spiritual lesson. The number three was often used for illustration. The expanding kingdom of heaven was likened to leaven which a woman hid in three measures of meal. Another parable highlighted the tenet of being a good neighbor and it identified three who passed by a wounded man; a priest, a Levite, and the good Samaritan. The parable to highlight the tenet that persistence is needed in prayer, showcased a friend who visited another friend at midnight seeking three loaves of bread for a friend who had visited unexpectedly. Though it was late, his persistence and the friendship they had was a stronger bond that overruled any inconveniences. The parable of the fig tree that bore no fruit for three years was used to highlight spiritual unfruitfulness. The parable of the three lost things: lost sheep, lost coin, and lost son. This highlighted spiritual loss, and the joy and triumph of being found and restored back to God. The parable on stewardship highlighted three servants who were entrusted with monetary blessings.

- *Peace offering (Lev 7:18)*—if eaten on the third day after being sacrificed it would not be accepted and became an abomination.
- *Pilgrimage Festivals (Exod 23:17)*—three major feast festivals that required all males to attend in Jerusalem: Passover or Pesach, Feast of Pentecost or Shavuot, and Feast of Tabernacle or Sukkot.
- *Purification after childbirth (Lev 12:4)*—according to Levitical laws, a new mother who gave birth to a son was required to go through purification an additional thirty-three days.
- *Ten Commandments (Exod 20:5)*—the second commandment denounces idolatry. God warns of punishment to the third and fourth generation.
- *Virtues*—three theological virtues: faith, hope, and charity (love.)

Bible Characters

- *Abimelech (Judg 9:22–23,43)*—a notorious ruler who reigned three years, then God sent an evil spirit between him and the men of Shechem. Divided his men into groups of three and ambushed the people of Shechem.
- *Abraham (Gen 15:9—18:2—22:4)*—God instructed him to sacrifice three animals, each three years old. Three men visited him, thought

to be angels. On the third day he arrived at Mount Moriah, the place God told him to sacrifice Isaac.

- *Absalom (2 Sam 18:14)*—killed by Joab with three arrows that pierced his heart.
- *Amos 1:3-11—2:1-6—4:7,12*—judgment on several nations, God did not withhold for three or four transgressions. God withheld rain three months before the harvest. Three areas people will run seeking the word in the last days: sea to sea, north to east, and to and fro.
- *Ananias and Sapphira (Acts 5:7)*—three hours apart they died for lying to the Holy Spirit.
- *Baalam (Num 22:32—24:10)*—blessed Israel three times. Struck his donkey three times.
- *Belshazzar (Dan 5:25)*—three words of judgment against him via a bloodless handwriting on the wall: mene, tekel, and upharsin.
- *Cornelius (Acts 10:3,7-8)*—Had a vision of an angel of God at 3 pm (ninth hour.) Sent three men to Joppa to call for Peter.
- *Daniel and his friends (Dan 1:5-7—3:12,23—5:29—6:10-12—8:1—10:1-3)*—Some of the Jewish captives were given the kings food for three years. Daniel and his three notable friends did not eat the king's food: Shadrach, Meshach, and Abednego. The three friends did not bow down to worship the golden image and were thrown into a fiery furnace. King Belshazzar offered to make him third in the kingdom. Prayed three times a day. A decree passed to ban worship for thirty days unless worship was given to the king. He had a vision in the third year of King Belshazzar. He had a vision of an angel in the third year of King Cyrus. Fasted for three weeks.
- *David (2 Sam 5:4-5—6:1—18:2—23:8-11—24:12-13)*—thirty years old when he began to reign and reigned for thirty-three years. Thirty thousand men chosen to take the Ark of Covenant to Jerusalem. Divided army in groups of three. Three mighty men were named in his army: Adino, Eleazar, and Shammah. God gave him three choices to choose his punishment for carrying out a census, as his motive was not pure—seven years of famine, three years fleeing from his enemies, or three days of pestilence.
- *Elijah (1 Kgs 17:21—18:1,34—19:11-12—2 Kgs 1:13-14; Luke 4:25)*—stretched himself over a sick child three times and cried unto

the Lord who restored the child. Prophesied of no rain for three and a half years. Three times he instructed the people to pour water on the sacrifice. God visited him on Mount Horeb and three events unfolded: strong wind, earthquake, and a still small voice. Three times fire came down and consumed the army of King Ahaziah.

- *Esther (Esth 4:16—8:9—5:1)*—called a three-day fast after the death decree was made against the Jews. In the third month, King Ahasuerus reversed the death decree. On the third day she went in to see the king to intervene for the Jewish people.

- *Ezekiel (Ezek 2:10—5:2,12)*—God delivered a scroll via a hand in which three things were written: lamentations, mourning, and woe. God instructed him to cut his hair and separate it in three parts: a third was to be burned in the midst of the city, a third was to be smitten with a knife, and a third scattered in the wind. These were three prophetic representations of Israel: a third was to die with pestilence and famine, a third was to fall by the sword, and a third scattered by the wind (dispersed from their homes.)

- *Ezra (Ezra 8:15—10:8)*—children of Israel camped in tents for three days on journey from Babylon to Jerusalem. Proclamation made that whoever did not gather in Jerusalem in three days would be forfeited from the congregation.

- *Gideon (Judg 7:7,16)*—three hundred men in the army who lapped the water were the chosen ones. Divided army of three hundred men into three groups.

- *Hannah (1 Sam 1:24)*—three bullocks offered as sacrifice when Samuel her son was dedicated to God.

- *Hezekiah (2 Kgs 20:5)*—God told him to go unto the house of the Lord on the third day after his healing.

- *Hosea (Hos 6:2)*—appeal to Israel to return to the Lord who will raise them up on the third day.

- *Ibzan (Judg 12:9)*—judge in Israel who had thirty sons and thirty daughters.

- *Isaiah (Isa 20:3)*—God's servant who walked naked and barefoot three years as a sign and wonder upon Egypt and Ethiopia.

- *Jacob (Gen 31:10)*—dreamt of three rams that were ringstraked, speckled, and grisled.

- *Jair (Judg 10:4)*—judge in Israel who had thirty sons who rode thirty colts and had thirty cities.
- *Jehoiakim (Dan 1:1)*—in his third year as king of Judah, Nebuchadnezzar, king of Babylon besieged Jerusalem.
- *Jeremiah (Jer 22:29—32:24—38:10,14—43:11)*—City fell to Chaldeans by three means: sword, famine, and pestilence. Thirty men freed him from the dungeon. King took him via the third entry of the house. Three curses against Egypt: "death to death," "captivity to captivity," and "sword to sword."
- *Jesse (1 Sam 17:13)*—three eldest sons joined Saul in battle: Eliab, Abinadab, and Shammah.
- *Job (Job 1:20—2:11)*—three friends; Eliphaz, Bildad, and Zophar.
- *Joel 2:19,23,28,30*—God promised to restore three things: corn, wine, and oil. God promised three outpourings: the rain, the former rain, and the latter rain. God promised to pour out the Spirit upon three groups: sons and daughters to prophesy, old men will dream dreams, and young men shall have visions. God will reveal three wonders in the heavens: blood, fire, and smoke.
- *John (Rev 1:19—14:2)*—three things Jesus told him to write about: things that he saw, things which are, and things that shall be. Heard three voices in vision from heaven: as the voice of many waters, voice of great thunder, and the voice of harpers harping.
- *Jonah 1:17*—three days and three nights in the whale's belly.
- *Jonathan (1 Sam 20:20,41)*—three arrows shot which was a signal for David as he hid from Saul. Three times David bowed before Jonathan.
- *Joseph (Gen 40:10-23—41:46—42:17)*—thirty years old when he appeared before Pharaoh. Dreamt of three branches and three baskets, which were interpreted to be three days. Placed his brothers in prison for three days.
- *Joshua (Josh 1:11—8:3)*—three days journey to cross Jordan into the promised land. Thirty thousand men of valor chosen to fight.
- *Judas (Matt 26:14-15)*—thirty pieces of silver was the pay he received to betray Jesus. Three hundred pence, the price Mary's oil could be sold for, as he berated her for using it to anoint Jesus.

- *Mary, mother of Jesus (Luke 1:56)*—visited her cousin Elisabeth for three months, who was pregnant with John, who was the forerunner of Jesus.
- *Micah (Mic 6:8)*—three things God requires: to do justly, love mercy, and humility.
- *Mordecai (Esth 8:15)*—three colors on royal garment: blue, white, and purple.
- *Moses (Exod 2:2—3:18—19:1,11—32:8; Deut 4:41,45—34:8)*—three months old when his mother hid him from Pharaoh's death decree. Told by God to take a three-day journey into the wilderness and make a sacrifice unto God. The Israelites journeyed from Egypt to Sinai in three months. God came down on the third day on Mount Sinai. Three thousand slain for worshiping the golden calf. Appoints three cities of refuge. The Mosaic law had three categories: testimonies, statutes, and judgments. Thirty days of mourning when he died.
- *Noah (Gen 6:10,15–16)*—three sons: Shem, Ham, and Japheth. God instructed him to build an ark with three decks, measuring three hundred cubits long, fifty cubits wide, and thirty cubits high.
- *Obededom (2 Sam 6:11)*—three months the Ark of the Covenant remained in his house and God blessed him and all his household.
- *Patriarchs (Lev 26:42)*—three generations: Abraham, Isaac, and Jacob. These three names appear together thirty-three times in the Bible (KJV.)
- *Paul/Saul (Acts 9:9,15—19:8—28:11-12,17; 2 Cor 11:25—12:8)*—lost sight for three days. Fasted for three days. Three groups God told him to bear witness to: Gentiles, kings, and children of Israel. Three months preaching in Ephesus. Three months on Isle of Melita. Three days in Syracuse. Third day after arriving in Rome he called the chief of the Jews together. Three times he is beaten with rods and three times shipwrecked. Three times he prayed asking God to remove his infirmity.
- *Peter (Luke 9:33—22:61; John 21:15-17; Acts 11:9-11)*—three tabernacles he offered to make on the mount of transfiguration for Jesus, Moses, and Elijah. Three times he denied knowing Jesus, after the cock had crowed three times. Three times Jesus asked him, "lovest thou me?" Three times God gave him a specific vision. Three men came to visit him shortly after his vision.

- *Pilate (Luke 23:22)*—three times he stated that he found no fault with Jesus to warrant crucifixion.
- *Rahab (Josh 2:16)*—told spies to hide in mountains for three days from their pursuers.
- *Samson (Judg 14:11-12,19—15:4,11-12)*—warrior and a judge. His parents brought thirty companions to his feast. He posed a riddle offering thirty sheets and thirty change of garments as prizes. Slew thirty men after the spirit of God came upon him. Three hundred foxes tied by their tails with fire torches and sent into the Philistine's cornfields. Three thousand men bound him and brought him unto the Philistines.
- *Samuel (1 Sam 3:8)*—three times God called his name but he thought it was Eli the priest.
- *Saul (1 Sam 10:3—11:8,11—24:2—31:6)*—Samuel anointed Saul and advised him that he will meet three men on the plain of Tabor going up to God to Bethel (House of God): one with three kids, another with three loaves, and the other with a bottle of wine. Saul numbered the children of Israel and there were three hundred thousand and thirty thousand men of Judah. Saul divides Israelites in three companies before battle with Ammorites. Saul took three thousand men in search of David. Saul was killed along with his three sons on the same day.
- *Solomon (1 Kgs 4:32—5:16—6:11-12—9:25)*—third and last king of the united kingdom of Israel, which included Judah. Spoke three thousand proverbs. Three thousand three hundred chosen to rule over the people. Three things God required of Solomon; "walk in my statutes, and execute my judgments, and keep all my commandments." Three times a year he offered sacrifice to God. Three books of the Bible attributed to him: Proverbs, Ecclesiastes, and Songs of Solomon.
- *Zechariah (Zech 1:19—13:9)*—three kingdoms scattered: Judah, Israel, and Jerusalem. One third of Israel to be refined in fire.

— Appendix B —

Trees and the Roles They Played

Trees have played important roles throughout various Bible accounts. Jesus used nature and symbols in his parables to convey his messages. However, he was not endorsing pantheism, which is idolatry. Nature points to a Creator. We ought to worship God the Creator and not the creation (nature.)

Noah Built Ark of Wood

It was the ark that saved Noah and his family. It was their sanctuary on water. It preserved life and allowed for the regeneration of humanity.

> Gen 6:14—"Make thee an ark of gopher wood; rooms shalt thou make in the ark, and shalt pitch it within and without with pitch."

The Sanctuary in the Wilderness

The Sanctuary in the wilderness held the presence of God in the Ark of the Covenant. It preserved spiritual life for the children if Israel.

> Exod 25:10,23—"And they shall make an ark of shittim wood, two cubits and a half shall be the length thereof, and a cubit

and a half the breadth thereof, and a cubit and a half the height thereof. Thou shalt also make a table of shittim wood, two cubits shall be the length thereof, and a cubit the breadth thereof, and a cubit and a half the height thereof."

Exod 30:1—38:1—"And thou shalt make an altar to burn incense upon, of shittim wood shalt thou make it. And he made the altar of burnt offering of shittim wood, five cubits was the length thereof, and five cubits the breadth thereof, it was foursquare and three cubits the height thereof."

Jesus Describes the Kingdom of Heaven as a Tree

The kingdom of heaven is likened as a tree, a sheltered sanctuary of refuge to preserve eternal rest.

Matt 13:31-32—"Another parable put he forth unto them, saying, 'the kingdom of heaven is like to a grain of mustard seed, which a man took, and sowed in his field, which indeed is the least of all seeds, but when it is grown, it is the greatest among herbs, and becometh a tree, so that the birds of the air come and lodge in the branches thereof.'"

Jesus was Crucified on a Tree

A tree became the crossroads where mercy and justice intersected; an emblem of the sanctuary of salvation.

Acts 5:30—"The God of our fathers raised up Jesus, whom ye slew and hanged on a tree."

Jesus Had Employment Working With Trees (Wood)

It is fitting to note that Jesus while on earth was a carpenter (Matt 13:55.) The Hebrew word for carpenter is *kharash* which means craftsman. A carpenter works with trees (wood.) Christ came to earth and worked as a carpenter and molded and shaped wood—like man whom God formed with his own hands. A symbolism of God who is a personal hands-on God that desires a personal intimate relationship with mankind.

Appendix B

Zechariah's Vision of Carpenters

> Zech 1:18–21—"Then lifted I up mine eyes, and saw, and behold four horns. And I said unto the angel that talked with me, 'what be these?' And he answered me, 'these are the horns which have scattered Judah, Israel, and Jerusalem.' And the Lord shewed me four carpenters. Then said I, 'what come these to do?' And he spake, saying, 'these are the horns which have scattered Judah, so that no man did lift up his head, but these are come to fray them, to cast out the horns of the Gentiles, which lifted up their horn over the land of Judah to scatter it.'"

In the historical context, God showed the prophet Zechariah his four appointed carpenters who were his agents, who would restore his people and rebuild the temple of the Lord. In a spiritual context, God sent his son Jesus, who became a carpenter, to restore mankind back to God and to rebuild his spiritual temple within mankind. Christ also came to "fray" or crush the serpent's head as was prophesied in the garden of Eden (Gen 3:15.) In an eschatological context, there is a spiritual warfare between God's remnant church and the little horn, which is the antichrist beast power. This little horn power, as is revealed in the books of Daniel and Revelation, is the alliance of papal Rome which is aligned with the dragon (Satan), and the false prophets. This alliance will seek to persecute the saints of God, modern-day spiritual Israel (Rev 16:13—13:15.)

> Fun Fact: The word kharash occurs thirty-three times in the Masoretic text of the Hebrew Bible. The word carpenter replaced the word treewwyrhta (tree wright) in the early 1300s.

— Appendix C —

Comparative Look at Revelation 14 and Psalms 96

Revelation chapter 14 documents the three angels' messages. These apocalyptic end-time messages were given by inspiration of the Holy Spirit to the apostle John while exiled on the Isle of Patmos during anti-Christian persecution under Roman Emperor Domitian in the late first century (AD 95 to AD 96.) Psalms 96 was written by David when he brought the Ark of the Covenant up to Jerusalem, circa 990 BC to 1000 BC. David brought with him thirty thousand chosen men of Israel (2 Sam 6:1.) Psalms 96 was sung as a hymn. Singers were instructed by David to sing this psalm every afternoon until the temple was constructed and the Ark placed inside (1 Chr 16:23–33.) In Hebrew this psalm is known as *Shiru Lashem* which translates "Sing to the Lord," and repeats the word "sing" three times. These three instances alluded to the three daily prayer services when Israel sang praises to God. "O worship the Lord in the beauty of holiness," was the clarion call to return to the worship of the one and true living God. This parallels the first angel of Rev 14:7 whose loud cry echoes David's call. Though they were written centuries apart, there are striking similarities between Psalms 96, which was sung three times a day and the three angels' messages of Revelation 14. The common themes include the true God versus false gods, true worship versus false worship, how to worship God, judgment, and the sovereign rulership of God.

- *Fear God and give glory*—David declared that the true God was to be "feared above all gods." The first angel similarly proclaimed, "fear God and give glory to him." The word glory is indicated three times in Psalms 96 and once by the first angel. The word fear is mentioned three times—twice by David and once by the first angel.

- *True God/true worship*—David declared that the true God is the Creator who made the heavens. The first angel similarly proclaimed that the true God is the one who made the heavens, earth, sea, and fountains of water. The word worship is declared once by David and mentioned three times by the three angels.

- *False worship/false gods*—David declared that all gods of all nations were false and idolatrous. The second angel defines this as Babylon, polluted wine, and spiritual fornication.

- *Gospel to the whole world*—David called for a declaration of God's glory and wonders among all people, even among heathens. The first angel similarly called for the gospel to be preached to every nation, kindred, tongue, and people.

- *Judgment*—David declared three times that God shall judge the world. The first angel also loudly and similarly declared that God's judgment had come.

- *Sovereignty*—David declared that God is great. Honor, and majesty was before him, he reigneth. The first angel also declared God as being the supreme creator, ruler, and judge.

David was thirty years old when he began his reign. Similarly, Jesus was thirty years old when he began his ministry. David's love for God was the motivation for bringing the Ark of the Covenant to Jerusalem. The Ark held the presence of God, and he desired that it had a permanent home and a place where true worship would be established. Similarly, it was Jesus' love for the Father and for mankind that brought him to earth. Jesus embodied the presence of God and the motivation for bringing God's presence to us was to restore mankind back to the Father—to establish worship in spirit and in truth. David's call to worship was a foreshadowing of the three angel's messages. This end-time clarion call is the most urgent and imperative message for all inhabitants of the earth as we near the second coming of Christ. A final call to return to true worship of the one true God, the Creator of the heavens, earth, and the seas.

Comparative Look at Revelation 14 and Psalms 96

Ps 96:1–9,11–12—"O sing unto the Lord a new song, sing unto the Lord, all the earth.
Sing unto the Lord, bless his name, shew forth his salvation from day to day.
Declare his glory among the heathen, his wonders among all people.
For the Lord is great, and greatly to be praised, he is to be feared above all gods.
For all the gods of the nations are idols, but the Lord made the heavens.
Honor and majesty are before him, strength and beauty are in his sanctuary.
Give unto the Lord, O ye kindreds of the people, give unto the Lord glory and strength.
Give unto the Lord the glory due unto his name, bring an offering, and come into his courts.
O worship the Lord in the beauty of holiness, fear before him, all the earth.
Let the heavens rejoice, and let the earth be glad, let the sea roar, and the fulness thereof.
Let the field be joyful, and all that is therein, then shall all the trees of the wood rejoice."

Rev 14:6–7 First Angel's Message
"And I saw another angel fly in the midst of heaven, having the everlasting gospel to preach unto them that dwell on the earth, and to every nation, and kindred, and tongue, and people. Saying with a loud voice, 'fear God, and give glory to him, for the hour of his judgment is come, and worship him that made heaven, and earth, and the sea, and the fountains of waters.'"

The common themes in the above scriptures call for a return to the worship of the true God who is the Creator. There is only one true God and all others are idols. The first angel also announces the beginning of judgment.

- Give glory to God
- Give praise to God
- Fear God
- The false gods of the nations are idols
- The true God is the Creator of the heaven, sea, and earth
- Worship the true God

- Hour of God's judgment has begun

    Ps 96:13—"Before the Lord, for he cometh, for he cometh to judge the earth, he shall judge the world with righteousness, and the people with his truth."

    Rev 14:8 Second Angel's Message
    "And there followed another angel, saying, 'Babylon is fallen, is fallen, that great city, because she made all nations drink of the wine of the wrath of her fornication.'"

The theme of the investigative phase of judgment is proclaimed by the first angel. The second angel picks up this theme and highlights the judgment against false worship (Babylon.) This is the sentencing phase of judgment. Babylon (false worship) is judged and "is fallen is fallen." This is repeated twice. "For he cometh, for he cometh," referring to the Lord is repeated twice. This juxtaposition and repetition shows the certainty of God's exacting judgment against false worship—spiritual Babylon that intoxicated the world with false doctrines, i.e., the dragon, the beast, and false prophets.

    Ps 96:10—"Say among the heathen that the Lord reigneth, the world also shall be established that it shall not be moved, he shall judge the people righteously."

    Rev 14:9-10—"And the third angel followed them, saying with a loud voice, 'if any man worship the beast and his image, and receive his mark in his forehead, or in his hand, the same shall drink of the wine of the wrath of God, which is poured out without mixture into the cup of his indignation, and he shall be tormented with fire and brimstone in the presence of the holy angels, and in the presence of the Lamb.'"

These verses highlight the theme of the executive phase of judgment and punishment against Babylon (false worship), and those who choose to accept the antichrist system and the mark of the beast. It speaks directly to those who align with false worship, which will be completely destroyed. The eternal and everlasting kingdom of God will reign.

— Appendix D —

The Investigative Judgment

The first angels' message heralds the beginning of the investigative judgment. There are three phases of judgment; investigative, sentencing, and executive. The investigative judgment began in the Most Holy Place in heaven in 1844. Jesus is still in the Most Holy Place. After probation ends, Jesus will move from the Most Holy Place to the Holy Place. In this second compartment he will carry out the sentencing phase and finally when the seven last plagues are poured out, the executive phase of judgment begins upon the earth, just before the second coming of Christ to earth (outer court.) How did God reveal to human agents that the investigative judgment had begun in 1844? In the early nineteenth century passionate Bible students, pastors, and truth seekers garnered a deep interest in prophecy and in the advent, the second coming of Christ. They were from different religious backgrounds, denominations, and countries. Having done exhaustive studies of the books of Daniel and Revelation, they concluded that the second advent would occur in October 1844. So convinced they were, that many sold cherished earthly possessions and eagerly awaited that day with anxious expectations. When time elapsed, they quickly realized that there must have been a misinterpretation of the prophecy of Daniel chapter 8 regarding the 2300 days. This feeling of dejection was coined the "Great Disappointment." Some abandoned the movement except a few, a remnant that regrouped and with fastidious re-examination of the prophecies, and with prayer, they sought from God deeper light. One of the members of this remnant group was a Baptist farmer named William Miller.

> "As I was fully convinced," says Miller, "that all Scripture given by inspiration of God is profitable (2 Tim 3:16); that it came not at any time by the will of man, but was written as holy men were moved by the Holy Ghost (2 Pet 1:21), and was written 'for our learning, that we through patience and comfort of the Scriptures might have hope' (Rom 15:4), I could but regard the chronological portions of the Bible as being as much a portion of the Word of God, and as much entitled to our serious consideration, as any other portion of the Scriptures. I therefore felt that in endeavoring to comprehend what God had in His mercy seen fit to reveal to us, I had no right to pass over the prophetic periods." The prophecy which seemed most clearly to reveal the time of the second advent was that of Dan 8:14; "unto two thousand and three hundred days, then shall the sanctuary be cleansed." Following his rule of making Scripture its own interpreter, Miller learned that a day in symbolic prophecy represents a year (Num 14:34; Ezek 4:6); he saw that the period of 2300 prophetic days, or literal years, would extend far beyond the close of the Jewish dispensation, hence it could not refer to the sanctuary of that dispensation. Miller accepted the generally received view that in the Christian age the earth is the sanctuary, and he therefore understood that the cleansing of the sanctuary foretold in Dan 8:14 represented the purification of the earth by fire at the second coming of Christ. If, then, the correct starting point could be found for the 2300 days, he concluded that the time of the second advent could be readily ascertained. Thus would be revealed the time of that great consummation, the time when the present state, with "all its pride and power, pomp, and vanity, wickedness, and oppression, would come to an end"; when the curse would be "removed from off the earth, death be destroyed, reward be given to the servants of God, the prophets and saints, and them who fear His name, and those be destroyed that destroy the earth." With a new and deeper earnestness, Miller continued the examination of the prophecies, whole nights as well as days being devoted to the study of what now appeared of such stupendous importance and all-absorbing interest. In the eighth chapter of Daniel he could find no clue to the starting point of the 2300 days; the angel Gabriel, though commanded to make Daniel understand the vision, gave him only a partial explanation. As the terrible persecution to befall the church was unfolded to the prophet's vision, physical strength gave way. He

could endure no more, and the angel left him for a time. Daniel "fainted and was sick certain days ... and I was astonished at the vision, but none understood it." Yet God had bidden His messenger, "make this man to understand the vision." That commission must be fulfilled. In obedience to it, the angel, some time afterward, returned to Daniel, saying, "I am now come forth to give thee skill and understanding ... therefore understand the matter, and consider the vision."(Dan 8:16,27—9:22-23,25-27.) There was one important point in the vision of chapter 8 which had been left unexplained, namely, that relating to time—the period of the 2300 days; therefore the angel, in resuming his explanation, dwells chiefly upon the subject of time; "seventy weeks are determined upon thy people and upon thy Holy City ... know therefore and understand, that from the going forth of the commandment to restore and to build Jerusalem unto the Messiah the Prince shall be seven weeks, and threescore and two weeks; the street shall be built again, and the wall, even in troublous times. And after threescore and two weeks shall Messiah be cut off, but not for Himself ... and He shall confirm the covenant with many for one week, and in the midst of the week He shall cause the sacrifice and the oblation to cease." The angel had been sent to Daniel for the express purpose of explaining to him the point which he had failed to understand in the vision of the eighth chapter, the statement relative to time—"unto two thousand and three hundred days, then shall the sanctuary be cleansed." After bidding Daniel "understand the matter, and consider the vision," the very first words of the angel are, "seventy weeks are determined upon thy people and upon thy Holy City." The word here American Reformer translated "determined" literally signifies "cut off." Seventy weeks, representing 490 years, are declared by the angel to be cut off, as specially pertaining to the Jews. But from what were they cut off? As the 2300 days was the only period of time mentioned in chapter 8, it must be the period from which the seventy weeks were cut off; the seventy weeks must therefore be a part of the 2300 days, and the two periods must begin together. The seventy weeks were declared by the angel to date from the going forth of the commandment to restore and build Jerusalem. If the date of this commandment could be found, then the starting point for the great period of the 2300 days would be ascertained. In the seventh chapter of Ezra the decree is found, verses [twelve to twenty-six.] In its completest form it was issued by Artaxerxes, king of Persia, 457 BC. But in Ezra 6:14 the house of the Lord at Jerusalem is said to have been built "according to the commandment ["decree," margin] of Cyrus, and Darius, and Artaxerxes king of Persia." These three kings, in originating, reaffirming, and completing the decree, brought it to the perfection required by the prophecy to mark the beginning of the 2300 years. Taking 457 BC, the time when the decree was completed, as the date of the commandment, every specification of the prophecy concerning the seventy weeks was seen to have been fulfilled. "From the going forth of the commandment to restore and to build Jerusalem unto the Messiah the Prince shall be seven weeks, and threescore and two weeks"—namely, sixty-nine weeks, or 483 years. The decree of Artaxerxes went into effect in the autumn of 457 BC. From this date, 483 years extend to the autumn of AD 27. At that time this prophecy was fulfilled. The word "Messiah" signifies "the Anointed One." In the autumn of AD 27 Christ was baptized by John and received the anointing of the Spirit. The apostle Peter testifies that "God anointed Jesus of Nazareth with the Holy Ghost and with power" (Acts 10:38.) And the Savior Himself declared, "the Spirit of the Lord is upon me, because He hath anointed me to preach the gospel to the poor" (Luke 4:18.) After His baptism He went into Galilee, "preaching the gospel of the kingdom of God, and saying, the time is fulfilled" (Mark 1:14–15.) "And He shall confirm the covenant with many for one week." The "week" here brought to view is the last one of the seventy; it is the last seven years of the period allotted especially to the Jews. During this time, extending from AD 27 to AD 34, Christ, at first in person and afterward by His disciples, extended the gospel invitation especially to the Jews. As the apostles went forth with the good tidings of the kingdom, the Savior's direction was, "go not into the way of the Gentiles, and into any city of the Samaritans enter ye not but go rather to the lost sheep of the house of Israel" (Matt 10:5–6.) "In the midst of the week He shall cause the sacrifice and the oblation to cease." In AD 31, three and a half years after His baptism, our Lord was crucified. With the great sacrifice offered upon Calvary, ended that system of offerings which for four thousand years had pointed forward to the Lamb of God. Type had met antitype, and all the sacrifices and oblations of the ceremonial system were there to cease. The seventy weeks, or 490 years, especially allotted to the Jews, ended, as we have seen, in AD 34. At that time, through the action of the Jewish Sanhedrin, the nation sealed its rejection of the gospel by the martyrdom of Stephen and the persecution of the followers of Christ. Then the message of salvation, no longer restricted to the chosen people, was given to the world. The disciples, forced by persecution to flee from Jerusalem, "went everywhere preaching the word." "Philip went down to the city of Samaria, and preached Christ unto them." Peter, divinely guided, opened the gospel to the centurion of Caesarea, the God-fearing Cornelius, and the ardent Paul, won to the faith of Christ, was commissioned to carry the glad tidings "far hence unto the Gentiles" (Acts 8:4–5—22:21.) Thus far every specification of the prophecies is strikingly fulfilled, and the beginning of the seventy weeks is fixed beyond question at 457 BC and their expiration in AD 34. From this data there is no difficulty in finding the termination of the 2300 days. The seventy weeks—490 days—having been cut off from the 2300, there were 1810 days remaining. After the end of 490 days, the 1810 days were still to be fulfilled. From AD 34, 1810 years extend to 1844. Consequently, the 2300 days of Dan 8:14 terminate in 1844."[1]

The early Bible prophecy students, pastors, and truth-seekers, though disappointed that Jesus did not return in 1844 were later given the interpretation of Dan 8:14, "unto two thousand and three hundred days, then shall the sanctuary be cleansed." The cleansing of the sanctuary meant that in heaven, Jesus moved from the Holy Place into the Most Holy Place to begin the cleansing of the heavenly sanctuary, which is the investigative phase of judgment. This was the beginning of the review of the records of sin.

---

1. White, *The Great Controversy*, 325–28.

— Appendix E —

Timeline of the 2300 Year Prophecy

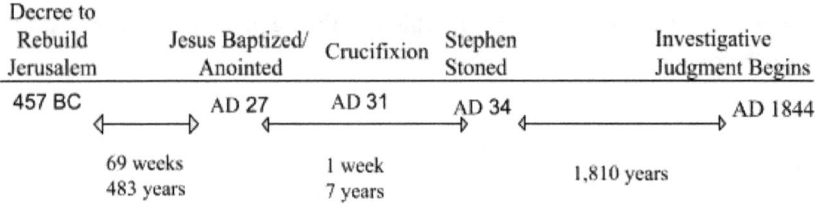

— Appendix F —

The First, Second, and Third Temple

Ark of Covenant. Rebuilt Temple (Solomon). New Jerusalem

Many are looking for an earthly man-made third temple as a sign that will precede the second coming of Christ. The hypothesis and anticipation is that this third temple will be erected in Jerusalem to replace the temple that was destroyed in AD 70 at the hands of the Romans. It is also interesting to note that that the "One World Religion Headquarters" or the "Abrahamic Family House" is slated to open in 2022 in Abu Dhabi. This is a joint venture between Pope Francis and the Sunni Muslim leader, Sheikh Ahmed el-Tayeb, who both signed a global peace covenant dubbed, "Document on Human Fraternity for World Peace and Living Together." There will be three buildings; a mosque, a synagogue, and a church.

God's desire has always been to abide with man and be present in a tangible way and not be represented by an impersonal physical edifice. Therefore, the third temple will not be a man-made earthly temple but will be the heavenly temple that will descend from heaven (Rev 21:2.) There are three notable temples that held and embodies the presence of God; the Ark of the Covenant in the sanctuary in the wilderness, Solomon's temple, and the heavenly temple.

When

First dwelling—sanctuary in the wilderness where the presence of God dwelt in the Ark of the Covenant; fifteenth century BC (circa 1444 BC.) Moses was instructed by God to build this temple which was a replica of the heavenly temple.

Second dwelling—Solomon's temple, where the presence of God dwelt in the Ark of the Covenant; tenth century BC (957 BC.) It was destroyed by the Babylonians in 586 BC.

Third dwelling—New Jerusalem, holy city; exists in heaven from eternity.

Where

First dwelling—wilderness of Sinai after the exodus of the Israelites from Egypt to Canaan (Exod 15:17—25:8)

Second dwelling—Jerusalem, Mount Moriah (2 Chr 3:1)

Third dwelling—will descend from heaven to Mount of Olives, Jerusalem (Act 1:11–12; Zech 14:4; Rev 21:2)

Who Shown/Told

First dwelling—Moses, law giver (Exod 25)

Second dwelling—Nathan, the prophet (2 Sam 7)

Third dwelling—John, the revelator (Rev 21)

How Shown

First dwelling—in person by God (Exod 25)

Second dwelling—vision by God (2 Sam 7)

Third dwelling—vision by the Holy Spirit (Rev 21:10)

Where Shown

First dwelling—Mount Sinai (Exod 24:15-16—25:8)

Second dwelling—Jerusalem, while Nathan lived in King David's kingdom

Third dwelling—Isle of Patmos; mountain in vision while John was exiled (Rev 1:9—21:10)

Stories/Apartments

First dwelling—three compartments: outer court, Holy Place, and Most Holy Place

Second dwelling—three stories in height. Three units: porch (ulam), Holy Place (heikal), and Holy of Holies (debir)

Third dwelling—not mentioned in Scripture

Wall

First dwelling—wall of curtain; 1500 square cubits (Exod 26:1-2—27:18)

Second dwelling—wall of Solomon/Jerusalem (1 Kgs 3:1)

Third dwelling—wall around; 1500 miles (12,000 furlongs) in perimeter (Rev 21:12,16)

Twelve Tribes of Israel

First dwelling—twelve tribes camped around sanctuary; there were four groups of three. Judah, Issachar, and Zebulun camped on the east. Reuben, Simeon, and Gad camped on the south. Ephraim, Manasseh, and Benjamin camped on the west. Dan, Asher and Naphtali camped on the north (Numbers chapter 2)

Second dwelling—twelve bronze oxen held up the bronze basin (laver) on their backs; three looking north, three looking west, three looking south, and three looking east (1 Kgs 7:25)

Third dwelling—twelve tribes' names on gates: three gates on the east, three gates on the north, three gates on the south, and three gates on the west (Rev 21:12-13)

Cherubim/Angels

First dwelling—cherubims of gold over the Ark of Covenant; images of cherubims on curtains and veil (Exod 25:18—26:1,31)

Second dwelling—cherubims of gold in Most Holy Place; images of cherubims carved on walls and doors (2 Chr 3:10;1 Kgs 6:29,32)

Third dwelling—angels at each of the twelve gates of city; angles around the throne of God (Rev 5:11—7:11—21:12)

Palm

First dwelling—Israelites encamped by waters next to seventy palm trees (Exod 15:27)

Second dwelling—palm carvings on walls and doors (Ezek 41:18-20)

Third dwelling—palm is a sign of triumph and victory. Palms are waved in the hands of the redeemed in heaven at the second coming of Christ (Rev 7:9,15)

Bibliography

Gibbons, James Cardinal. *Faith of Our Fathers*. Baltimore, MD: John Murphy Company, 1876.

The Jewish Chronicle. "Ahavah." October 2008. https://www.thejc.com/judaism/jewish-words/ahavah.

Korpel, Marjo C.A., "Fit for a Queen: Jezebel's Royal Seal." https://www.biblicalarchaeology.org/daily/biblical-artifacts/inscriptions/fit-for-a-queen-jezebels-royal-seal/.

Livy, Titus. *History of Rome*. Book 1. 15th century. Translated by Rev. Canon Roberts. London, UK: J. M. Dent and Sons, Ltd. 1905.

Rendelman, Daniel. "Ahavah: Hebrew Word Study." https://myemail.constantcontact.com/Hebrew-Word-Study—Ahavah.html.

Rudd, Steve. "Six Trials of Jesus." https://www.bible.ca/doctrine-six-trials-of-jesus-3-jewish-guilty—3-roman-innocent.htm.

White, Ellen G. *The Desire of Ages*. Silver Spring, MD: Ellen G. White Estate, (1898) 233–34. https://www.ellenwhite.info/books/ellen-g-white-book-desire-of-ages-da-23.htm.

———. *Early Writings*. Silver Spring, MD: Ellen G. White Estate, (1882) 126, 262. https://www.ellenwhite.info/books/ellen-g-white-book-early-writings-ew-32.htm; https://www.ellenwhite.info/books/ellen-g-white-book-early-writings-ew-63.htm.

———. *The Great Controversy*. Silver Spring, MD: Ellen G. White Estate, (1858) 325–28, 418–564. https://www.ellenwhite.info/books/ellen-g-white-book-great-controversy-gc-18.htm; https://www.ellenwhite.info/books/ellen-g-white-book-great-controversy-gc-23.htm; https://www.ellenwhite.info/books/ellen-g-white-book-great-controversy-gc-25.htm; https://www.ellenwhite.info/books/ellen-g-white-book-great-controversy-gc-35.htm.

———. *Last Day Events*. Nampa, ID: Pacific, (1992) 183–87.

———. *Letters and Manuscript*, volume 17. Silver Spring, MD: Ellen G. White Estate, (1902) 173. https://m.egwwritings.org/en/book/14067.9055001; https://m.egwwritings.org/pl/book/93.279.

———. *Life Sketches of Ellen G. White*. Silver Spring, MD: Ellen G. White Estate, (1915) 95. https://egwwritings-a.akamaihd.net/pdf/en_LS.pdf.

———. *Maranatha*. Silver Spring, MD: Review and Herald, (1976) 176. https://egwwritings-a.akamaihd.net/pdf/en_Mar.pdf.

———. *Qualifications for the Worker*. Silver Spring, MD: Review and Herald, 1895. https://m.egwwritings.org/en/book/821.14260#14260.

———. *The Story of Patriarchs and Prophets*. Silver Spring, MD: Ellen G. White Estate, (1890) 58. https://www.ellenwhite.info/books/ellen-g-white-book-patriarchs-and-prophets-pp-3.htm.

www.ingramcontent.com/pod-product-compliance
Lightning Source LLC
Chambersburg PA
CBHW071232230426
43668CB00011B/1403